have no co~~~~~~~~~~~~~~~~~~~~~~meth-
ods for cre~~~~~~~~~~~~~~~~~~~~~~ your
target empl~~~~~~~~~~~~~~~~~~~~ you.
What Jimi Hendrix was to the ~~~~~~ Perry
is to job hunting. I cannot recommend this book
highly enough."

Kevin Donlin, Creator,
TheSimpleJobSearch.com,
Co-Creator, The Guerrilla Job Search
Home Study Course

"Job hunters don't need to be told the 'what' of job
hunting, they want and need to know the 'hows'
They are all in here and then some and, just as
important, conveyed with the energy and passion
of someone who not only knows what he's talking
about, but truly believes it. You will too."

Dave Opton, Founder and CEO,
ExecuNet

"This new book lays out a straightforward and detailed 'plan of attack' for every step of a job search—
from planning to negotiating the offer. The insights
and insider knowledge of the recruitment industry
that *Guerrilla Marketing for Job Hunters 2.0* offers
establishes it as an indispensable tool for job seekers to land the interview and secure the job of their
dreams. Going into a job search without this book
would be like going into battle unarmed."

Gautam Godhwani, CEO,
SimplyHired.com

"This book is brilliant. Packed with stories, examples, and tactics to help you at any point in your
job search—this book is all about landing a real job
with intense competition in a minimal amount of
time. An absolute must read."

Jason Alba, CEO, JibberJobber.com

"If you're a college student looking for an internship or a recent graduate looking for an entry-level
job, then you'll understand from even a quick skim
through *Guerrilla Marketing for Job Hunters 2.0* that
it will be as indispensable to your job search as your
textbooks were for your classes. In tight job markets,
the competition for the best positions is especially
fierce, and every candidate will be looking for an

edge. If you want to get the edge over your competition, then you need to get this great new book."
Steven Rothberg, Founder,
CollegeRecruiter.com job board

"David Perry truly understands how changes in information and communication technologies have created new opportunities and pitfalls for the job seeker. Stand out from the crowd and truly shine by illuminating your most important talents to the broadest audience—in a cost effective fashion. Stop wasting time and start with this book."
Sam Zales, President, Zoom Information, Inc.

"If you are ever tempted to think, 'I know all that' when it comes to the job search, read this book. As a former director of Career Services at a major university, this book is a humbling reminder that even 'experts' need refreshers and new insights to stay relevant. Thanks to technology, the tools and techniques to assist with self-marketing strategies are constantly changing (evolving). This book not only allows you to stay in the game, but it helps you get ahead of the game when it comes to marketing you."
Dawn Brown, author, *That Perception Thing!*

"David Perry calls his co-author, Jay Levinson, the '5-star general of guerrilla marketing.' Perry is the drill sergeant. He kicks butt. In the army, his squad would lose the fewest men. In the job wars, his men and women beat the opposition and gain the position. If a career victory is what you're after, follow Perry."
Tony Patterson, Editor and CEO,
SCAN/scansite.ca News Leader for the Ontario Technology Corridor

"This book provides readers with valuable information that will enable them to stand above the crowd and secure the best suitable employment. A wealth of information extends into areas that I will be able to utilize in my business, because in a way, I am always applying for the 'job' of being a trusted advisor to potential clients."

Milan Topolovec, BA, TEP, CLU,
RHU, President & CEO, TK Group,
www.thetkgroup.com

"The technology of job hunting has changed. If you blinked, you may have missed it. Unless you fully understand how to use modern tools to market yourself, you'll be at a disadvantage. In this book, David reviews the old axioms of job hunting that still apply and introduces new techniques that have become just as important."

Rick Dalmazzi, President & CEO,
VoIPshield Systems Inc.

"*Guerrilla Marketing for Job Hunters 2.0* is a *must-have* manual for the serious career professional. David brings his strong sales perspective to the job-hunt strategy. Follow his process. Don't compromise. Leave your emotions in the bedroom and let his 'system' do the work. David leaves out the fluff and academics leaving us with fast-paced advice and lots of free 'go-to' resources that he uses to execute the system himself. I'll be providing a copy of *Guerrilla Marketing for Job Hunters 2.0* to all my sales clients. David's approach applies to the deal hunter as much as it does the job hunter."

Terry Ledden, Sandler Training

"This much-needed sequel to *Guerrilla Marketing for Job Hunters* puts the tools of the Internet at the fingertips of the searcher! Advice on social networks, blogs, special web sites, and interactive promotion is laid out for all to use. In today's troubled economy, it would pay every employee—not just those who are currently looking for a job—to become familiar with this book. One of the benefits of the process is that it will help you appreciate your own strengths and skills and your value as a person—not a bad side effect from an exercise that is, after all, devoted to your future!"

Barry Gander, Senior Vice President,
CATA Alliance

"David has looked at the process of job hunting in a completely out-of-the-box approach, and why not? The automotive industry says this is no longer your father's car, so your approach to looking for a job is no longer the way your father looked for one either. It's about the two-way street of value. Your future employer needs to value your skills just as you need to value their appreciation of them, and David's book is about the whole process."

Allan Zander, CEO, Data Kinetics,

"I have been working with David as an employer and a client for the last 10 years. David has always had a singularly unique recruiting style, not the usual methodology of matching a requirements check box to a resume. David dropped the conventional rules and found me someone who truly fit the environment based on common sense and has matched me to the right employer the same way. David is the first recruiter who is concerned about the whole ecosystem around the match to employee and employer, and he tells it like it is. His latest book reflects his unique approach and gives the job searcher real tools, examples, and the mental support needed when looking for employment. Very pragmatic and a how-to approach for the knowledge worker."

Charles Duffett, Senior VP and CIO
Adviser, Canadian Advanced
Technology Alliance

"A must read. A useful and effective tool for all economic times. Once you start reading, it's hard to put it down."

Rick M Sabatino, Financial Director,
Camp Fortune/Mont
SteMarie/Fortune Cinemas/Ski
Banff Norquay

"You can look for a job the old-fashioned way—send or upload your resume and apply for all the jobs you find online—and wait, and wait, and wait some more, to see if you get a response. Or, you can be brave and try job searching differently. Given today's job market, anyone not willing to try something different is going to be in trouble.

There are fewer job openings and more candidates for every single opening. On top of that, there are more very qualified candidates for each position, and hiring managers can afford to be very selective. In order to compete, you need to stand out from the crowd and get noticed. If you don't want to be one of those job seekers who has applied for hundreds of jobs without a single response, *Guerrilla Marketing for Job Hunters 2.0* will help. This book takes you outside the job-seeking box and provides tips, advice, and tactics for job hunting. These job-search strategies really work, and the book includes real-life stories from job seekers who have successfully used them to find their next job."

Alison Doyle, About.com Guide to
Job Searching, jobsearch.about.com

"Dave never ceases to amaze me with his ability to adapt the latest marketing trends to the job-search procedure. Bravo, Dave! This book is even better than the last one."

Mark Hanley, Director of
Operations, Kingston Economic
Development Corporation

"The job-search paradigm has shifted, and you can either play by the new rules or go the way of the dinosaurs. The bold, cutting-edge search strategies found in *Guerrilla Marketing for Job Hunters 2.0* will position you to exploit the system and demolish the competition. I know, because it's how I coach my clients to win!"

Cindy Kraft, CPBS, CCMC, CCM,
CPRW, JCTC, The CFO–Coach

"It doesn't matter how brilliant you are or how exceptional you are at your job. If you are not getting yourself in front of the right people, the hiring decisions makers, you will be overlooked. David Perry and his *Guerrilla Marketing for Job Hunters 2.0* will give you the ammunition to get noticed. Don't get lost on the battlefield, win the war."

Donato Diorio, CEO, Broadlook
Technologies

GUERRILLA MARKETING

FOR

JOB HUNTERS 2.0

GUERRILLA MARKETING

FOR

JOB HUNTERS 2.0

1,001 Unconventional Tips, Tricks, and Tactics for Landing Your Dream Job

JAY CONRAD LEVINSON
DAVID E. PERRY

WILEY

John Wiley & Sons, Inc.

Published by John Wiley & Sons, Inc., Hoboken, New Jersey.
Published simultaneously in Canada.

Back cover photo: Daniel Houle

For general information on our other products and services or for technical support, please contact our Customer Care Department within the United States at (800) 762-2974, outside the United States at (317) 572-3993 or fax (317) 572-4002.

Wiley also publishes its books in a variety of electronic formats. Some content that appears in print may not be available in electronic books. For more information about Wiley products, visit our web site at www.wiley.com.

Library of Congress Cataloging-in-Publication Data:

Levinson, Jay Conrad.
    Guerrilla marketing for job hunters 2.0 : 1,001 unconventional tips, tricks, and tactics for landing your dream job / Jay Conrad Levinson, David E. Perry.
        p. cm.
    Includes index.
        ISBN 978-0-470-45584-5 (pbk. : acid-free paper)
    1. Job hunting.   2. Career development.   3. Vocational guidance.
I. Perry, David, 1960 Jan. 12–   II. Title.
    HF5382.7.L4653 2009
    650.14—dc22   2009004125

Printed in the United States of America.

10 9 8 7 6 5 4 3 2 1

You know who you are, David Perry, and you know how much heavy lifting and fiery hoop diving you've had to do. I also owe acknowledgments to Frank and Ginger Adkins, who are currently walking the walk; to Jeremy Huffman, who has reached his destination already; to Christy Huffman, who has the journey ahead of her and will benefit from the words in these pages; and to Joshua Huffman, who searched for the perfect job and found it while looking in the mirror.

J. C. L.

Twenty-eight years ago a beautiful young woman took a chance on me. We quickly became best friends. We were married 6 years later. Anita Martel and I became business partners 2 years after that when she suggested selling her family home and investing the proceeds of her inheritance in us, thereby starting Perry-Martel International Inc., our executive search firm. The backbone of our relationship has always been the love we have for each other and her unconditional confidence in me. Thank you, Anita, I love you, appreciate you, and am honored in every way to be your partner. You are an inspiration as a mother, wife, and partner.

D. E. P.

Contents

Foreword

Do you know why Jay Conrad Levinson and David Perry use the word *guerrilla* in the titles of all their books and talks? The answer is that guerrillas pursue conventional goals in unconventional ways. Guerrillas, like the achievers who read *SUCCESS* magazine, have a better perspective on reality than their conventional opponents who tend to pursue their dreams by the book.

Never before have guerrillas had such a competitive advantage. In the job market, doing things "by the book" is a fairly certain path to disaster and frustration—unless you operate according to the principles and insights in *this* book. This book ushers you into the land of conventional goals attained, to reality as it is, rather than as it was. It guides you to a new world that remains unknown to other job hunters—a world in which guerrillas reign supreme. It has been said that in a dog-eat-dog economy, the Doberman is king. We're in that kind of economy right now—and the guerrilla is king.

It takes a lot to be a true guerrilla, and this book provides a lot to accomplish that goal. Wanting to be a guerrilla is part of the job, but the heavy lifting of becoming a guerrilla is in being a master of details. Where do you learn those details? The answer is in the pages ahead. It's not necessarily an easy answer, but it's a correct answer.

You absolutely must be aware of how the job market has changed dramatically just in the last decade. This is not your father's generation; it is yours. But it only belongs to you if you have the wisdom and awareness of the guerrilla. You'll gain those invaluable attributes if you soak up that wisdom and become aware of today's realities. This book was written both to help you open doors to jobs others dream about and to show you how to get one.

To many, getting the job of their dreams is close to impossible. But guerrillas are experts at learning the art of the impossible. Their knowledge of what is really happening in the job market transforms the impossible into the probable. Lightning has been captured in these pages. Minds will be changed. Lives will be changed. Light will illuminate the way.

Can all that really happen with just a book? It's a beginning. If you're not a guerrilla job hunter, we wish you success, but if you are a guerrilla job hunter, we *predict* success.

Are you ready to design your life on purpose and live the best years ever? Start right now!

To your SUCCESS,

Darren Hardy
Publisher
SUCCESS Magazine
www.SUCCESS.com

Acknowledgments

Sage Schofield knows what she's done, Seth Pickett is our Official Man on the Streets, and Natalie Smith continues to lead by spirit.

Acknowledgments are also due to Steven, Michelle, Heide, Elexa, Hayley, Zachary, Austin, Blake, Ava, Alyssa, Leighton, and John Thomas for being so darned cute.

And of course, my life and my search are more fruitful because of my new bride, Jeannie Levinson, and my constant daughter, Amy Levinson.

J. C. L.

I am truly grateful for the generous contributions made by friends and colleagues.

The recruiting industry, by its very nature, attracts mavericks, evangelists, and pioneers. It has been my good fortune to work alongside and share ideas with some of the finest in the business, including many who contributed to this book. My deep thanks go out to Lauryn Franzoni, Bill Humbert, Beth H. Kniss, Ross Macpherson, Shari Miller, Jim Moens, Dave Opton, Sally Poole, Paul Rector, Jill Tanenbaum, Deanna J. Williams, John Sumser, David Braun, Jason Alba, Peter Clayton, Jason Davis, Laura Dierker, Donato Diorio, Kevin Donlin, Allison Doyle, James Durbin, Stephen Forsyth, Willy Franzen, Glenn Gutmacher, Mark Haluska, Daniel Houle, Dave Howlett, Harry Joiner, Michael Kelemen, Cindy Kraft, Joseph Lanzon, Ross Macpherson, Patrick McConnell, Anita Martel, Matt Massey, Dave Mendoza, Shari Miller, Joseph Nour, Steve Panyko, Allan Place, Darryl Praill, Jim Reil, Steven Rothberg, Dennis Smith, Gary Smith, Simon Stapleton, Jim Stroud, Penelope Trunk, Bill Vick, Kevin Watson, Tom Weishaar, and Allan Zander. You will benefit immensely from the insights of this powerhouse of professionals.

When I started my executive search firm with my wife and business partner, Anita Martel, my marketing budget for the entire year was $20. As luck would have it, I stumbled across an interesting book called *Guerrilla Marketing* by Jay Conrad Levinson (Boston: Houghton Mifflin, 1989) that promised to reveal hundreds of ways to stretch my marketing budget and get results. Indeed, I owe my early successes in recruiting to Jay's ideas. Little did I know that 17 years later Jay would write the Foreword for my first book, *Career Guide for the High-Tech Professional* (Franklin Lakes, NJ: Career Press, 2004), and later ask me to coauthor this book. To guerrilla marketers, Jay Conrad Levinson is a 5-star general. He is also a true gentleman. I am honored to write alongside him.

I was 8 years old when I discovered *SUCCESS* Magazine. Each issue was a revelation, stuffed with state-of-the-moment advice and spiked with interviews of the brightest businesspeople in the world. I drank the Kool-Aid, and I've never missed an issue since 1968. So, as you can imagine, when Darren Hardy, the new publisher of SUCCESS agreed to write the Foreword—I was ecstatic! You would be wise to join millions of other top performers and keep SUCCESS on your nightstand as you pilot your new career.

I have Christa Martel-Perry to thank for providing the "drill instructor" themed original artwork. Daniel Houle shot the photo on the back cover.

Mark J. Haluska, my friend, colleague, and business partner in recruiting, contributed his blood, sweat, and cheers to this book. Following a remarkable career in the military and in public service, Mark has become a first-class headhunter. His insight into the minds of hiring managers, his knowledge of all things recruiting, and his off-the-wall sense of humor have been invaluable.

Kevin Donlin helped to expand the offering with the formation of the Guerrilla Job Search Boot Camp™. A great business partner, he's a pleasure to work with—except for all the excess energy.

To my business partners in RecruiterPix (Kevin Watson, Daniel Houle, Steve Panyko), the job board attached to the GM4JH.com web site—thanks. But we know it was Jerri Panyko who managed to corral the four of us long enough to complete the task. Jerri, you're my hero!

All the people at John Wiley & Sons were a pleasure to work with, including Christine and Beth. I want to single out Shannon for suggesting the idea for *Guerrilla Marketing for Job Hunters 2.0* and shepherding it through the editorial process. What a breath of fresh air she has been.

Many thanks to Megan Quinn at Google for steering me through the permissions process so we could use all the Google screen shots that make the book easier to follow. Google is a trademark of Google Inc.

To my father Fred Perry who patiently read and reviewed all my first drafts in spite of having a life of his own . . . thanks!

To the tens of thousands of job hunters and hundreds of clients I have worked with over the years—thank you. Without you, my life would not have been nearly as interesting.

To Christa, Corey, Mandy, and Shannon Martel-Perry who put up with my modified schedule to get the second edition out on time—Thanks.

Last, to my darling wife who picked up the slack in our executive search practice and made sure none of our clients' projects fell through the cracks—you're a life saver. Thanks, I love you.

D. E. P.

Warning

This is the book some headhunters didn't want written!

I know what to say and how to say it to get employers to make hiring decisions. I know all the tricks of the trade to turn finding a job into a logical and systematic process—I discovered almost all of them the hard way—and I am going to share them with you so that you don't need to go through the same agonizing trial-and-error experiments I did. In my 22 years as an executive search professional, headhunter, recruiter, and placement counselor, I have negotiated more than $174 million in salaries. BUT, and there's always a "but," don't waste your time if you're one of the millions of people who dream of "hitting it big," and becoming a "high-roller" by winning the lottery, but who never actually buy a ticket! This book is definitely not for you.

With us you actually have to get in the game and work. There are no silver bullets! I hope that's not you I hear groaning, "Then why did I buy this book?" Why? Because there is a well-honed process we can teach you if you want to learn it and work it—but *YOU* actually have to do the work yourself.

Do you want to take charge of your life and advance your career on purpose. Yes? Then this book is absolutely for you. Read on.

■ DON'T PANIC!

We'll show you how to headhunt your next job and exactly how to work effectively with friends, colleagues, strangers, and headhunters so they can help you, too.

Full speed ahead!

Introduction

We only live once, and most of our time is spent at work, so it's vital that we are allowed to feel good about what we do.

—Sir Richard Branson, Virgin Group

In the spring of 2006, Allan Zander and Daryl Praill were celebrating. After helping triple their company's valuation, taking it from worst to first among competitors—56 months ahead of plan—their company had just been acquired for the highest earnings' multiple in their industry's history. How were they rewarded for their incredible efforts?

They were laid off, of course.

Undeterred, Praill and Zander immediately went on the offensive, and teamed up with the headhunter who had originally recruited them to the opportunity. Together, they identified 38 companies that could use their skills. They launched a marketing campaign fashioned after the best principles in the book *Guerrilla Marketing for Job Hunters*.

They were packaged and sold as a "team" into a marketplace with 65 percent unemployment. Would you say, "tough job market"?

Yet, within weeks, they had:

➤ Developed a list of targeted employers using 2 free web sites, ZoomInfo and LinkedIn;

➤ Designed a direct mail campaign based on methods never used in job hunting;

➤ Created 2 Guerrilla Resumes using unconventional tactics to get attention;

➤ Built an eye-grabbing web site;

➤ Launched an elegantly effective blog using Google;

➤ Released a series of radio-quality podcasts;

➤ Issued press releases to local newspapers;

➤ Created a unique market niche by distributing white papers to CEOs;

➤ Rolled out a public speaking program; and

➤ Launched a targeted e-mail and fax campaign.

... All without spending a penny!

Very quickly, Praill and Zander landed 18 interviews, got 11 call backs, and received 7 job offers from choice companies.... NEVER HAVING READ A NEWSPAPER, SURFED A JOB BOARD, GONE TO A NETWORKING EVENT, OR SPENT A PENNY ON CAREER COUNSELORS!

Unbelievable—yet true!

For me personally, the campaign was both a knee-jerk reaction to their having been "right-sized" after the acquisition as well as an opportunity to showcase the Force Multiplier Effect in action. My friends thought I was nuts. No author or job-hunting guru had ever tested their methods in a public forum. No wonder, then, that influential career podcaster Peter Clayton jumped at the chance to interview the 3 of us as we progressed through what amounted to the first *Guerrilla Job Search Boot Camp.*

■ SO WHY THE SECOND EDITION?

For job hunters, a lot has changed in the 4 years since the book debuted in 2005—mostly technology. For example:

➤ When I wrote about an upstart social networking site with lots of promise named LinkedIn, they barely had 25,000 members. I was member 113,709. Today it's a household word. (No other job-search book teaches you that recommendations you post on LinkedIn can entice recruiters to read your profile and call. Of course, there's more to LinkedIn's success than this and we cover it all.)

➤ Likewise, ZoomInfo had less than half a million profiles. Today, any successful job search strategy needs to start with claiming your ZoomInfo profile or making one.

➤ Using Google was a novel tactic, used only by recruiters. Now Google must be a major weapon in your job search arsenal.

➤ Podcasting? The technology had barely been invented.

➤ Blogs were "the voice of the people" and a minor annoyance to mainstream media. Nowadays "real" journalists troll blogs for story ideas.

➤ Monster and CareerBuilder *were* the largest jobs boards (and still are). Now there are also 42,000 micro-boards and you need an efficient way to use them (introducing SimplyHired.com).

➤ MySpace and Facebook didn't exist. Recruiters hang out there all day long now.

In April 2009, MySpace had more than 280 million members; Facebook more than 100 million. When compared to the social networking site MySpace, CareerBuilder and Monsterboard (the 2 best branded job boards) were 45th and 46th, respectively, in web site traffic. Yet in the midst of all this change, most people are still looking for opportunities the way they did 5 years ago. This has serious implications when you're trying to find a job and/or be found by recruiters.

You must think and you must act—differently. Don't worry. We'll show you how!

■ WHAT'S DIFFERENT ABOUT THIS BOOK?

There are 2 key breakthroughs:

1. Our step-by-step marketing-based approach
2. The Force Multiplier Effect

➤ Our Step-by-Step Marketing-Based Approach

Every job search is a sales and marketing campaign. The successful job hunter identifies prospective companies; contacts them by phone, mail, and/or e-mail; and meets in person to convince them to make a job offer. This is no different from what an insurance agent or mortgage broker does to get new clients—it's sales and marketing. Intuitively we all know this.

Yet, the vast majority of job-search books are written by people with no background in sales or marketing—academics, human resource professionals, and career coaches.

By contrast, Jay and I have forgotten more about sales and marketing than most job search experts will ever learn. This is not to brag—being tops at sales and marketing in the career space is like being the tallest midget in the sideshow.

Yet, Jay and I do stand out, with sales and marketing backgrounds unlike any other writing team in the career space today.

Jay is the father of *Guerrilla Marketing*, the best-selling marketing series in history, while I started a successful recruiting practice by making up to 150 cold calls per day, telephoning busy executives, and handling rejection after rejection. My prospecting and closing skills were forged after a year-long baptism by fire and this has helped me negotiate more than $174 million in salaries since 1986.

➤ The Force Multiplier Effect

In *Guerrilla Marketing for Job Hunters: 400 Unconventional Tips, Tricks, and Tactics for Landing Your Dream Job,* job hunters were introduced to the Force Multiplier Effect, the military discipline of using multiple tactics at the same time to create synergy—and overwhelm the target. In modern warfare, it's a proven process of dominating the enemy to win.

Guerrilla Marketing for Job Hunters 2.0 is the sequel designed to help you organize and launch your own Force Multiplier Effect. It explains in step-by-step detail how to use the newest social networking sites and digital tools to perform a precession-guided job search and all-out job-hunting assault on a targeted list of ideal employers. Every tactic in the original book has been put to the test. There is 53 percent new information in this edition. It's all based on feedback from job hunters who bought the book and the newest techniques used by recruiters and employers.

Guerrilla Marketing for Job Hunters 2.0 is filled with worksheets and exercises that make it drop-dead simple for the reader to find a job fast. There are detailed before-and-after sample resumes and cover letters, as well as proven ideas you *can use* to tailor the strategies and tactics to your individual situation.

■ YOUR FAST LANE TO SUCCESS

The quickest way to success is to read the entire book from cover-to-cover—twice. The first time helps you appreciate how all the ideas can fit together and understand why some tactics are strategy specific. The second read is where you start to combine strategies and tactics to customize your personal Force Multiplier Effect. You can't do this piecemeal.

You could jump from chapter to chapter like the stereotypical male driver who wastes time "looking" for his destination, instead of pulling over and asking for directions. Take my advice: in this economy, you don't have time to waste. Follow our map by reading the book from cover-to-over as directed. It's faster!

■ HOW THE BOOK IS SET UP

Each chapter builds on the previous chapter, starting with an understanding of how the changing economy affects you, through to personal branding, resume lingerie, Recruiter*nomics,* and landing the interview and negotiating your package.

Special Benefits

➤ *Drills:* Exercises to stimulate out-of-the-box thinking.

➤ *War Stories:* anecdotes about employing Guerrilla Marketing techniques to land a dream job.

➤ *Guerrilla Tactics:* Dozens of tips and tricks to hasten your hunt.

➤ *Guerrilla Intelligence:* Vignettes by prominent bloggers/ authors designed to boost your creative resolve. They represent the best-of-the-best from the multibillion dollar recruiting industry. Their names are household words in my industry. Each is a thought leader. Many are speakers, trainers, and successful authors. They've been brought together for the first time between the covers of this book because of the unprecedented changes in the employment market. You will quickly learn about the tools and tactics used by successful recruiters to find you and how to apply them in your job-hunting strategy.

Extra Bonuses

➤ *Software:* Links to free software and other special offers like a contact management system—all of which are designed to accelerate your job hunting.

➤ *Web Site and Blog:* State-of-the-moment tactics and articles on social networking through www.gm4jh.com.

➤ *Job Board:* Fully functional and completely anonymous job board where you can profile your accomplishments and have recruiters find you. And you don't need to take down your profile when you find a job—just put it on "do not disturb" or keep the offers coming. It's anonymous and your boss will never know. The job board is provided by www.Recruiterpix.com.

➤ *Back Page:* To help you get hired even faster using this book, there is a collection of free job-search resources waiting for you at the end of the book.

■ WHAT'S IN IT FOR YOU

The keys to landing your dream job, *Guerrilla Marketing for Job Hunters 2.0,* shows you how to take full advantage of strategies and job-hunting techniques that *are not* available as free information on the Internet and were previously only known by a handful of insiders.

You will discover how to:

➤ Leverage ZoomInfo, LinkedIn, MySpace, Facebook, and other social networking sites to take advantage of "the secret lives of top recruiters."

➤ Build a specialized resume that is fun to read, speaks the language of employers, and proves every claim.

➤ Target a job that plays to your strengths and abilities—a job you would do for free, if you weren't getting paid!

➤ Design, launch, and execute a multimodal job-hunting campaign based on the same success principles used by General Norman Schwarzkopf in Operation Desert Storm.

➤ Understand how to articulate your unique strengths in resumes, letters, e-mail, and interviews (while avoiding the typical "resume speak" or "interview babble" that causes hiring managers to guffaw).

➤ Learn how to present your skills in creative new ways that stand out in today's hyper-competitive job market.

➤ Employ little-known search engine optimization tricks used by top headhunters (who have to make placements or starve).

➤ Zero in on the best jobs, at the highest salary—fast—because you'll know exactly what hiring managers really want (this transforms you from "pest" to "guest" in the minds of employers).

Employers will literally be begging to hire you because the book will:

➤ Guide you through a simple method to pick your most marketable skills in 30 seconds or less (as a result, every resume, cover letter, and conversation you send will cut through the noise in any job market like a hot knife through butter).

➤ Lead you through the process of crafting a resume that connects directly to your ideal employer (based on 100 years of principles used in advertising copywriting).

➤ Build a LinkedIn, MySpace, Facebook, and/or ZoomInfo profile that gets found and read, and makes the phone ring with interview offers.

➤ Demonstrate how to use innovations like Google-Local to identify employers.

➤ Detail 21 alternate ways to land an interview, with action steps that you won't find anywhere online.

➤ Include a pre-interview worksheet to structure your research, a daily plan, and a scorecard that enables you to track your progress.

➤ Show you how to start work before you're hired and prove your ability by demonstrating your skills right there in your next interview.

■ WELCOME TO YOUR FUTURE

Guerrilla Marketing for Job Hunters 2.0 is about managing your career as a professional services provider: how to brand yourself, increase your value, and build a rewarding career. We detail how you can mount a multipronged plan of attack that outflanks the competition—that will separate you from the pack quickly and put you on top always—but you have to get on the field.

Guerrilla, this is your Super Bowl, and you know there can be only one winner. Play with your head and your heart. Give this everything you've got and let us know about your successes.

GUERRILLA INTELLIGENCE

Hiding in Plain Sight

John Sumser

Things have really changed. Knowing exactly what you want is more important than ever. In the last generation, you could "parachute" into your new job. Today, it's a guerrilla war . . . clear, focused, targeted, and opportunistic.

While you weren't looking, job hunting became a direct marketing exercise. "Who you know" matters less than "who knows

(continued)

you." The transition between one job and the next is a matter of how quickly you can acquire and harness attention. You are now required to know what you want and where to get it. You are in charge of manufacturing your own luck.

Employers are buried in a sea of resumes they don't want or like. If they acquire yours from a job board, they may consider you an "active job hunter." That's a bad thing. Huge volumes of unwanted and indistinct resumes mean that you have to simultaneously stand out and look like you're not trying to be seen.

That is the essence of a guerrilla job-hunting campaign.

Have you noticed that it gets harder to make sense out of the world every day? The Internet created explosive growth in information sources. Each offers an opinion screaming for your attention. Survival depends on choosing among the sources.

Information overload affects everyone. Our organizations know more and more about themselves. They are less and less able to utilize that knowledge.

The workplace contains members of 4 four generations. Differing preferences for differing communications technologies drive the vast gulf between them. Collaboration and file sharing, the favorite tools of the young, look like cheating and stealing to their elders. The ever-present texting and social networking seem rude and unproductive to the technologically illiterate.

Several things make the workforce older with each passing day. The United States (and the entire industrialized world) produces fewer offspring than it takes to keep the population constant. As a result, the average age of workers in the economy rises continuously. More elders stay at work. Changes in finance, housing, and pensions raise the real retirement age. The differing generational perspectives cloud the certainty needed to make productive decisions.

New technology flows relentlessly into our lives. Cell phones became ubiquitous in under a decade. Universal Wi-Fi dominates public spaces, including your car. Computers merge with phones to create an omnipresent connectedness. Old media dies; new media replaces it. Disruption and change define the era.

Amid all of this, we find our work. The orderly processes of the last generation are evaporating as quickly as newspapers. Old industries disappear while new ones explode on the scene. Looking for work means finding people we want to work with.

It means helping them find us. Guerrilla job hunters stand out from the crowd with purpose.

The goal is disarmingly simple: identify and build relationships with the kind of people who either do what you want to do or want you to do it. Let them know you are available, better than competent, creative, and persistent. Demonstrate your value. Demonstrate it again.

The problem is always the opportunity. Today, so much has changed, from demographics to technology, that getting simple things done can be confusing. An environment like that rewards people who are clear about what they want. It pays big benefits to people who persist. Environments with great potential are confused and noisy.

You are on your own. Exhilaration, autonomy, and self-direction are now the necessities, not the consequences. You find your next engagement by being distinct from the noise.

John Sumser is the CEO of Two Color Hat, a company devoted to the development of Recruiting Strategies. Visit him at www.johnsumser.com. See him on LinkedIn at www.linkedin.com/in/johnsumser.

Chapter 1

Why You Need to Become a Guerrilla Job Hunter

The New Global America

It's not the strongest of the species, nor the most intelligent, that survive; it's the one most responsive to change.

—CHARLES DARWIN

Under siege from layoffs, outsourcing, offshoring, rightsizing, downsizing, and bankruptcies, America is in the midst of a profound business transformation. It is the result of developments in information and communications technologies, changing human values, and the rise of the global knowledge-based economy. The sheer complexity and technical sophistication of business has transformed the job market. Business is becoming knowledge based and technology intensive.

Knowledge workers are the backbone of the United States. They are employed in all sectors of the economy, most prominently in the information technology and communications sectors, but also to a growing extent in health care, manufacturing, education, finance, natural resources, defense, and government—in any field that requires innovation to sustain competitiveness. Competitive advantage is rooted in the new ideas of these skilled workers.

Twenty to forty million Americans change jobs every year. Already reeling from the struggling economy, competition for the remaining jobs is tougher than ever, the rules for getting jobs have changed, and global competition ensures that the rules will change again tomorrow. Many people needlessly drift in and out of dead-end jobs because they don't know which industries have a future or how to present their value in the right terms to the people who have the authority to hire them.

To succeed in this new job market, you must have a plan. Your plan must be clear and detailed in every way. It must also be:

➤ Clever
➤ Results driven
➤ Marketing oriented
➤ Inexpensive to execute
➤ Realistic
➤ Achievable

No government agency, educational institution, or think tank has a genuine crystal ball to make a call on the future; there are simply too many unknown factors when it comes to industry and job creation. One thing is certain, whether you are employed but unhappy, or unemployed and in need of a new opportunity, as a job hunter you are at a strategic fork in the road.

■ THE NEW GLOBAL THEATER

The United States is again at a major crossroads in history. The current "jobless" recovery is a consequence of the economy's rapid evolution from a natural resources- and manufacturing-based economy to a knowledge-based one. We are witnessing the first economic recovery in what has become a full information economy.

For most of the twentieth century, a recession was a cyclical decline in demand—the result of excess inventory that needed to be sold off. People were temporarily laid off, inventory backlogs were reduced, and demand would snap back quickly. As product demand increased, workers returned to their preexisting positions in factories, or they found an equivalent job with another company.

Over the past few years, dramatic advances in information technology have allowed companies to establish tightly integrated demand and supply chains, and to outsource manufacturing and low-end service jobs to save money. Rightly or wrongly, many of the jobs that have entirely disappeared from North America have reappeared in India, China, and Latin America. Rather than furloughs, many people were let go, forcing them to switch industries, sectors, locations, or re-skill to find a new job.

If job growth now depends on the creation of new positions, you should expect a long lag before employment rebounds. Employers incur risks in creating new jobs and require additional time to establish and fill positions. Investment in new capital equipment is no longer a pendulum swinging from recession to recovery and back again.

Instead of resources or land, today capital means human capital. It doesn't take a shoe factory to go into the shoe business these days. Nor do you need raw materials or fleets of trucks. Nike became a shoe industry leader by concentrating on the value-producing capacity of its employees for design, marketing, and distribution know-how. The real capital is intangible: a person's knowledge level, combined with an aptitude for application.

■ WHY YOU NEED TO BE A GUERRILLA

With a radically smaller pool of skilled workers and the increased demand for profits, the original War for Talent of the late 1990s has morphed from a quantitative to a qualitative one, best described as the War for the Best Talent by author Peter Weddle in *Generalship: HR Leadership in a Time of War* (Stamford, CT: Weddle's, 2004). The old "bums-on-seats" mentality of many employers is quickly being replaced by "brains-on-seats."

Faced with stiffer competition and tougher hiring requirements, companies of every sort are becoming single-minded about productivity and bottom-line performance. Consequently, competition for jobs is increasing as management seeks and hires only those persons who appear to have the most potential for helping to boost the company's profits. For many companies, employees are now viewed as a variable cost—hence the term *human capital*—to remain "on the books" only as long as they continue to produce. Looking for an old-fashioned job like the one Dad used to have is a waste of your time—jobs are temporary in the new economy—henceforth you always need to be looking for the next opportunity.

The people who market their talent the best will win!

■ OFFSHORING AND AMERICA'S FUTURE AS A GLOBAL INNOVATOR

During the 2008 presidential election, both President Bush and Democratic presidential candidate Senator Barack Obama had a lot to say about the future of offshoring and what the practice of shipping jobs overseas means for the U.S. economy. Even after the election, Republicans and Democrats disagreed on this subject.

The macroeconomics will be argued for some time to come. As a guerrilla job hunter, you need interest yourself only in the microeconomic impact of offshoring and how it affects your career—in short, which jobs are likely to disappear over time and what industries are likely to benefit. If you think "By America" legislation will save your job—don't bet on it. There are many issues that will take time for President Barack Hussein Obama II to work through Congress, though personally I'm confident he will.

Your job is at risk to offshoring if:

➤ It can be broken down into many smaller tasks that can be redistributed to lower skilled, lower paid workers.

➤ Your company's profits are under constant assault by low-cost competitors.

➤ Someone else with a high-school education can do your job with less than a week's training.

Here's what you can bank on:

➤ The offshoring trend won't stop anytime soon.

➤ Companies will continue to maximize profits and reduce costs.

➤ The government will not solve your career problems—at best it will provide limited retraining assistance.

■ SKILLS THAT WON'T BE OFFSHORED

➤ Leadership Skills

Self-confessed team players are often regarded as "followers" or "hangers-on" by senior management. I know you have been told: "We are supposed to be team players." The human resources department may have told you that, but there's a difference between leaders who can follow others, and those people who always need to follow others. My advice to you—forget about buying another power tie, instead invest in a course on leadership and look for opportunities to test your newfound skills within the company or outside as a volunteer. The ability to lead will be the number one requirement for guerrilla job hunters.

➤ Project Management Skills

Develop the fine art of managing people and projects. Learn how to deal with customers, work with vendors, and interact with management in ways that satisfy the needs and objectives of the organization. This elusive talent is of great value and will support the notion that you are becoming a person who is of great value to your organization. My advice: look into a formal accreditation through the Project Management Institute (www.pmi.org/info/default.asp).

➤ People Skills

If you become the person who can pull teams together, support communication, and make things happen, that will help make your position and perceived value within the organization more visible and support the argument that leaving your job intact is a good business decision. My advice: learn to be likable and how to work a room without looking like a self-obsessed shark.

➤ Communication Skills

Writing and public speaking are critical skills whether you are representing your company or merely trying to sway your boss. A public speaking course will have you on the podium and in the limelight faster than any other single action you can take. Your value and confidence will increase dramatically. My advice: join a Toastmasters networking group near you today.

➤ Sales Skills

There are many jokes about salespeople: what do they really do besides lunch and golf? Bring in the business, that's what, and today that's everyone's responsibility. New business is the lifeblood of every business. When you become known as a rainmaker, the chances of your job being offshored diminish dramatically. My advice: become great at it. Start with a few books like *Five Minutes with VITO* by David Mattson and Anthony Parinello (Beverly Hills, CA: Pegasus Media World, 2008), and *Speak to Win: How to Present with Power in Any Situation* by Brian Tracy (New York: AMACOM, 2008). Devour those books and then take a formal course.

■ JOBS THAT WON'T BE OFFSHORED

There are some jobs that, at the moment, just can't be offshored. Can you imagine offshoring your personal financial planning to a stranger in some foreign country? Are you going to fly to a foreign country just to see a doctor or check yourself into a hospital? Is a salesperson from Asia likely to travel to your home or place of business to sell you insurance, a new car, computer, or clothes? Unlikely.

There is a clear pattern here. Many jobs, because of their personal or "intangible nature, cannot be offshored. Baby boomers are the wealthiest generation ever and scores of new jobs will be created because of their obsession with youth, advances in medicine, bioengineering, and security.

The security issues that were exposed by the 9/11 terrorist activities have spawned whole new industries as the United States looks to secure its borders from terrorists. The banking, travel, agriculture, energy, medical, and other industries vital to our social and economic well-being are vulnerable and not likely to be leaving our shores anytime soon.

This quote from Michael Mandel sums up what's happening:

> The war between the intangible and tangible sectors of the U.S. economy is over—and intangibles have won. Since the economy went into recession a year ago, the industries producing or distributing physical or tangible goods—including construction, manufacturing, retail trade, and transportation—have lost an astounding 1.8 million jobs. That includes a decline of 260,000 jobs in the much-beleaguered auto industry and its dealer network, and a drop of 300,000 in residential construction employment. (BusinessWeek, December 9, 2008)

President Obama's stimulus package in the United States is primarily aimed at the tangible market, which will encourage growth in the intangible market as well. Understanding which jobs are not likely to be offshored and why can help you make informed career choices. I strongly suggest you read *The Rise of the Creative Class: And How It's Transforming Work, Leisure, Community, and Everyday Life* (New York: Basic Books, 2003) if you're having trouble picking an industry with a future.

Industries that won't be offshored include:

➤ *Energy:* There will be an increased push to find new sources of energy. There will be more demand for the people who search for, mine, and develop new sources as well as for people to manage marketing and sales, accounting, human resources, and technology, and the list goes on. Look to California to lead the way in electric cars.

➤ *Preventive health care:* This is a hot area for growth right now and it will continue for years to come as the baby boomers age. The demand for workers applies to all levels and to suppliers as well. Here's something to think about. The cover story in *BusinessWeek*, September 25, 2006, concluded, "Since 2001, the health-care industry has added 1.7 million jobs. The rest of the private sector? None."

➤ *Security:* In addition to antiterrorism needs, there is growing concern among companies to protect their greatest asset: information. Additionally, employers are increasingly concerned about the backgrounds of people they are hiring, which will give rise to investigative services.

➤ *Military:* Need I say more? The demand will increase as will the educational requirements for people looking for the jobs in communications and intelligence.

➤ *Government:* At every level—municipal, state, and federal—demands will only get bigger. Leadership will be in high demand as will bilingualism in many jurisdictions.

➤ *Insurance:* The more uncertainty there is in a society, the greater the demand for insurance. Providers will continue to need sales agents, claims adjusters, researchers, customer service people, accountants, and lawyers.

➤ *Consumer financial services:* As more people own homes, cars, and so on, demand is increasing for loan agents and title company workers. With losses growing in company-sponsored 401(k) plans, more people are taking greater control over their retirement savings and seeking investment counselors and brokers to manage their money.

➤ *Agriculture:* Farms employ hundreds of thousands of people in almost every capacity imaginable, from marketing and public relations professionals to genetic scientists (www.usda.gov/wps/portal/usdahome).

➤ *Biotechnology/pharmaceutical:* Greater need for prescription drugs will increase demand in these sectors. As more and more money is dedicated to gene and cloning research, opportunities will grow in the biotech industry.

The prospects in your area of the country will vary, but this list provides a snapshot of what will be happening around the country.

■ YOUR SIX CAREERS

William Bridges, author of *JobShift—How to Prosper in a Workplace without Jobs* (Philadelphia: Perseus Books Group, 1995), contends that the United States is undergoing a process of "dejobbing"—an end to the traditional job as we know it. "The old pattern of hiring and keeping large numbers of full-time, long-term workers on the grounds that they may be needed in the future is harder and harder for companies to do," Bridges says.

Twenty-five years ago, the U.S. Labor Department looked at the workforce and at trends in the job market and announced that people will have as many as 5 or 6 careers in their lifetime (*Anything Goes! What I've Learned from Pundits, Politicians, and Presidents*, by Larry King, New York: Warner Books, 2000). Who would have thought they'd get that one right! I certainly wouldn't have, yet I am a prime example.

I started my career in retail, moved into banking, and then into executive search and placement, all before I was 25. Twenty years later, I am still in the executive search and placement industry, but even that career has evolved from a specialty in retail to the construction and property management industries and now into the high-tech marketplace. You could even argue that writing a book is yet another career.

Not long ago, society expected an individual to spend a lifetime at one company. Those expectations have changed. Now you are expected to change jobs every few years.

To thrive in this environment, you need to adopt a guerrilla marketing mindset. You need to think of yourself as a tightly knit package of capabilities—a value-added product to sell around the globe.

■ GUERRILLA MARKETING IS THE KEY TO YOUR SUCCESS

I can tell you from personal experience that the most qualified job hunter is rarely the one who wins. The positions invariably go to the person who does the best job at positioning himself or herself as the solution to an employer's problem.

The dramatic changes we are witnessing in the marketplace mean that the tried-and-true methods of finding a job will no longer suffice. They should remain a solid part of your plan, but they don't provide an adequate amount of exposure to potential employers.

In 1997, Tom Peters introduced the concept of Brand U in his book *Re-Imagine!* (London: Dorling Kindersley, 2003). At the time, self-branding was an assertive marketing concept best reserved for high-flying techies and senior executives who wanted to maximize the financial returns of their biggest asset—their career. Today, personal branding is a matter of survival.

Becoming a guerrilla job hunter is the only way to consistently move your career forward. The market is geared toward those who effectively brand and market themselves as the ultimate commodity across multiple distribution channels. Winning the War for Talent requires you to become a guerrilla job hunter.

GUERRILLA INTELLIGENCE

Emotional Intelligence and Your Career Portfolio

Anita Martel, RGR

Having an up-to-date emotional intelligence assessment has become one of your greatest assets in your job search strategy. Why? Because by doing so you've reduced the risk the hiring manager has in hiring *YOU*.

An emotional intelligence assessment gives you concrete and valid evidence that complements your resume and provides tangible proof to a potential employer. Hiring managers are risk averse, and by making their job virtually risk free you have just given yourself a leg up on the competition. The added plus to having your emotional intelligence assessed is that you can speak with complete confidence during an interview. You gain valuable insight that you can use to your benefit. By knowing your strong points, you can further build on them and use them to position yourself advantageously. In addition, by knowing your weaker points, you can specifically concentrate on improving them. It is strongly recommended that you retake the test at 2- to 3-year intervals to reevaluate your progress over time.

In the workplace, an ever-increasing number of employers are choosing to use emotional intelligence assessments to ensure a greater fit of potential and current employees within their company culture. It is becoming more and more obvious to today's companies that their workforce can no longer be managed in the traditional style. That is, today's employee is no longer

(continued)

just a part of the puzzle that completes the big picture but has become the process with which to do it. Organizations are now filled with highly educated knowledge workers that as a team have become this process. This is in essence what will give one company a distinct competitive advantage over another, and today's companies are specifically looking for that edge.

On the personal side of things, none of us live in a vacuum, and we can clearly see how our personal life always ends up trickling into our professional life at one time or another. We develop relationships with everyone around us. How well we manage those relationships can have a significant impact on both our professional as well as our personal lives. Having vibrant, healthy relationships has become the core competitive advantage in today's workplace.

So what exactly is emotional intelligence? "Emotional intelligence is the unique repertoire of emotional skills that a person uses to navigate the everyday challenges of life" (Multi-Health Systems, 2008). It is the awareness of one's emotions and the ability to use those emotions to strengthen one's performance. Simply put, emotional intelligence is often referred to as common sense or street smarts.

Research has demonstrated that an individual's emotional intelligence is often a more accurate predictor of success than that person's IQ. No matter how intellectually intelligent someone is, their success is still governed by how well they can communicate their ideas and interact with their peers. As opposed to IQ, which is said to be set early on in life, your emotional intelligence can be substantially strengthened and developed with appropriate training and thus can be improved considerably. Since emotional intelligence is elastic, those who lack it can gain it, and those who have it can augment and develop it further.

Many emotional intelligence tests exist on the market and all claim to be the best. I have researched a great number of them and keep coming back to one in particular. The BarOn EQ-I assessment is by far the most comprehensive on the market. It assesses interpersonal and intrapersonal skills, stress management, adaptability, and general mood with many other areas within these categories. Several different reports can be generated including a leadership one, and its versatility allows individuals to track and work on their emotional intelligence. A company wanting to have an accurate predictor of best performers or a comparison/fit for potential employees can also use it. It is used worldwide, can be produced in several different languages, and has been scientifically validated. It can be taken online and completed in about 40 minutes. You receive a clear and easy-to-read written interpretation of your results, recommendations on what to do to increase your emotional intelligence, and a debriefing session with a certified administrator.

Remember, you are creating your career portfolio and whatever you can add to it that will put you a step ahead of the competition is essential. All good career portfolios include a summary resume, a thorough detailed resume, a number of references, and an up-to-date emotional intelligence assessment.

Anita Martel is a partner of Perry-Martel International and a Certified BarOn EQ-I administrator. She is devoted to helping leaders, individuals, and teams increase their effectiveness and attain their full potential. For more information or to take the test, e-mail anitam@perrymartel.com.

Part

I

Your Guerrilla Mind

Chapter 2

Personal Branding Guerrilla Style

Shape Up Your Brand with Attitude

If Christopher Columbus had turned back, no one would have blamed him. Of course, no one would have remembered him either.

—UNKNOWN AUTHOR

Embrace this fact: it's rarely the best qualified person who wins the most coveted position. Instead, it is often the person who "packages" themself best to meet the needs of employers. This all comes down to how you look on paper initially and the attitude you bring to your job search. You have 100 percent control over both. We'll discuss branding guerrilla style first, then your attitude.

■ "YOU INC."—YOUR PERSONAL BRAND

More than ever in our history, huge value is being leveraged from smart ideas and the winning technology and business models they create. In the years to come, as companies strive to hire fewer but better people, employers will try harder than they ever have to attract and retain smart, boldly entrepreneurial overachievers. In the new world of work, value is not salary—not for the employer, not for you. With millions of dollars at stake, an employer's search for an employee will be value-focused, not salary-driven.

15

As a job hunter, you need to comprehend that the production of value is the most important criterion for an employer when hiring. Articulating your value is your key to successful job hunting; it separates you from all the other job hunters. Understand, value is not salary; worth does not flow from a job title. Knowing what's important to a company means looking beyond job descriptions and compensation tables, especially today when sudden changes and uncertainty are the norm.

You need to comprehend:

➤ What value is a company expecting from an employee's contribution?

➤ How do you communicate your value to an employer?

Especially for management and senior positions, companies are rarely looking to fill in a box on a standard employee recruitment form; they are looking for something nebulous and more important. They are searching for a person who can deliver a quality, not a quantity, someone who can explode outward from an open-ended initiative-driven space.

Qualities are difficult to find, measure, or test, and you don't find these qualities by searching for specific salary levels—the qualities that make up the new value table are money-resistant, as initially explained in *Career Guide for the High-Tech Professional: Where the Jobs Are Now and How to Land Them,* by David Perry (Franklin Lakes, NJ: Career Press, 2004). The new value table (Table 2.1) goes beyond skill sets and resumes.

In its simplest form, Table 2.1 represents the base elements of your personal "brand." Building your brand—making a "name for yourself"—need not be expensive.

➤ Create Your Brand Guerrilla Style

Personal branding is not about projecting a false image. It is about understanding what is unique about you—your accomplishments, experience, attitude—and using that to differentiate yourself from other job hunters. Your brand is your edge.

Do you buy generic beer, clothes, cars? Do you buy any no-name large ticket items at all? Not likely. If you are like most people, you buy a brand because of the security and peace of mind that come from the quality and reliability of a known brand. Employers do the exact same thing when they hire people.

Table 2.1 New Value Table™

Employer's Value Requirements	Your Quality That Counts
Create new intellectual wealth for my company; add to my intellectual assets.	A consuming desire to make something new; to cut a new path rather than take a road.
High-energy enthusiasm for the job, regardless of the hours worked.	Work is a game—an integral, vibrant part of his or her life.
Not only is money not the most important issue—it's beside the point.	Internal pride to leave a "legacy signature" on their work, rather than strive for a paycheck.
Enduring performance.	An ability to stay and finish the race, because not finishing is inconceivable emotionally.
"Think around corners" to solve problems creatively.	Have an inner voice saying "There's always a way [to create a technology fix: make a deal]."
Bring up-to-date professionalism into every fray.	Contain a desire to grow professionally—to become the best person he or she can be: invest in themselves.
Ever-increasing contribution.	The key to inner pleasure is recognized as making an individual contribution.
Identify and develop values for your company.	Instinctive grasp and exploitation of today's real value: the intangible capital of brand image, staff talent, and customer relationships.
Challenge the status quo.	Willingness and courage to speak the truth when you see a conflict.

Personal branding is critical for guerrilla marketers because:

➤ Employers are looking for results.

➤ Your results demonstrate your qualities, which satisfy an employer's value requirements.

➤ Employers won't buy generic employees.

➤ Employers will buy the intangible qualities implied by your brand (you are like Nike, too).

➤ How to Create Your Brand

Personal branding is about making yourself stand out so that people trust you and are interested in you. Guerrillas do this by leveraging their previous employers' brand (names, slogans, and logos) to create an identity that is memorable and desirable to the people they want to reach.

For your cover letter, this means naming the projects you worked on or the clients you sold to. Be specific. Be detailed. Sell the sizzle *and* the steak.

For your resume, it may mean taking the logos (with permission, of course) of the companies you worked for or the product you developed and placing them on your resume for extra punch. Nothing will get an employer's attention faster than a well-known brand's logo, especially if it is a competitor or a coveted account (this reaction is known as the "halo effect").

What would make the person reading your resume take notice of you? Could it be your training at another company? Might it be the companies you have sold to? Were you responsible for a major product that the employer might recognize? There are likely thousands of images you could use. You only want to put in 5, so choose the 5 your reader is most likely to be interested in. Putting in more than 5 makes it too crowded.

Table 2.2 is a list of suggestions for you to use in choosing your images.

Let's get right into how to choose your most marketable skills and write about your accomplishments to reflect your brand. We will use the output you produce in this section with the clever design of your resume(s) in Chapter 5. You will reuse the info in LinkedIn, Facebook, MySpace, and blogs.

■ EFFECTIVE BRANDING IS ABOUT SELLING WHAT MATTERS

This section is designed to help you do 2 things that are essential to branding yourself:

1. Determine your marketable skills, and
2. Find achievements that prove your claims.

The data you assemble here will help you write your Guerrilla Resume later (in the Chapter 5). DO NOT SKIP THIS STEP! In fact, if you can't find the time to do these 2 things, please stop reading now and ask for your money back—this book will be of no use to you.

Ready? Let's begin.

First, we will . . .

Table 2.2   Resume Image Suggestion List

Position Sought	Reader's Interest	Suggested Graphics
Sales	Who have you sold to? Are there any major accounts you know they would like to have or would recognize as difficult to get that would make you look like a superstar?	Logos of the companies you have worked for or the major customers you have sold. Perhaps a product you sold if it's more recognizable than the company's logo.
Engineering	Who have you worked for? What major product did you help design?	Logos of your employers or customers. A logo or photo of the product you designed.
Marketing	What brands have you helped create? Where have you gotten press coverage for your products? What trade shows have you worked?	Logos of your employers or of the newspapers or magazines you have had coverage in. Media quotes you were responsible for.
Finance	Have you done an IPO on Nasdaq? Have you secured funding from a major venture capital firm?	Logos of your employers or significant partners with whom you have negotiated.
Administration	How have you increased efficiencies?	Logos of your employers.

➤ Determine Your Marketable Skills

Your Guerrilla Resume will highlight your most valuable and attractive skills in such a way that employers are more likely to call you. So, what are your most marketable skills? Complete the following 2 exercises:

Exercise 1: What do you do well? What do you do better and more easily than other people? Is it the work you're doing now? Something you studied in school? A hobby? Take out a pad of paper and write down your answers, no matter how unrelated they are to work. The goal is to get your creative juices flowing.

Let's take a fictitious job seeker, Sally, and write down what she does well: public speaking, sales, client service, managing projects, solving computer problems, managing others, speaking French.

Exercise 2: What do you enjoy doing? What skills do you most enjoy using on the job or in school right now? What would you do even if you weren't paid? Write your answers down.

Here are Sally's answers to this second question: public speaking, bicycling, client service, solving computer problems, baking cookies, managing others, speaking French, serving as a Girl Scout leader, hiking, writing.

Now, you'll see that Sally's answers to question 2 produced a different set of skills from question 1. That's okay, but you will notice several skills that appeared in both lists. That's better than okay—that is exactly what we're after!

When you write down a skill that you enjoy doing (question 2), which you have also written down because you do it well (question 1), *highlight* it in some way.

Let's go back and highlight Sally's skills listed in response to question 2 that were also answers to question 1: *public speaking,* bicycling, *client service, solving computer problems,* baking cookies, managing others, *speaking French,* serving as a Girl Scout leader, hiking, writing.

For Sally, our fictitious example, the skills she does well *and* enjoys doing are: public speaking, client service, solving computer problems, and speaking French.

Pretty simple, huh? By answering these 2 questions, Sally now knows more about herself than roughly 90 percent of job seekers who don't know what they do well or what they want to do.

Now, complete this exercise for yourself. Write down your answers to questions 1 and 2, then underline those skills found in both lists. These are skills you do well and enjoy doing. You may come up with 3, 4, 7, or more skills.

You're almost done. Now, choose the 2 or 3 skills you think will be most attractive to the hiring authority reading your resume. These are your *most marketable skills*. They will form a skeleton around which you build your entire Guerrilla Resume.

WARNING

This is the most important step in the process of writing your Guerrilla Resume. Do not go on without completing this exercise. Stop. Do it now. Write now!

Why? Because once you know what your most marketable skills are, you can highlight your most relevant experience, which will help you find the job that's best for you. It all flows in order, like painting your garage—first the prep work, then the painting.

Okay, now we're ready for the second part of this 2-step process.

➤ Find Achievements That Prove Your Claims

What achievements/accomplishments prove the marketable skills you listed? For each skill, write down at least 3 things you did that you're proud of along with their specific results.

Use facts. Be specific. The more exact the better—figures, dates, percentages, and so on. What have you done to increase productivity, profits, efficiency, sales, and so on? Your achievements can be from paid or volunteer employment, school projects, or even hobbies. As long as they're relevant to the work you want to do, you may include them in your resume.

Here are some more examples to illustrate what you should or shouldn't write for achievements.

First, here's what NOT to write. These nonspecific achievements prove *nothing*:

➤ Managed numerous projects to success.

➤ Provided sales and customer service to house accounts.

➤ Wrote reports and correspondence for busy executives.

Now, here's what to write. These specific achievements *prove* your skills:

➤ Managed 100 percent of 27 projects to successful completion in 2006, finishing an average of 10 days early on budgets ranging up to $256,850. Built and led teams of up to 34 staff.

➤ Increased sales $456,000 in 1 year by managing and developing 34 house accounts.

➤ Saved $52,000 after writing 3 employee manuals that standardized operations. Also wrote more than 85 reports for a team of 23 executives, meeting all deadlines.

See the difference?

It may help to interview yourself as a newspaper reporter would, and ask yourself a series of questions (Why, How, When, Who, What) about the things you've done that you're proudest of.

For example, let's say that in your last job you overhauled an Oracle database. For most job seekers, they would stick this phrase in their resume: "Cleaned up Oracle database."

And then ... nothing would happen because language like that tells readers nothing at all about your value on the job. The phone won't ring because employers won't be interested.

Instead, ask yourself questions about your achievements, like these:

➤ *Why* were you assigned to clean up the database?

➤ *How* did you do it?

➤ *When* did you do it?

➤ *Who* did you do it for?

➤ *What* happened as a result of your efforts?

Your answers will often lead to surprising results, which will serve as the basis for a very powerful Guerrilla Resume.

Example Answers

➤ *Why* did I clean up the database? One of our clients was ready to take their business elsewhere because a database we built for them kept failing.

➤ *How* did I do it? By working 12-hour days for 2 weeks straight.

➤ *When* did I do it? In 2006.

➤ *Who* did I do it for? Our company's #1 client, which represented $14 million in annual revenue.

➤ *What* happened as a result of my efforts? The client was happy and stayed with us.

Now, here's how you can rewrite the boring statement—Cleaned up Oracle database—to include the specific results of your actions: "Helped retain $14-million account by working 12-hour days for 2 weeks to clean up Oracle database for firm's top client in 2006."

See the difference?

A few sentences like these are all you need in your Guerrilla Resume to make the phone ring with interview requests from employers who are anxious to meet you.

I think you'll agree that this is powerful stuff. It really is easy to uncover specific results in your work history by asking yourself these questions.

Here are 2 shortcuts to help you create a list of achievements for inclusion in your resume.

➤ Shortcut 1

Write down all the *money you've saved or generated* for employers in every job. What have you done to increase overall profits in your current and prior jobs? *Be specific!*

Do NOT write, "Sold products and met quotas." Write, "Sold $516,750 in 1 year while exceeding all quarterly quotas by an average of 21 percent."

Do NOT write, "Produced substantial savings." Write, "Saved $45,890 in 45 days."

➤ Shortcut 2

You may find it difficult to quantify your work in terms of dollars. You may even find it impossible. If so, try to come at it from a different angle.

Write down everything you've done to *increase efficiency* or *save time.* Time is literally money to employers. Perhaps you wrote an employee training manual, or created a way to back up data faster each night, or devised a way to speed up shipping out on the loading dock. Anything and everything is fair game here.

The key is to figure out exactly how many hours you saved per week, then assign a dollar value to those hours. Then annualize that figure to get the highest, most impressive number. This requires you to do one very important thing: you must *do the thinking* for the reader of your resume. It's your responsibility as the author of your resume to connect the dots for the reader. Make it easy for the reader to picture you as an excellent employee without thinking.

For example, say you created a process that saves 10 hours a week. How much does your employer pay someone to do what you just automated? If it's $10 an hour, add another 30 percent to cover insurance and other benefits, and you'll get a figure of $13 an hour. Multiply that by 10 hours per week and you've just saved $130 per week, $520 per month, $27,040 per year.

So, you can write this eye-catching sentence in your resume: "Saved $27,040 annually by automating widget process."

Now, here's the fun part. When you save $27,000 here and $27,000 there, pretty soon you're talking real money. Include all these money totals in your Guerrilla Resume.

When you fill your Guerrilla Resume with specific achievements that are quantified in dollars, guess what? You turn yourself from just another job seeker, crying "Please give me a job!" to a walking, talking, blue-chip stock, who says: "Hire me at $50,000 and I can deliver a 400 percent return on your investment because I've routinely saved $200,000 annually at my prior jobs."

While ordinary job seekers are crying out, "Please give me a job!" your resume will be saying, "Hiring me is like buying money at a discount." Other job seekers come across as supplicants, begging for work, while you come across as a superhero minus the cape.

Put another way, you will put an immediate halt to the "apples versus apples" comparison that employers make when considering ordinary job seekers. It's now "apples versus oranges"—and you're the only orange. You're changing the rules of the game and putting them in your favor—kind of like picking up a Monopoly board and tipping all the money, hotels, and houses into your lap.

Nice, eh? And it all starts when you stop thinking of yourself as an ordinary job seeker and start thinking of yourself as a living, breathing investment.

Here's a final tip on how to uncover the dollar value for good things you've done on the job. It's this: don't be afraid to call up current and former coworkers to ask for help. You may not know how much money your top client brought in last year or what the budget was on the X-14 project you managed, but someone in the accounting or marketing department might. Leave no stone unturned in your search for accomplishments.

Let me reemphasize this critical point: when you do the thinking for the reader and include specific results in your Guerrilla Resume, good things will happen in your job search.

If you do nothing more than use the instructions in this chapter to come up with at least 3 solid, specific achievements for each job you've held, you will immediately improve your resume. You should start getting more calls from employers to interview. And you will have received full value for your purchase of this book.

But this is only the beginning. You're not just going to improve your resume. You're going to create an eye-popping Guerrilla Resume and cover letter that will produce rapid results in your job search in Chapter 5.

GUERRILLA INTELLIGENCE

Social Media and the Guerrilla Job Hunter
Dennis Smith

Why is our brand such an important part of our job-searching efforts? Because our personal brand creates a strong, consistent association between us and the perceived value we have to offer an employer.

And, like it or not, our brand precedes us in the interview process. That's right. Think of it this way: long before the wide-eyed hunter focuses his scope on the massive profile of the hairy beast, he hears the thumping sounds of the gorilla (Note: Gorilla, not Guerrilla) methodically beating his chest in the jungle. The gorilla-noise (and his reputation) precedes the inevitable meeting.

Similarly, you—like all job seekers—send signals to prospective employers. They precede you—by a jungle mile. However, the difference between the aimless job hunter and the guerrilla job hunter is this: *a carefully crafted brand.* It whets the appetite of the potential employer, laying the foundation for a dynamic, chest-thumping interview supported by well-defined facts of goals smashed and lessons learned.

Besides a knock-your-socks-off *Guerrilla Resume,* there are few tools as compelling as social media to help the guerrilla

(continued)

job hunter spread the word about his or her carefully crafted brand. Spanning 29 countries and 17,000 Internet users, recent research by Universal McCann found that almost 60 percent of Internet users are members of an online community such as LinkedIn, YouTube, Facebook, or WirelessJobs.com. Even more mind-blowing: 78 percent of Internet users read blogs (up from 66 percent in the previous study). No longer confined to the realm of the college set, today's online social networks are an extremely powerful platform to connect with colleagues and industry professionals. As someone once said, "If you are not online, you don't exist."

Chances are, then, long before you arrive for a personal interview, your hiring decision makers will look you up online. *Will they find you?* If so, what will they find? Are you sharing your knowledge in professional forums? Connecting with like-minded professionals who share your passions? Establishing yourself as the resident expert in your profession? Is your resume up to date? Does it match the profiles you highlight in your social networks? Who is in your network? And most importantly, does your online persona really reflect the brand you've been working so hard to create?

A lot of questions—all worth asking. Undoubtedly, this information works together to represent your online digital footprint. More importantly, it contributes to how a potential employer "sees" you. As a savvy guerrilla job hunter, you understand this, and you can carefully position yourself to be "findable" online.

Need an easy place to start? Here are 10 social media activities that will help you—even if you are an Internet novice—join the online conversation and begin spreading the word about YOU:

Online Networks

1. Look for online networks that share your career focus, volunteer interests, geographical area, professional associations, or alma mater. Join them, offer to guest post on their blogs, participate in their forums, and share your expertise.

2. Get a LinkedIn account for your professional network. Then, create a group on LinkedIn focused on your profession (e.g., "Wireless Jobs" group has 11k+ members). Invite the experts in your profession to join the group.

3. Get a Facebook account (smart job hunters use the massive demographics of Facebook [100M+] to their benefit). Ditto with Twitter (use it to follow the online conversations about your profession—your company—YOU).

4. Check out podcasts and iTunes and listen to thought leaders—not just in your professional arena, but in other areas as well.

5. Get a StumbleUpon.com and/or Digg.com account for voting, and a *del.icio.us* account for social bookmarking.

Blogs

6. Create a blog and begin interacting with and reaching out to your target audience (e.g., CrunchWireless.com).

7. Comment on other people's blogs. This is a great way for others to get to know you, especially when your ideas are pertinent and meaningful.

8. Promote others—their blogs, articles, and ideas—on your site.

9. Don't let your blog go static. Keep it fresh with a daily mix (or at a minimum, 3 times a week) of information, opinion, interviews, and lists. Throw in an occasional self-recorded YouTube video and you'll cement your brand quickly in the eyes of your audience.

10. Subscribe to Google's web-based feed reader to keep up with the blogs and news pertaining to your industry (reader.google.com).

Tim Sanders said, "In the twenty-first century, our success will be based on the people we know." Guerrilla job hunters get this—and because they understand that relationships serve as a predictor of our success, they include social media as a standard part of their job-search strategy.

Make no mistake—no other investment opportunity can compare with the global reach of the Internet in your efforts to evangelize the value of your brand. Social media will help you use the power of the network to gain opportunities and build relationships. In other words, it will help you get the

(continued)

attention—your brand in the crosshairs—of the people with whom you need to connect.

_____

Dennis Smith web site address: www.WirelessJobs.com e-mail link: dennis@ wirelessjobs.com.

Okay, put the exercise and results away for now. We'll be using them soon enough, but first let's talk about what really matters most when you're job hunting: attitude.

■ ATTITUDE CHECK

Employers want to hire positive people as much as they need to hire people who are competent. If you have both characteristics, the employer's decision becomes obvious. Most employers I know, including yours truly, would rather have an employee with a great attitude and some related work experience, than a more experienced one with a poor attitude. Why is that, and how do you show it?

➤ The Importance of a Can-Do Attitude

Attitude rates bigger than ever with interviewers these days because employers are facing a future of constantly accelerating change and need to look aggressively for ways to expand, grow, and stay in business. They are seeking job hunters who can have a positive impact on the company's results. Employers want employees who:

➤ Believe they can change the impossible into the possible.

➤ Do things better, smarter, and faster as a natural force in their life.

➤ Can find new ways to accomplish something without a map.

➤ Will relentlessly search until they find a way.

Interviewers spot "can-do" people immediately. They're the ones who can describe the obstacles they faced and how they overcame them—in fine detail. Can-doers are also quick to admit they haven't been victorious every time, but they analyze each failure and take away valuable lessons from it. That's what employers are hoping for, and they'll make every effort to hire job hunters who can demonstrate that they have gone the extra mile, who are ready to shoulder a little more responsibility when needed, and who do not automatically expect to be rewarded for it.

Most employers have had the pleasant experience of hiring a job seeker who had something nebulous they couldn't quite put their finger on, but that encouraged them to hire the inexperienced person with a bounce in his step, and a desire to win. Every employer who has done that is bound and determined to find the next diamond in the rough—where the rough is the experience, not the attitude.

Employers hire people because they want to grow their business. If you approach your job search with a negative attitude that conveys you just want a paycheck, employers will pick it up quickly and react accordingly.

Guerrillas leap tall buildings . . . because their attitude proclaims "can-do," and they do not let the naysayers of the world get them down. Pop singer Chris Daughtry sold 2.4 million of his self-titled album after losing out to Taylor Hicks on season 5 of American Idol. He continued to push forward and found the success he wanted. Daughtry's a role model for the can-do attitude.

You must decide right now to accept all setbacks as temporary. If you were good enough to be interviewed at a company, then you doubtless have what it takes to land a similar position with another company. It is your attitude in reaction to an event that colors your success.

GUERRILLA INTELLIGENCE

Job Hunting and Dating

Dave Howlett, RHB

Looking for the perfect job is like searching for that perfect partner. Some of the best job and love matches are set-ups. So how on earth can you get people to say nice things about you when you aren't in the room? How can you be confident they'll smile and say, "Hey, I know someone who would be a great match!"

Recently I chatted with an executive assistant who works at a large wealth management firm. She told me she had been with

(continued)

the company 3 years. She confided that she had been referred by a friend who also worked there. I asked her if she also had friends she would also refer into the company.

"Some of them," she replied.

"Why wouldn't you refer all of your friends?" I enquired.

She shrugged, "I guess some would embarrass me."

You Need to Make Others Look Good

Word-of-mouth and referrals happen when your friends know you aren't going to embarrass them. If you possess "an interesting personality," it's likely your friends won't bring up your name. Think about it; they can envision their friend (or boss) saying, "Who the heck referred this person?" The real issue is that your friends are too polite. They won't tell you your pants are 1 inch above your ankles and that your jokes are offensive. So take some guerrilla control.

Memorize 2 questions and start asking them to everyone: "What is it I do well? If I could do one thing better, what would it be?" Keep a journal and look for trends. A client told me his greatest takeaway from one of my workshops was "Never turn down a breath mint." Remember, your friends have been interviewing you for years; they know exactly what you need to do to improve. You just need to get them to complain to your face.

Assume Everyone Is Intelligent

Ask any woman how she feels about going on a second date with a guy who went on and on about himself and then acted in a rude manner with the waiter. A managing director told me she talks with her front-office staff after interviewing a consultant/job seeker. She trusts her staff to inform her how you acted around people you didn't think were worthy of your courtesy. That's indicative of how you will "fit" into her company. Who do you consider beneath you?

Have a Passion for What You Do

I have divorced friends who have a habit of making unkind comments about their ex and about marriage in general. "All women are after my money." "Men are such pigs." Then they ask me to keep an eye out for any dating opportunities. I am honestly reluctant to do this. Dumped from your last job? Worked for a psychotic boss? Feeling sorry for how your life has turned out? Find a good friend (or a counselor) to discuss your troubles. But *don't* use your next date or your next job interview to moan and vent.

Get Over Yourself

Pastor Joe Palusak is an extraordinary guy I met 7 years ago. Joe ministered to the needs of police and firefighters at the World Trade Center after 9/11. He shared with me a sentence that I have said aloud each week since then: "You would care less what other people thought about you if you knew how little time they spent thinking about you." Write this down and keep it on your desk.

In job seeking and date seeking, the days seem like weeks and the weeks seem like months. You start to think, "She didn't return my call because of something I did," or "They didn't like my resume and that's why they're not calling." Don't give up because one person or one company doesn't get back to you right away. Until I hear a client say, "No, we don't need you this year," I always assume they are busy doing other things (and it's not about me).

You've got too much time on your hands. Get over yourself. Keep busy, keep the pipeline filled, volunteer at a school or immigrant-assistance program and put your experience and knowledge into helping others. Join a Toastmasters group and meet amazing and motivated people. (www.toastmasters.org). How would you answer this question on your next date/job interview? "So, you got divorced 2 years ago, what have you been doing since then?"

One Last Thing

Start asking couples how they met. Start asking employees how they got their job. You'll find a lot of similarities. Opportunities are around us every day. Treat job hunting like looking for a date. Make other people look good and they'll send leads your way. Then tuck your new business card inside your wedding invitation.

Dave Howlett is founder and managing director of www.realhumanbeing.org. RHB hosts seminars on networking, sales, and company culture. He can be reached at dhowlett@realhumanbeing.org.

■ HOW TO STAY MOTIVATED

Everyone acknowledges that rejection is a fact of life when you are job hunting. It pushes all the wrong buttons—not once—but sometimes hundreds of times. What is even worse than the rejection letters is dead silence—the lack of acknowledgment that you even exist. The fundamental truth of job hunting is that it's not pleasant. It is all about being rejected and ignored. Eventually the stress gets to everyone. You can lessen the sting and develop that critical can-do attitude by taking the following 4 empowering steps.

➤ Step 1: Take Charge of Your Job Hunt

Only you know your strengths and weaknesses. Only you know what you really enjoy doing. Only you know where you want to work and why. Only you know how you can help a prospective employer. Only you can articulate your interests and strengths in a cover letter and resume. Don't let anyone else do your resume or your cover letter. You need to do it yourself. You can ask people to review it but it must come from you—even if you are receiving outplacement counseling. Come interview time, you need to mirror the person you have portrayed on paper or you will strike out. You can sell yourself better if you own every word on the page.

➤ Step 2: Adopt a Tough Mindset

Surround yourself with positive people. Get rid of anyone who sympathizes with your plight and is eager to commiserate. You do not need sympathy. You need support, and there is a huge difference. Supportive, helpful, optimistic family, friends, and reputable professionals remind you of your strengths and give needed encouragement and feedback. Sympathizers zap your energy and self-esteem. Staying inspired requires the input of inspiring people, so find a trusted confidante who can help you polish your presentation, provide moral support, and strategize.

➤ Step 3: Stay Focused

You need to feed your opportunity funnel in the same way that salespersons feed their sales funnel: so many leads, so many calls, so many interviews. Like a good salesperson, you need to track and record your efforts. You must keep a record to show yourself that you are making progress. If you can visually see progress, you will have an extra incentive to keep at it. If you've completed 10 calls today, then record it. If you have sent out a batch of networking letters, note that, too. I encourage my friends to chart their accomplishments on the wall as I do because "seeing is believing." Note how many interviews you've scheduled, calls you've made, callbacks you've noted, and research you've completed. It is critical to be able to view your job-hunting funnel to ensure you have adequate leads to provide a steady supply of interviews.

➤ **Step 4: Think Positive**

As Henry Ford once said, "Whether you think you can or whether you think you can't, you're right." It is important for you to believe you'll succeed. You must convince yourself, through your own self-talk, that you are successful. Write out positive affirmations about your job-hunting skills such as the following:

➤ I interview well.

➤ I come across with confidence in interviews.

➤ I find the perfect positions that use and grow all my talents.

Keep your statements in the present, not the future tense. Read your list every day. Post it at eye level as a subliminal motivator. You can be your own worst enemy or your biggest fan. Give yourself credit for what you've completed and don't beat yourself up over what you haven't yet accomplished. Work at a steady pace with your end goal in mind. Your new job, and the burst of self-esteem that comes with it, will be worth all the effort. I'm not kidding. Start doing this right now.

Guerrilla Tips

➤ *Regard every "no" as a "not today" and a step closer to "yes."* This book explains how to repackage and repitch yourself until the persuasion works.

➤ *Monitor your self-talk.* Only you have the power to change your attitude and your perspective. Keep a vigilant eye out for negative self-talk. Notice what you are saying to yourself as you move through your search. Your mental dialogue can boost your esteem or drag you down.

➤ *Measure yourself by your own standards.* Avoid comparing yourself with others. People aren't going to tell you things are tough in their lives. When you ask how they are doing, they usually will say, "Great, never better," which will make you feel like crap. That's just their game face; they are not doing any better than you are. You are the only person you need to please. If you stick with your plan, you will achieve success.

➤ *When someone suggests you try something new—do it.* Guerrillas aren't afraid to try new things and fail. I recently had a woman tell me that none of my ideas would work, although she hadn't tried even one of the 50 suggestions I gave her—which might explain why she has been unemployed for 2 years.

➤ *Stay healthy.* Get enough sleep, eat well, and exercise. A brisk walk at noon will burn off the "blues" and ward off the flu. See your doctor if you are always sad. If it is wintertime, you may not be getting enough sunlight.

➤ *Be social.* Get out and see your friends and don't talk about your job hunt all the time, but do let people feed you leads and encourage you.

GUERRILLA INTELLIGENCE

Sally Poole

After hiring and working with this employee for about a year, she told me what she did to get the job. She was almost destitute, living in a new town where she knew no one, and had no way to produce a resume. So she thought to herself, "Where are there plenty of unused computers that I might use?" She came up with an idea and called the local school district to find out the name of the superintendent. Then she called a nearby school, told them she was the superintendent's niece from out of town, and could she use a computer to type up a report for school? They actually escorted her to the computer room, she typed up her resume, printed copies, and got out quick. I liked her tenacity, her way of getting work done in a creative way. That woman would let nothing stop her, not even being dirt poor. She is still one of my best employees.

Sally Poole, Poole Advertising LLC, www.pooleadvertising.com.

■ THE MOST COMMON CAUSES OF FAILURE AND HOW TO AVOID THEM

It is the little things that trip you up when you are job hunting. You know, the inconsequential details like knowing what job you want or expecting other people to do your job hunting for you. Here are the 4 biggest mistakes and how to avoid them.

➤ Mistake 1: Fuzzy Goals

To wage an effective job-hunting campaign, you need to know your marketable skills and where you can sell them. Starting a job search before you know the job you want and what you have to offer will end in frustration. Employers expect you to be able to tell them how you can contribute. They don't want to figure it out for themselves, and that is not in your best interests anyway. If you are going to expend the effort to find a new job, then take the time to do it right. Target your efforts toward a job you want—or you'll likely be job hunting again very soon.

The Solution
The answer to fuzzy goals is self-assessment. If you can't do this yourself, find a career counselor and invest in yourself. More important than telling you what salary you can command, career counselors will help you understand the following:

- ➤ Your likes and dislikes,
- ➤ Your unique marketable skills,
- ➤ The transferable skills that you enjoy using most,
- ➤ Your most prominent personality traits, and
- ➤ The working conditions and people environments you most value.

To do this on your own, read *Claiming Your Place at the Fire: Living the Second Half of Your Life on Purpose,* by Richard J. Leider and David A. Shapiro (San Francisco: Berrett-Koehler Publishers, 2004). The following web sites also have tools you can use to help discover your purpose:

- ➤ Stephen Covey's 7 *Habits of Highly of Effective People* (New York: Free Press, 2004), Mission builder tool www.franklincovey. com/missionbuilder/index.html.
- ➤ The Inventure Group at www.inventuregroup.com.

➤ **Mistake 2: Procrastination**

I had a colleague 20 years ago who lived to reorganize his office. He had the most meticulous desk and working area I have ever seen. He would do anything to avoid making marketing calls. Daily he would regale his colleagues with the elaborate tracking systems he built to log how many people he interviewed. I felt totally inferior because my office was a living, breathing disaster. It was only after I left to start out on my own that I discovered that during the time I billed $758,000, he billed $5,000. You need to be able to find your files, but don't let that block finding your dream job. There is a huge difference between activity and results—$753,000 if my math is correct.

The Solution
Admit you are terrified at the prospect of failure. Most people live in constant fear that someone else is going to find out that they are not really as good as they say they are, so you are in good company. It is all in your head—literally; fear of failure and fear of rejection cause many people to build the perfect resume or cover letter over and over and over again—but never send it. You have to complete the process by putting the resume in the mail and following up by telephone. The sooner you start, the sooner you will finish. Recognize that activity still matters, as long as it is the right activity that moves you closer to your goals. Here are a few truisms to keep in mind if you are procrastinating:

➤ You were hired for your last job without a perfect resume.

➤ If you increase the quality (targeting of employers) and the quantity (sending resumes and calling to book interviews), you will experience explosive results.

➤ 25 million people change jobs in the United States every year, which represents:

— 68,681 successful job hunters every day

— 2,861 per hour

— 47.6 every second

That means that 364 days per year, while you are poring over the latest revisions to your resume, thousands of lesser qualified people are getting hired.

For years, I thought that there must be some magic words other recruiters were using to pull their deals together. I read dozens of books on sales techniques that all offered similar advice: if you enlarge your funnel, you will increase your results.

➤ Mistake 3: Relying on Others Too Much

Job hunting is a do-it-yourself activity. There is just no way around it. Unlike baseball, you can't substitute a pinch hitter, yet many people rely exclusively on personnel agencies and executive search firms. This "let-the-other-guy-do-it" approach puts the burden of responsibility on others who, in most cases, neither know you nor care about your future.

The Solution

You need to develop your battle plan for approaching employers. You need to choose your target companies and coordinate your approach personally. You don't get to send in troops. You're it. You need to be on top of all the details of your job search, personally, every minute. Nothing less than your total commitment to your own success will do. Your campaign should include a cross section of weapons and tactics, including:

- ➤ Networking
- ➤ Targeted marketing
- ➤ Newspaper classifieds
- ➤ Job boards
- ➤ Newsgroups
- ➤ Third-party recruiters

➤ Mistake 4: Lack of Preparation

There is nothing worse than a candidate who comes to an interview unprepared. Job hunters who haven't taken the time to research the company appear more interested in themselves than in the challenges of the job. I have seen many people disintegrate before my eyes when a client has asked a question as simple as, "So besides what David has provided to you, what do you know about our company?"

The Solution

Look at the hiring process from the other side of the desk—from the employer's perspective. Employers want to know that you've gone out and looked at their industry and understand where they're going. Research, research, research—and then match your experience to their needs. Ask yourself, "What do they need a new hire to provide for them?" Then practice answering typical questions like, "Why should we hire you?" with answers that show how your skills and experience will solve their problems.

➤ **Summary**

As a guerrilla job hunter, you now know what you need to avoid doing. The solutions involve common sense and are easy to implement, so don't procrastinate.

■ THE MOST POWERFUL WAY TO CHANGE YOUR RESULTS

When you realize that the basic aim of every company is to stay in business, you can begin to position yourself as a solution to their need to create and serve the customers who keep them in business, instead of focusing on your need for a job. Most people understand this intellectually but fail to act on it because on the surface it seems too simple an explanation.

"Solution selling" is in vogue all across the United States for a very good reason—it works. In solution selling, you begin by understanding your customer's business and therefore the need for your product to create a solution. You emphasize the benefits that the buyer needs. You know what the buyer needs because you have researched the company to discover its "pain points."

When salespeople focus on solution selling, they increase the value of their products and services because their product is not viewed as just another list of features like those of every competitor. As a job hunter, you increase your value exponentially when you focus on the employer's needs.

For example, 2 equally qualified accountants apply for a job in the accounting department of a growing company. Job hunter A researches the company and discovers the company plans to do an initial public offering. In his cover letter and resume, he emphasizes his experience with publicly traded companies. Job hunter B, who is equally qualified, sends in a standard cover letter and resume.

Job hunter A gets the call, and in the interview discusses the company's needs against the backdrop of his experience. The results are predictable—job hunter A gets hired and job hunter B is never even considered.

Job hunting can actually be that simple, yet all too many job hunters, even those adept at marketing, focus on their needs and not the employer's. Think about what you have to offer the company in light of its ability to serve its customers and grow.

■ THE THREE RS OF SUCCESSFUL JOB HUNTING

In grade school, we learned the Three Rs—Reading, wRriting, and aRithmetic. Those were our most important lessons [okay, so I'm dating myself here]. For job hunters, Research, Relevancy, and Resiliency will result in an interview.

➤ Research

As a job hunter, you need to research and determine:

➤ Which are your marketable skills?

➤ Which industries/companies should you target that use those skills?

➤ What are the specific needs of each company in your target market?

➤ Who is in a position to hire you in those companies?

➤ What is the best way to approach them?

Your research will determine the way you approach people. We talk more about research later in the book.

➤ Relevancy

Your offer (skills) must fit their needs. It has to solve the employer's issues, not yours. It is not about you. At the core, employers only want to know 3 things about you:

1. Can you make me money?
2. Can you save me money?
3. Can you increase our efficiencies?

As global competitiveness increases, employers will be looking for all three. Later in the book, we show you how to express your relevancy—value—to an employer.

➤ **Resiliency**

Resiliency is the ability to spring back from disappointment and keep moving forward. This is the quality that keeps guerrillas focused on their goals and driving forward. Adopt a positive mindset no matter what. Guerrillas always look for the positives even when people and events are clearly indicating they should not.

───────────────── A WAR STORY ─────────────────

Mark J. Haluska

Gary Smith [not his real name] is a highly skilled jack-of-all-trades when it comes to residential carpentry and construction. Some years back when interest rates went through the roof, the result was a severe slowdown in new home building. As a result, Gary was laid off. Being the proud person that he is, he refused to accept unemployment compensation. Besides, it never covers the bills. Gary decided to take the matter into his own hands in an unusual way.

Gary started driving around to all the area building supply companies to find out where any new home construction sites might be located. This piece of detective work quickly provided him with several places to target. That very day, he found one that seemed to have plenty of work in progress. So the next morning by 7 AM, he just showed up at the work site, coffee thermos and lunch pail in hand, and a tool belt on his waist.

As the crew started to work, Gary decided he would just help himself to being useful. He began the morning by offering to help the crew unload the morning delivery trucks. When that was done, he started to help haul shingles up on the roof and then proceeded to nail shingles.

During the first coffee break, Gary asked one of the people he was so generously helping, "Where's the boss?" To which he received the reply, "The boss never shows up before 11 AM."

When coffee break was over, Gary crawled back up on the roof and started nailing more shingles. The crew boss finally showed up and after about 2 hours, finally asked Gary, "Who are you?" To which Gary replied, "My name is Gary Smith, and I am a carpenter. I thought maybe you could use some help around here." The boss responded, "Gary, we're not hiring right now, so give me your number and if I need help I'll call you."

Now Gary being a guerrilla said, "What the heck, the day is more than half over, I had nothing planned for the day so let me just finish out the shift at no cost to you, and when we're done for the day, just let me know how I did."

The construction site boss said, "Hey, it's your nickel, but I never agreed to pay you."

The shift over, Gary asked how he did and the boss said, "You did a good job. I see that you are a steady worker, so just leave me your phone number and I'll call if I ever need you."

Now most people would simply leave it at that and wait for the phone to ring ... but not Gary!

The next day he showed up at 7 AM again with his tools, thermos, and lunch pail in hand. He worked for 4 hours, then the site boss showed up but did not notice Gary up on a roof until the noon lunch break. The site boss said, "Gary, I told you yesterday I did not need help right now, but I would call you if and when I do; you really need to pack your things and go home."

Now Gary kicked it up a step and said to the foreman, "I know, it's just that I started this roof yesterday, and I just want to see the roof finished. It'll be fully installed by the end of today's shift. I just don't like to leave any project undone."

The boss walked away mumbling to Gary that he was not getting paid; he had not been offered a job and if he wanted to work for free he was foolish, but this would be the last time, "Go ahead, but don't be here tomorrow."

At 7 AM the next morning, Gary arrived at the job site, jumped right in, and started the whole process over. This particular day, the boss did not show up at all and Gary proceeded to work the whole shift, for no pay.

Day 4. Same routine for Gary, but this time the boss showed up at 11 AM as usual. He immediately spotted Gary working away and called him down off the roof. He said in a somewhat loud manner, "I thought I told you I would call if I needed you, now go home."

Gary was ready for it and went for all the marbles. He responded to the foreman, "I've been here four days now. I have proven to you and your crew I am a Class A carpenter. I am unemployed right now with nothing else to do, so since you don't get here until 11 AM each day, I am going to be here at 7 AM and stay here until you throw me off the work site."

At this point, the foreman threw in the towel, wrote down an address, and told Gary, "Go to this address, this is our home office. Fill out the paperwork and be here tomorrow at 7 AM ready to work." Gary is still with the construction company. Today, he is a foreman.

Let me qualify the preceding story by noting that it occurred before liability insurance, workmen's comp, and federal illegal alien hiring laws. These would have forced the foreman to dismiss Gary immediately. I wouldn't try this one in today's litigious economy.

Compliments of Mark J. Haluska, executive director, Real Time NetWork, www.rtnetwork.net.

Chapter 3

Your Guerrilla Job-Hunting Strategy

Think Like a General—Work Like a Sergeant

> The general who wins a battle makes many calculations in his temple before the battle is fought. The general who loses a battle makes but few calculations beforehand. Thus do many calculations lead to victory and few calculations to defeat: how much more no calculation at all! It is by attention to this point that I can foresee who is likely to win or lose.
>
> —Sun Tzu, *The Art of War*

Unlike the one-size-fits-all strategies in most job-hunting books, the balanced approach in *Guerrilla Marketing for Job Hunters 2.0* blends the best of networking, target marketing, warm-calling, and public relations into a cohesive framework for success. Strategy underpins every suggestion in this book.

Networking is not always the answer: neither are direct marketing and job boards. Instead, consider combining several tactics with the correct weapons to create a force multiplier effect. It can lead to victory—your dream job. This section shows you how to think like a general, plan your strategy, marshal your resources, and then how to work like a sergeant and execute that strategy.

■ WHY YOU NEED A PERSONAL MARKETING STRATEGY

As Sun Tzu said 2,500 years ago, "many calculations lead to victory and few calculations to defeat." Before you begin job hunting, you need to craft a personal marketing strategy that will guide your efforts. This game plan includes the details about whom you will approach, how you will approach them, and what weapons you will need to use.

As a professional recruiter, I know firsthand that all employers have a salary range they like to work within for every position. Once the most suitable candidate is found, it is my job to negotiate a deal that is acceptable for both parties. In nearly all cases, the difference between the lower and the upper end is $20,000—and I am not talking about executive level candidates here. I am referring to midlevel managers where the salary band can run from $30,000 to $50,000 per year.

Your marketing strategy will determine not only whether you get an interview, but also where you fit in that range. If you market your skills as a commodity, you'll be lucky to even land the job, and you will be paid at the bottom end. However, if you market and present yourself as a "you-can't-do-without-me" solution to the employer, you will start near *the top* or more. Over the course of your lifetime earnings, this can easily amount to an extra $800,000 to $1 million in salary.

There are hundreds of books that explain how to sell yourself in an interview, but you need to get the interview first. To do that, you need to understand what employers are seeking in a candidate.

Being great at your job is not enough anymore. People have to know you are one of the best if you want to advance in your chosen profession. As technology continues to shrink trade barriers and offshore competition increases, North American employers will have more options, and there are likely to be many other candidates who are just as good as you.

The bar for job hunters was raised during the last recession. Indeed, many companies will opt to make no decision rather than risk making a poor hire.

■ SKILLS EMPLOYERS BUY

You need to position yourself in a different way. You need to emphasize those qualities that will let you leapfrog over other competitors. The following qualities will land you at the front of the hiring line:

➤ Leadership skills
➤ Communication skills

> ➤ Bias toward action
> ➤ Passion
> ➤ Cultural compatibility

➤ Leadership Skills

At every level of organizations, employers are hiring leaders who can galvanize talented people toward ambitious goals and motivate them to succeed. Employers today don't need another "team player." Team players are often afraid to voice their opinions. Who wants another hanger-on? Every company in the United States is battling the clock to stay in business, increase market share, and meet the demands of their shareholders. In this environment, you must convince an employer that you will have a positive influence on their ability to win and that you are an integral part of their solution. If you can't communicate your personal commitment and drive through your words and actions in the interview, you won't be their first choice. Be a team leader instead.

➤ Communication Skills

Your ability to communicate a clear vision for your group must be far above average. Unclear writing and lumbering speaking skills rarely indicate sharp thinking, whereas clarity and concise expression are favorable signs. Slang expressions may work well on the factory floor but they will not impress customers or your prospective boss. Employers hire articulate candidates before all others. People don't have the time to interpret what they think you said. More and more, companies are requesting that candidates prepare presentations and deliver them in front of the hiring board. This is especially true in sales and marketing roles, but it also extends down to line positions on the shop floor.

➤ A Bias toward Action

Because companies are hiring fewer but better qualified people, they are pushing decision-making authority down the chain of command. Today, a manager may need to make a decision that a few years ago might have been approved by a management committee. So no matter what level of employment you are seeking, do not be afraid to ask the hard questions and make tough decisions. You must demonstrate your ability to take action with limited or imperfect information.

➤ Passion

Clients often ask me to find someone with "fire in their belly"—that is, employer speak for passion. Employers know that many employees coast through life preferring to be safe rather than sorry in their career. I have had the great fortune to work with brilliant technical people who are also passionate about what they do and want to leave their mark on the world. They challenge others to stretch and open their minds to new possibilities. Passionate workers envision what is possible, not just what is. They have a zest for life and a sense of urgency that infects everyone around them. Show an employer that you have that spark and they will hire you over more experienced candidates any day!

➤ Cultural Compatibility

By the year 2010, the cumulative codified knowledge of the world will double every 11 hours. What you go to bed knowing at night will be outdated by daybreak. Shelf life for knowledge is the same as that for a banana. To succeed today, a company's employees must share knowledge freely, a concept that is foreign to most organizations, where people hoard knowledge to safeguard their jobs.

In the upcoming book, *Building Organizations That Leap Tall Buildings in a Single Bound* (Ottawa, ON: Totem Hill), Ron Wiens, Ken Sudday, and I focus on how to build a corporate culture that produces a winning bottom line by focusing on the organization's Relationship Intelligence (RI). The authors explain that the ability of employees to trust is a measure of the organization's RI. Companies with high RI will succeed because they can build new knowledge and therefore new products and wealth on a constant basis. In contrast, companies that have low RI and hoard their knowledge will fail.

As a job hunter, you cannot risk being viewed as "political" or as "playing games." Managers who play politics have a devastating impact on their organization regardless of their personal performance. The winning companies are the ones whose players play for the good of the whole. They know how to fight and disagree with each other but they do so not for personal gain but for corporate gain. The paradox is that managers who play this way end up with the fattest personal bottom line.

That is just the beginning of what is expected. Particular qualities and attributes dominate each hiring level, and you need to be aware of the different interests that govern each. We go into greater detail in Chapter 12, when we discuss face-to-face interviews.

■ THE HIDDEN JOB MARKET AND WHY IT IS HIDING

Okay, so it is a misnomer. The hidden job market isn't really hidden. It is just not in plain sight. It is called the hidden job market because of the way jobs are created and filled.

Most jobs are created in a company in one of 3 ways:

1. The company is growing.
2. Someone quits, leaving a vacancy.
3. Someone is being replaced, and the employer does not want the employees to know about it.

When the company is growing, the owner, president, or someone else may know they need to make a new hire, but they haven't initiated any measures to find someone. They may not have had the time. They may not quite have the budget. They may not want to go through the hassle of advertising and interviewing. So while the need is real, the job itself remains hidden in the hiring manager's head.

When someone quits, managers will first consider eliminating the job. If that is not feasible, they will look inside their organization to see if there is an employee they can promote into the role. If they can't find anyone, they'll likely ask their coworkers for referrals. If that doesn't work, depending on the size of the company, they may run an ad through HR, or hire a headhunter. They may even run it on a job board or in the newspaper as a "company confidential" box ad. Companies will contact a headhunter when secrecy is required because the recruiter can conduct a search without anyone ever knowing.

In all cases, the job remains hidden to the outside world for weeks if not months; hence the term hidden job market. The only successful way to access this market is to reach the hiring managers before they opt to go the advertising or HR route. The bulk of this book revolves around creative and effective ways to reach hiring managers who are just waiting to hear from you.

The hidden job market is your private laboratory to test out the best methods for finding your dream job.

➤ Cracking the Hidden Job Market

For most people, the Internet is a mess. It suffers from too much information and too little structure. Most people looking for a job online quickly get overwhelmed with the quantity of responses from a search engine. Headhunters use the following types of Internet searches to find new job openings, and you can do the same thing:

> ➤ Target competitors.
> ➤ Obtain referrals from associations.
> ➤ Conduct Internet searches.

Here is how to reverse-engineer what recruiters do, so that you can target your next employer.

Target Competitors

The easiest place for a recruiter to sell your skills is to a direct competitor or at least someone who is in your industry. Go to www.hoovers.com. Enter the name of the company and hit the "capsule tab." This will give you a snapshot not only of the company but also of its competitors. You can play the competitor's competitors game all day at Hoover's and never finish. Go in looking for what you need and don't waste your time playing with the technology. This is a very rich resource.

There are 2 other key organizations you can also try: www.edgar-online.com and www.herring.com.

Obtain Referrals from Associations

The next best way to research an industry is through its associations. The best site to find the association most related to your interests is the American Society of Association Executives: www.asaenet.org. All I can say about this site is wow! I recently visited it so I could e-mail a colleague in New York a place to start her search for an accounting job. I did a keyword search on "accounting" that brought back 244 hits. By refining it to just include those in the state of New York, I received 15 hits that ranged from American Association of Hispanic Certified Public Accountants to the Society of Insurance Accountants. Clicking on Society of Insurance Accountants gave me their address and phone number. The site runs the gambit from "Accounting" to "Youth organizations" and represents more than 300 industries. It is a great place to start.

Conduct Internet Searches

By far the best way to discover new opportunities is by doing structured search engine queries. And it is fairly easy to do. Here is how to do targeted research to find companies and the people who can hire you.

Develop a Target List of Companies

Here is an example using Google.com to search for work in advertising in New York:

➤ When you do targeted research, generally you concentrate on an industry or a geographic preference (in this example, New York City). Use whatever city you like.

➤ We need to find the names of all the advertising companies in New York. There are easy ways to do this using the Internet. Go to www.google.com and type the following words in the advanced option in Google: advertising, new york, directory, conference. You are instructing Google to search for a directory of advertising firms in New York or a conference on advertising held in New York. We want this information to obtain leads to companies.

Your text needs to be filled in as shown in Figure 3.1.

The results returned when you hit the search button will be similar to those shown in Figure 3.2.

At the time I did this search, the first result was for a conference held in New York for the advertising industry. The next 2 hits are both for directories of advertising companies in New York, complete with Web addresses, phone numbers, profiles, and more.

Find People Who Can Hire You

Once you have a target list of companies, you need to find out the names of the people who can actually hire you. Go to each company's web site and gather names. If you are lucky, every web site will provide the complete identification of all their senior executives, including names and sometimes e-mail, too. Web information should be

Google™ Advanced Search		
Find results	with **all** of the words	advertising
	with the **exact phrase**	new york
	with **at least one** of the words	directory conference
	without the words	

Figure 3.1   Google advanced.

Google™

Web   Images   Groups^Newl   News   Froogle   **more »**

advertising   directory OR conference "new york"   Search   Advanced Search
Preferences

Web   Results **1 - 100** of about **11,300,000** for **advertising directory**

Tip: Find maps by searching for a street address with city or zip code

AD:TECH - The Event for Interactive Marketing
... 15-17, 2005 How was AD:TECH **New York** 2004? ... yourself why thousands of marketing and
advertising executives make ... There's nothing like leaving a **conference** with a ...
www.ad-tech.com/ - 29k - 15 Jan 2005 - Cached - Similar pages

> **Conference** Sessions By Day
> ... **Conference** Sessions By Day. ... Track 2: **Advertising** & Promotion (Sponsored Revenue Science,
> Hosted by AdAge ... Craig Calder, Chief Evangelist, **New York** Times Digital. ...
> www.ad-tech.com/sessions_byDay.asp?reqEvent=7 - 86k - Cached - Similar pages
> [More results from www.ad-tech.com]

Advertising Directory of **New York**
... **New York Advertising Directory**. Home :: **Advertising** ::
ADD YOUR SITE Select A City or County. ...
new-york.uscity.net/Advertising/ - 101k - Cached - Similar pages

New York State > Manhattan > **Advertising** in the Yahoo! **Directory**
... SITE LISTINGS. AJ Ross Creative Media - **advertising** and marketing agency specializing
in medical, real estate, and senior living industries. ...
dir.yahoo.com/.../Business_and_Shopping/ Business_to_Business/Marketing_and_Advertising/Advertising/ - 20k - Cached

---

Figure 3.2   Google target directories.

up-to-the-minute accurate, but if you have any doubts, make a phone call to confirm it.

Once you have the name of the individual who is one rung up the ladder from the job you want, you need to process the name through Google again. This time you put the first and last name in the first box and the company name in the third box. This will produce a list of press releases and news articles in which that person is mentioned, as well as conferences he or she has attended. Read an article or two and clip something memorable, so that when you send a letter, you will be able to say, "I read your article in ... about ... which prompted me to write." Very powerful.

Guerrilla Tips

➤ If you get too many search results, here are ways to narrow your search.

➤ If it is outside the geographic area you are interested in, try putting in area codes instead of cities to localize the results. Area codes are a more exact means of honing in on a city.

➤ New York City consists of several boroughs, so if you do a 212 area code you will not pick them all up: you will need to search on 718, 917, and 347 to cover the whole city. If you were to just do a city search for New York, you would probably miss 75 percent of all the jobs.

If you used Google, your computer screen would look like the one shown here:

■ OTHER SOURCES OF INFORMATION

Other sources of information on who can hire you can be obtained by referring to annual reports, 10(K) reports, and proxy statements. You can look up the phone numbers in Standard & Poors or another large general directory, or call toll free information (800-555-1212). Annual reports provide valuable organizational information, division and subsidiary data, locations, names, titles, revenues, numbers of employees, discussions about strategy and growth plans, and sometimes even photos of employees.

10(K) reports are required by law to disclose names and titles of senior management, each executive's number of years with the company and a career summary, and his or her age. Age is relevant because shareholders have a right to know when key managers might be approaching retirement, which could materially affect the performance of the company. These reports often provide plant locations and define a company's lines of business. They must also state if anything could adversely affect the company's performance or stock price, such as a major lawsuit or pending environmental expenses.

Proxy statements are required to disclose the compensation paid to the 4 highest paid executives. Proxies also provide detailed background information on the board of directors. You can obtain hard copy of the annual report, 10(K) report, and proxy statement free by calling the company. Most companies post these reports on their web sites.

➤ **How to Have Fresh Leads Delivered to Your Inbox Daily**

You can subscribe to a vast number of free services that will bring information straight to your desktop. JustSell.com, for example, delivers a list of newly funded companies complete with the contact numbers for their executives. Nearly every newspaper available on the Web has a News Alert function. Subscribe to as many as you need to cover your interests:

➤ www.privateequityweek.com

➤ www.eetimes.com

➤ www.professional.venturewire.com

GUERRILLA INTELLIGENCE

How to Find the Best Jobs from the Hidden Job Market

Simon Stapleton

The best jobs aren't advertised in the newspaper or on the Web. Much like real estate, the best of the bunch are snapped up before they ever hit advertisements. If you scour job ad sites or the back pages of a paper, then you're really looking at the jobs the top people don't want. You're not in the domain of mediocrity, are you?

The truth is that the best jobs are created or shaped to capitalize on talent that has emerged from the labor pool, that is, *you*. These jobs didn't exist before a potential employer knew you existed because top jobs are created for unique people.

The art of searching the hidden job market is to have high-impact self-marketing, providing proof and authority of your claims, making connections within organizations, working on your relationships, and then tapping these connections to seek job opportunities. How?

It starts with first knowing which organizations and departments you want to work in. So draw up your list.

Then you need to create an in-your-face, hard-to-resist profile. This is your primary sales tool. It's unthinkable nowadays to consider anything but a "social profile" using Web 2.0 technologies such as the ubiquitous LinkedIn, which is the best of the bunch for this kind of search because it's primarily for business use. Build up your profile to capture your personal and career achievements, and you should especially emphasize your uniqueness.

The next step is to market to your potential employers by building relationships and joining groups associated with their organization. Introduce yourself and ask others what it is like working in their organization. Demonstrate curiosity in the organization's brand, culture, and values. Enter discussions and answer questions placed by its workers, to the best of your ability. Avoid going for the jugular and asking for work—that will come! Spend time building up your relationships and adjust your profile accordingly.

Once you've built quality relationships, it's time to decide which connections could become a potential sponsor in each organization. These folks will introduce you to managers in the departments you're targeting. Spend time working on these people and engage in conversations on subjects of mutual interest until you've hooked them in. You'll know when this has happened because they will begin to ask you questions about your current employment situation and about your future; you now have a sponsor. Remember, keep your profile adjusted appropriately.

Then, go all out on using these sponsors to push into your target department by using LinkedIn to ask for introductions to the hiring managers in it. Be charming, be direct, but don't be pushy.

Once you've been introduced, it's time to work the charm again and to build on these relationships that will bear the fruit of opportunity. Your profile, by this stage, should be well stocked with your unique skills and experience as well as credible points of reference and a history of engagement with employees in your target organizations; your self-marketing has the highest impact at this stage. Maintaining these relationships, and those with sponsors, is worth every second. At some point, an opening

(continued)

will arise or be created for you—and you'll be first in line. Like this whole method, the key is to be persistent, but not pushy. This isn't an overnight process, so you will need to keep working at it, but believe me this will pay off!

Last thought: the tools are there online, and free to use. But they become most effective when you have a process and structure to work with. By applying a bit of this know-how, you'll avoid the dross and get first sight of the very best jobs even before they exist.

Simon Stapleton is a leader and innovator in Information Technology, and he has made it his mission to help emerging IT leaders with their personal and career development. His blog is www.simonstapleton.com. He can be reached at simon@simonstapleton.com.

■ STRATEGIC TWISTS ON TRADITIONAL STRATEGIES

Most people use a few traditional strategies including:

- ➤ Newspaper ads
- ➤ Job boards
- ➤ Newsgroups

Although you shouldn't ignore these avenues completely, you should think of them as passive ways to find a job because they don't require a lot of work. The following tips will put you ahead of your competitors and at least double your odds of success.

➤ Newspaper Ads

The major daily newspapers are still a rich source of job openings and not just in the classified section. Careerbuilder.com is a product of Knight Ridder and the Tribune Company, which combined represent more than 130 newspapers. Careerbuilder is the vehicle I suggest my clients use because it has both national and local pull through the newspapers. Most major papers have their own online classified section in which jobs are archived. Go back through the online archives 30 to 60 days because many jobs are not filled the first time they are advertised:

➤ Post your resume if the site allows and enroll for the online classifieds Job Alert program, which notifies you of matches with your background.

➤ Always check the classifieds. Display ads, or the "Career Section" as it is commonly referred to, are very expensive, as much as 100 times more costly than the classified "word ads." Small- and medium-size companies use the classified section.

➤ Business journals are full of decision makers. To find the one in your city: www.bizjournalsdirectory.com or www.bizjournals.com.

➤ Review the "appointments" or "onward and upward" column for the names of recently promoted or appointed executives. Send them your resume.

➤ Find out where the recently hired people came from because their old company may now be in the middle of a search that is a perfect fit for you.

Most importantly, read the business and city sections to see what is going on in your town. Which companies are growing or announcing new products? They may be prime candidates for your skills. Years ago when I first got into the headhunting business, I was trained like every other recruiter in how to troll for leads. I read the classifieds every day and called the companies to see if I could help. My pitch was, "I have candidates who exactly fit your requirements," along with a bunch of other lame openers, and then I tried to overcome their objections to paying me to replicate their efforts ... with disappointing but predictable results.

I soon realized that by the time an employer advertised a position, it was too late to try to sell my services. I would be competing with their newspaper ad and dozens of other recruiters to fill that slot, and frankly I wasn't that good of a salesperson. I needed an alternative—fast! Sometimes you have to be careful what you wish for.

Quite accidentally, I read an article about a new office building being built. Still wet behind the ears and not realizing I was supposed to wait until they called us, I phoned the general manager and asked him if we could have coffee and talk about his project. The next day we spent most of the morning talking about the hurdles he faced in getting a team of construction guys together in time to complete the project. I volunteered to help and left with my first job order in hand. I knew nothing about construction, so I started calling my friends to see if any of them knew anyone in the construction business who would have coffee with me.

I found a guy who tutored me in the intricacies of hiring a construction manager: what to look for and where to look. I finished that project and was quickly hired to do 7 more. They put me on retainer, gave me a company credit card, and offered me access to the company jet.

All-in-all, I hired 37 people in 4 cities and never ran a newspaper ad—not once! Yet, I found the lead in the newspaper. So read between the lines of the business section and don't hesitate to call the president of a company you read about; he or she may be facing the same challenge as my first client. To this day, I still find the bulk of my projects by reading the business section, and I have little competition from other recruiters who are still getting their leads the old-fashioned way.

► **Job Boards**

According to John Sumser, the president of Interbiz.com, a firm that monitors the comings-and-goings in the electronic recruiting industry, there are approximately 42,000 different job boards. So, where do you start looking? First, there is no master list. Nor is there any way to register at more than one board at a time. To make matters even more interesting, Monsterboard, which at the time of my writing was the largest, has approximately 75,000 customers. With more than 10 million businesses in the United States, that means the industry leader has less than a 1 percent market share (www.interbiznet.com).

Job boards do not share information with each other, so you need to register with as many as you can find time for. Only those companies that pay a fee can post a job or review your resume. Some sites are so expensive they are only used by the Fortune 1000, so if you are looking for a job in a small business, you are better off using niche boards.

Register yourself at all the top job boards and you will cover 2 percent of the available jobs. The usual rule in marketing is that the top 20 percent of companies in an industry own 80 percent of the market. Not true here, obviously. You can find niche job boards for your industry by going to the Google search engine at www.google.com and typing in the words: "job board" and your niche (e.g., "retail" "construction" "software") and hitting the Google Search button. That command in Google will bring you a list of job boards specific to your industry. You can also find niche job boards by function (e.g., sales or accounting at www.theladders.com).

■ MAKE TECHNOLOGY WORK FOR YOU

The past 5 years have seen an explosion in technology that makes your job so much easier. Today, get more information faster than ever. Job aggregators, job alerts, news alerts are all readily available. Uncover potential job leads at the job aggregators, which are spider engines that go to all of the job boards (www.simplyhired.com, www.indeed.com, www.just-posted.com, www.jobster.com). If you haven't already done so, subscribe to them and sign up now. It's free. To research newly available jobs from company web sites, try www.hound.com.

SimplyHired is the largest of the aggregators. Besides supplying jobs directly to MySpace and Facebook, they have some amazing widgets and tools.

➤ Job Widgets

You can add their *MySpace Job Alerts* to your MySpace homepage to see the newest jobs daily. Likewise, their *Workin' It!* application on Facebook. *Job Search Widget* brings new jobs to your iGoogle homepage, your blog, or your computer's desktop. *Mobile Jobs* lets people on the go access millions of jobs from the palm of your hand—literally!

➤ Job Tools

You can save your search preferences and saved jobs in the *My Jobs* tab. Set up your own *e-mail alerts* to send jobs when and where you want. The *RSS Feed* sends the jobs you're interested in to you in real time, while the *Local Jobs* function lets you search by city block or other region. You can check *Salaries* and *Trends* as well. There are also numerous job-related *Forums* as well.

By taking advantage of these systems, you allow technology to work for you, saving you valuable time and resources. Being a guerrilla is all about making the most of every minute. Put these ideas to work today.

GUERRILLA TIPS

➤ Look for positions that are 1 or 2 levels above yours; they can give you clues to what is happening at a particular company and may hint at other positions that will soon be filled. When a company is looking for a new vice president of marketing, you can almost guarantee the new hire will realign the team he or she inherits. The same holds true for sales and engineering.

➤ Register at local job boards because most employers advertise and source candidates locally first.

➤ If you do not want to be bothered at home by recruiters, you should list an e-mail address as your main point of contact, preferably one you can cancel when you find a job.

GUERRILLA INTELLIGENCE

How Best to Use Job Boards
Steven Rothberg

Job boards have been around almost since the dawn of the Internet and became popular in the mid-1990s with the birth of some of today's biggest and best job boards. They're wonderful tools for both job seekers and employers, yet like all tools they can be dangerous in the hands of someone who misuses them. The following tips will maximize your chances of finding a great new job as quickly as possible.

Come, Use, Go Away
Although I'm the president and founder of job board College Recruiter.com and therefore have a vested interest in getting job seekers to use job boards, I also recognize that far too many job seekers spend far too much time on job boards. No one can use all or even most of them.

Just about every job seeker will be well served by using the big 3 general boards (Careerbuilder, Monster, and HotJobs), 2 or 3 niche boards that target your occupational field or experience level, and 2 or 3 niche boards that target your geographic preferences.

Once you find the general and niche sites that best fit your interests, go to each of them, register, apply to all of the advertised jobs for which you are qualified, and set up job match agents (sometimes called alerts) and then go away and don't come back until you receive an e-mailed alert telling you a job has just been posted. You should spend at most one day on the job boards and then at most an hour a week after that.

Keywords Matter When You Search
Virtually every job board allows candidates to search by a combination of keywords and geographic parameters. Are you

actually looking for a retail sales position in Manhattan? Then search using the keywords "retail sales" and the geographic parameter "Manhattan." Your results will be of much higher quality because most of the potential matches you'll see will actually be of interest to you.

Keywords Also Matter When You Apply

The trick is to get your resume noticed by the employer when they are reviewing resumes submitted for a job for which you are both qualified and interested. Rather than referring to your previous experience just as an "Account Executive," also include the word "sales" if that's what your function actually was. Rather than referring to yourself as a "Registered Nurse," also include the acronym "RN" because some employers will search one way and others the other way.

Fraud Alert

Protect yourself by posting your resume anonymously at the job boards that offer that option so that employers and fraudsters who search the resume bank can't see your name, e-mail, or other contact information. Better yet, patronize the small number of major job boards like CollegeRecruiter.com that do not sell resume searching access to employers so as to better protect the candidates who are using the sites.

Follow-Up

Keep track of the jobs to which you've applied. Follow up with each and every employer. Give them 4 or 5 business days to review your resume. Then e-mail or call using any contact information included in the job posting. If there is no such information in the ad, and there often isn't, then go to the employer's web site and use the Contact Us or other such page to contact the human resources office. All you want to know at this stage is if they received your resume and when they'll likely review it. Be polite but firm in getting that information. Any good employer should be able and willing to communicate that to you. If they tell you 5 business days, call or e-mail them back on the sixth business day to ask for an update and the timing of the next step. If they tell you that they'll be setting up interviews in 10 business days, then call or e-mail them back on the eleventh day.

(continued)

Keep repeating the process until you've been hired or excluded from consideration.

Steven Rothberg is the president and founder of CollegeRecruiter.com at www.CollegeRecruiter.com, the leading job board for college students who are searching for internships and recent graduates who are hunting for entry-level jobs and other career opportunities.

➤ **Newsgroups**

Newsgroups are my favorite way to find candidates because they are categorized by industry and specialization. There is literally a newsgroup for every occupation and they are free, so everyone from the Fortune 500 company to the corner store can use them. Yes, you can get a lot of crap, but the quality of jobs has been improving over the years. Headhunters use newsgroups far more than job boards because they are highly targeted, free, and used by the most astute guerrillas.

GUERRILLA TIPS

➤ You need to check and recheck newsgroups every 24 hours because jobs only remain on the site for approximately 24 hours.

➤ It is more efficient to search for jobs than to post your resume and wait for a call.

➤ There are far more jobs on the newsgroups than on job boards.

GUERRILLA INTELLIGENCE

The "Shotgun Blast" Approach

Dave Mendoza

A weak personal branding strategy, an ineffective e-mail protocol, and a lack of online due diligence will often adversely affect the quantity and quality of job leads and interviews.

The most common mistake of job seekers is the "shotgun blast" approach. Too often job seekers e-mail, mail, or call anyone and everywhere without a strategy other than hoping the law of averages will inevitably be in their favor. In an online world, however, recruiters can sense desperation or lack of care in the approach of a job seeker that can just as easily call their competence into question. For instance, if a sales candidate only wants to work in Chicago, but e-mails a recruiter in Denver who only works in semiconductor engineering—it becomes readily apparent the job seeker failed to take the time to perform minimal due diligence. Likewise, an ambiguous e-mail subject header such as "Does it make sense to chat?" without any context within the correspondence and without a resume attachment, not to mention a lack of context as to how the job seeker assumed relevance in the relationship, all at once suggests minimal regard for a recruiter's time. Recruiters are keenly aware that the most adept job seekers are equally capable as they are of utilizing online resources tools for efficient introductions. Subsequently, in cases where a job seeker shows a lack of proficiency with regards to online etiquette, or avoids the more efficient means of introduction, they instead inadvertently showcase their vulnerabilities. The job seeker has only effectively presented weaknesses rather than strengths in the ever-important "first impression."

It's Not What You Know, It's Who Knows You
The phrase "It's not what you know, it's who you know" is a phrase we learn early in life. We are most keenly aware of it when we submit our college applications and as we enter the workforce. Today, however, the emphasis of one's effort in effective networking is commonly misplaced. Social and professional networking used to be defined largely by power calls to foster candidate generation. Today, the emphasis is broader and in tandem; the effective phone call references the online connection as an introduction. Meaningful and sustainable networking relies on an emphasis of "knowledge transfer"—what you learn—in your associations and likewise a "benefit by association." The personal brand of job seekers are optimized best when they have developed an online presence that signifies

(continued)

particular areas of expertise within their respective skill discipline and within a certain industry. How a job seeker positions himself within this realm is critical to attracting employers via online search tools that can sort by industry, company, discipline, and organization. The successful job seeker is always cognizant of the refined and relevant mantra, "It's Not What You Know, It's Who Knows You."

Dave Mendoza is an award winning blogger, global speaker, and sourcing consultant. A corporate partner to RecruitingBlogs.com, he is one of the top 20 networkers worldwide on LinkedIn (www.linkedin.com/in/davemendoza/ www.sixdegreesfromdave.com).

■ PROMOTE YOURSELF

Many think answering newspaper ads and responding to postings on the Internet constitute a solid job search strategy. Nothing could be further from reality. In fact, you are likely to get depressed and frustrated within days if you adopt this as your major strategy. Guerrilla job hunters know that publicity—or self-promotion—is the only tried-and-true means of landing your dream job. Now is not the time to be shy. As we demonstrate in upcoming chapters, an active job-hunting campaign involves making direct contact with employers and headhunters on a daily basis.

Newspaper ads and Internet job postings should not be ignored, but they are of limited value because everyone else is doing it. Guerrillas venture upstream to get the prize fish. It requires a little more effort, but they find a fishing hole that no one else has discovered. Responding to newspapers is not a strategy; it is just another tactic.

In my experience, responding to newspaper ads gives you a 1 in 1,000 chance of landing a job. It is not unusual for an Internet job posting to attract 400 to 5,000 resumes. Do you like those odds? And who does the prescreening—the corporate recruiters or human resources department? Do you want them assessing your credentials? Still like your odds?

A WAR STORY

Jim Reil

In the mid-1980s, my cousin Randy Smith graduated from the theater program at the University of Victoria. He wanted to be a director, not an actor. He directed a few small productions in Victoria but then what? How could he start the kind of career he wanted?

In a newspaper, he read that the great American theater and opera director Robert Wilson was staying at the Hotel Vancouver in Vancouver, a ferry ride from Victoria. So Randy called the front desk and asked for Robert Wilson's room. He was put through, and Robert Wilson answered the phone. Randy said something like, "Mr. Wilson, I just graduated from theater studies and I want to study with you because you are the greatest living director in the world. I will do anything that needs doing so I can learn from you." A pause. Then Wilson said something like, "I've never got a call like this before. The answer is yes."

A short time later, Randy was on his way first to Italy and then to Germany, where Wilson was directing. Everyone who knew Randy was astonished. He was a shy, quiet person. But he had a great passion for theater and knew that it was his vocation. He ended up in senior management at the Vancouver Opera. His story will always be an inspiration to me.

Compliments of Jim Reil, jim@jimreil.com.

■ LOGISTICS—BUILDING YOUR WAR ROOM

Next to knowing what kind of job you want, there is nothing more important than being organized. You will need to compile research, track your job leads, schedule calls, follow up your interview activities, and send correspondence. While this may not sound like much, it is a lot to keep track of, and if you misplace or lose information, it could cost you your dream job.

Here is what I suggest. First, find a space in your home where you can be out of everybody else's way—an area that you can get other family members to agree is yours and yours alone. Having said that, I must add that the lack of space is no excuse for failure.

When I started looking for my second job, I was working full-time 50 to 70 hours per week. My workspace was the dining-room table in my dinky little apartment—until my best friend needed a place to stay. After he showed up, I put a filing cabinet in the trunk of my car with all my documents and resumes and a suitcase with 2 suits, 4 shirts, and 2 matching ties. I landed 14 interviews and 13 offers in a 4-week period.

> *The Ultimate Collection of Absolute Must Have Free Job-Hunting Tools—Download Them Now*
>
> ➤ *Jibber Jobber:* These days, no job is immune to cutbacks, downsizing, rightsizing, or off-shoring. Like a politician whose first job is to get reelected, your first responsibility to yourself and your future is to be continually looking for new opportunities. But who has the time to track down job leads and still have a life? Now you do with Jibber Jobber. It lets you manage a serious job search—while you focus on feeding your opportunity funnel. Very Guerrilla (www.jibberjobber.com/signup.php).
>
> ➤ *Natsjobs.com:* This is a must-have applet. Natsjobs.com searches over 328,173 web sites, including corporate, government, and major job boards in North America looking for unique jobs that suit your parameters. It then e-mails them to you so you can spend your time applying for jobs and not surfing the net looking. Think about it. Try to track 100 of your favorite companies. If you spend just 3 minutes per company, that's 5 hours a day—time you should be spending in interviews, not surfing (www.natsjobs.com).
>
> ➤ *Google Local:* Do you hate to commute? Want to relocate? If where you work is as important as whom you work for, you can limit your job search to a specific location. Google can help. At local.google.com you can search for employers and businesses in a specific area. Simply type in a business name or industry, as

well as your city (the more specific the better). Example: "advertising agencies near Detroit, MI." Take this string complete with the "" and put it into Google local. Always leave in the word "near" but play around with keywords and the city or address.

➤ *Message Tag:* Everybody loves e-mail. It's cheap, quick, and easy. But how many times do you find yourself wondering what happened to that message? Should I call to see if they got it or should I wait? You'll never wonder again. Don't let the technology derail your job search one more minute (www.msgtag.com/download/).

➤ *Phrase Express:* Filling in forms and/or remembering that ideal phrase you used last week will never be a challenge again. This free program can save you a lot of typing (www.phrase express.com).

➤ *Google Docs:* Ever need to change something in your resume at the last minute, or wish you could show a recruiter or prospective employer your portfolio? Google to the rescue again—this time with Google Docs www.google.ca/intl/en/options/. Make yourself 2 separate accounts, one for you to keep your private documents on and another which you allow employers or recruiters to view relevant material such as references, resume, transcripts, and sample projects. You will be able to access your account from the internet during your interview. You could show the employer your portfolio on the employers computer screen.

➤ *News Search Engines:* Keep on top of breaking news on your desktop. News search engines automatically collect stories from thousands of sites on the Internet. They then cluster the stories and photos into an online magazine format. It is like having CNN right on your desktop, but you get to decide what you want to see. The top news search engines are:

— Google News (news.google.com)

— Yahoo News (news.yahoo.com)

— Alta Vista News (www.altavista.com/news/)

— All the Web News (www.alltheweb.com)

— MSN News (msnbc.msn.com)

➤ *Google Alerts:* Even more impressive for my money are Google Alerts, *a service* available at www.google.com/alerts/. Essentially, these are updates delivered by e-mail once a day based on information you tell Google to watch for. Use it like the job board agents to establish daily feeds of the information you need. It's a fundamental tool and it's free.

➤ *eVoice:* Need a telephone number you can always rely on for free? Want to have a number in a different city because you're moving and employers will screen you out if they think they have to pay for your relocation? Want a phone your thoughtful children or roommate can't tie up? Then you need eVoice. Did I mention it'll deliver messages to your desktop (www.evoice.com)?

➤ *Grand Central:* if you're on the go and live on your cell, then you need to check out www.grandcentral.com by Google. It's your one-stop solution as a guerrilla job hunter: voicemail, e-mail, and a whole lot more to your cell phone.

GUERRILLA INTELLIGENCE

Guerrilla Googling and the Job Hunter's Dashboard
Amitai Givertz

Google's search engine has become an indispensible tool for everyone who spends any amount of time online. In the hands of a highly motivated operative, Google can be a job seeker's most powerful weapon.

When Google's various products and services are integrated for the single purpose of landing a job, that's "Googling." Using Gmail for sending off resumes; Google Docs for writing cover letters; Google Calendar for rescheduling the latest sorry-something-just-came-up-can-we-reschedule-the-interview-for-next-week-speaking-too-fast-to-catch-my-number-click is at best, ho-hum.

But when those same tools are applied for the sole purpose of gaining a competitive advantage to ensure your job search goals are attained, that's "Guerrilla Googling." What's more, while potentially quite dangerous, it's also a lot of fun.

Your Job Hunter's Dashboard
Guerrilla Googling is about replicating the enemies' process and systems to gather and monitor actionable intelligence so they can be engaged on the battleground of your choosing. All that is needed is a computer with Internet access and resolute determination.

A carefully chosen alias and password will give you access to your Job Hunter's Dashboard, a command-and-control center, if you will. And because Google is providing the platform, conceivably you could conduct your job search in places as far flung as the Smokin' Sadhu Cyber Café, Katmandu, or closer to home in the Kansas City Library.

Here are the first steps for getting your Dashboard up and running:

1. Create a Google account. Because we will be using this account for covert operations, choose an innocuous user name that cannot be traced back to you.

2. Register for the following services: iGoogle, Gmail, Google Reader, Google Docs, Notebook, Talk, and Google Sites. Other products and services will be added later.

3. If you'll be using a personal computer, you should also download the Google Toolbar and Google Desktop.

4. While you're at it, if you are not already using the Firefox browser, you should be. Firefox has a number of very useful extensions that will enhance your experience. Gmail Space, GMarks, Integrated Gmail, Google Date Keeper, and other add-ons will give you significantly improved results.

Next, sign into iGoogle where you'll see that everything you'll need to create a customizable homepage has been provided.

By configuring the various gadgets that are publicly available with some of our own creation, an innocuous iGoogle page can be transformed from something that's cool to something that is a mission-critical technology—your Job Hunter's Dashboard!

Armed with the same expertise as a top-notch recruiter, you can now wreak havoc by doing things like inserting yourself in the recruiting process before the recruiter even knows there is an opening coming down the pike.

Of course, we haven't discussed how to use Google Sites or Google Base to make your online resume easier for recruiters to find or how to text a recruiter who rarely, if ever, gets a resume delivered to his or her mobile.

We haven't discussed how to use Google for a soup-to-nuts direct marketing campaign or how to back up your most

(continued)

important files using your Gmail account. And we haven't mentioned yet that, with the exception of $0.51 paperback, all of this can be done without spending a dime.

Because all this and more can be achieved using a single Google account, and a well-managed command-and-control center, I hope you'll find some reason to explore these possibilities further.

Jump online and visit http://jobhunters.g-recruiting.com when you have a few minutes to spare. There you'll find a number of easy-to-follow tutorials that will guide you through the setup and configuration of your dashboard. You'll also find shortcuts and off-the-shelf gadgets that will save you time and effort as you get started.

All of the things described here can be achieved using Google products and services combined with a determination to get the job *you really* want.

Amitai Givertz is Principal, AMG Management Advisors. Fast becoming a central theorist and practitioner in twenty-first century online recruiting, Ami is widely recognized for his active participation in the ongoing debate on how social media, networking, and "2.0 values" can help advance the recruiting industry's progress in a fast-evolving world. He is the editor of RecruitingBlogs.com, a contributing editor on Recruiting.com, and sits on the Advisory Board for Kennedy Information's Recruiting Trends. Ami is also a member of the Human Capital Institute's Expert Advisor Panel, Internet Recruiting 2.0. Reach him at www.linkedin.com/in/amitai001.

■ MANAGING YOUR SCHEDULE AND PLANNING YOUR WORK

Looking at your job hunting as flextime or a mini-vacation is a mistake. If you want to succeed, you need to stay disciplined. I have met too many people who have said, "I'm going to take the summer off," only to be scrambling before winter comes. Good for you if you can do it, but while you are lounging by the pool, guerrilla job hunters are taking opportunities away from you. My advice: take 2 weeks off *after* you land your job.

Your full-time job is now looking for a job. Begin your day around 6:30 to 7:00 AM. That time of the morning, you will be free from distractions and many executives will be in their office waiting for your call (I'm kidding). They will be in the office trying to get a jump on their day's work, and you will be a nice distraction—after you learn how to talk to these people (discussed in Chapter 9, Fearless Warm Calling). It is also a mental conditioning exercise.

When you're job hunting, you need to maintain a regular day schedule. You must start your day at the same time every morning. You also need to finish on schedule and walk away at night or you'll quickly go nuts. My suggestion has always been to start at 6:30 AM working the phone and doing the related record keeping until 3 PM. At 3 PM, you start planning your activities for the next day and take any calls that come in from employers.

Balance your activity levels carefully. You need to plan your attack, and be immersed in the minutiae of your campaign on a daily basis. There is no point in firing off a thousand resumes and not following any of them up—because the follow-up is what gets you the interview. Nor is it sensible to forsake uncovering new opportunities while you are interviewing because you may not land any offers and then you will have to start from ground zero all over again.

Your day should be organized around calling employers to arrange interviews, networking, researching new opportunities, talking to headhunters, sending correspondence, and interviewing. To the best of your ability, you should establish a routine for your activities. You want to do high-stress things when your energy level is at its highest, and call employers when they are most receptive to a call.

If you wake up each day in a cold sweat, start your day by networking with your friends because they are more likely to be pleasant than will a complete stranger. If you have a heart of stone, you can begin calling employers first thing in the morning.

I have included an organizer in Appendix 1 for planning and monitoring all the essential components of your job search. I suggest you take it to your local photocopy center and have it copied onto an 11 × 17 sheet of paper. Keep this organizer on your desk:

1. Make the calls to employers to set up interviews first thing in the morning (6:00 to 8:00 AM). Employers will be easier to reach and are likely to be in a good mood because they haven't had time to spoil their day yet. You are a solution to the problems they had yesterday—a welcome distraction.

2. Next, move on to making networking calls to friends and associates to whom you've sent your resume. Put your effort where

the results are going to appear first. You also want to make these calls first thing in the day because generally you won't have been rejected by many people yet and your voice will project enthusiasm (if you have already been rejected, it likely wasn't work related).

3. Call recruiters next. Recruiters block out 8:00 to 10:00 AM for marketing calls, so although you want to get them early in the morning, don't interrupt those marketing calls ... after all, they could be marketing you.

4. Next, call those companies you identified yesterday as potentials.

5. Last, make a list of companies for tomorrow and start researching them on the web.

Some people think that getting an offer is the only indicator of success in job hunting, but they are wrong. Job hunting is a process with a beginning, middle, and end. If you nail the beginning and middle part early in the game, the end comes quickly.

■ THE GOLDEN SELLING HOUR(S)

If your calls are constantly being blocked by secretaries or receptionists, change your tactics. The best times to reach an executive are before 8:30 in the morning and after 5:30 PM. Most are at their desk early in the morning and leave late. Support staff generally only work from 9:00 to 5:00. When in doubt, call the main number until you don't get a receptionist.

GUERRILLA INTELLIGENCE

Common Ground—Online Job Searching for Women
Alison Doyle

When it comes to job searching and building your career, what you have in common outside of your job can be just as beneficial, or even more so, than what you have in common when it comes to your work, your career field, and your business connections.

I have Facebook friends who started out being friends on an e-mail list for working moms, back before Facebook existed. We're still in touch and those friends have helped boost my career and I've helped them with job searching.

Some of my closest LinkedIn connections became so partially because of job searching and career interests, but also because of other things we have in common—dogs with one group, politics with another, and our families with a third.

➤ *Discover your common ground.* One thing women do well is talk and it doesn't have to be on the phone or in-person. That dog connection has helped my book and my web site gain attention in a nationally syndicated column and on the Internet. How? The author and I became friends when our e-mails went beyond business and we discovered we were both "dog" people. A business relationship developed into a strong connection with someone who has helped my career immensely.

➤ *Expand your network.* Be open to accepting new connections and friends because you never know who might be able to help you in the future—perhaps referring you to a job list or providing a reference.

➤ *Join a group.* When you join a LinkedIn or Facebook group, you'll be able to add even further to your network. Join Facebook groups that have everything to do with what you're interested in outside of work, in addition to those that are career focused. Again, you'll have contacts that can assist when you need them.

➤ *Talk to your friends and contacts.* Pay attention to what your connections post. Add comments, share information, answer questions, and offer to help (networking works both ways—you get help and you provide assistance).

➤ *Share your situation.* When you're looking for a job and you're still employed, discreetly let your contacts know. Discreetly is the important part. I know one person who messaged all her LinkedIn connections including her boss to let them know she was job searching. Her boss wasn't amused and she ended up looking for a new job sooner rather than

(continued)

later. Message your friends and contacts privately to let them know. You'll be able to get advice, tips, job leads, references, and everything you need to job search effectively. If you are out of work, tell the world.

Alison Doyle is a job search and career expert with many years of experience in human resources, career development, and job searching. She has covered job searching for About.com (jobsearch.about.com) since 1998.

Chapter 4

Your Research Plan

Research: The Guerrilla's Competitive Edge

We will either find a way, or make one.

—HANNIBAL

Research is a guerrilla's competitive edge. It is an integral part of your job search. A company's web site and corporate marketing materials are designed to promote the best possible image; by learning a few clever research skills, you will be able to uncover and assess information that ordinary job hunters won't have. This information will help you make informed career choices.

Most job hunters think that reading a company's web site is all the research they need to do before a job interview—but they are wrong. Guerrillas know that it is only a start. In fact, it is not even where most guerrillas will start. When an interview is imminent, guerrillas will visit the company's web site and those of their chief competitors. Then they Google the company for:

- ➤ Articles
- ➤ Personal and corporate blogs
- ➤ Company newsletters
- ➤ Industry newsletters
- ➤ News clips
- ➤ Speeches or keynote presentations
- ➤ Membership in associations
- ➤ Resumes of former employees

The research skills discussed in this chapter enable you to fully research any industry or company any time, anywhere, and show you how to direct-source jobs like a headhunter. These 2 skills give you the inside track. You will be able to fill your opportunity pipeline full of jobs that other job hunters will never know exist.

■ YOUR RESEARCH BUDGET

Time, not money, buys the best research. Most of the information you need is available free through your local library or online. There certainly is a lot of information that you can buy, but usually these reports are summaries of information you can find yourself with a little digging if you know where to look. You won't learn these techniques anywhere else.

The basis for all good research starts with understanding what you need to know. You want to understand the intricacies of the industries that interest you and how to best position yourself—not just into your new job—but also into a succession of jobs that you can parlay into a 5-star career. To accomplish this, do your research in 3 steps:

1. Identify which industries you want to, or are qualified to, work in.

2. Locate which companies in those industries are of interest.

3. Evaluate who has the authority in those companies to hire you.

➤ Researching an Industry

To select an industry to research, you need to know which industries employ people with the skills you are marketing. Skills assessment can be tricky if you don't have access to a career counselor or career coach. Don't fret; the fastest, most effective way to determine which industries use your skills is to visit America's Career InfoNet online at www.acinet.org.

Go to their home page. Click on 1 of 2 sections depending on where you are starting your search: (1) Skills Profiler (if you are a new grad or career changer), or (2) Industry Information (if you know which industries you want to explore).

Skills Profiler
If you need to get a better understanding of the industries that use your skills because you are just starting your career or want to switch

Menu Search
Select an industry sector.

11 - Agriculture, Forestry, Fishing and Hunting
21 - Mining
22 - Utilities
23 - Construction
31 - Manufacturing

Search

Figure 4.1   Industry sectors.

careers, start with the Skills Profiler. It has a menu-driven assessment tool called "Skills Explorer" that will tell you, in about 5 minutes, which occupations and industries employ your skills. This is the most comprehensive tool of its kind on the Internet, and it is free. Not only will this easy-to-use tool tell you which industries use your skills, but when used in conjunction with the Industry Information tools that are available on the site, it will identify opportunities in your city or town that match your skills. Even if you already have a strong sense of what you want to do and where you want to do it, don't pass up the opportunity to consider all your possibilities.

Industry Information

The Industry Information section includes a menu-driven tool that allows you to look inside an industry and see which sectors employ those skills. If we use the Industry Information tool to look at the construction industry, here's what we find:

First we select "Construction" as our industry (see Figure 4.1).

We find the subsectors shown in Figure 4.2: Subsectors defined.

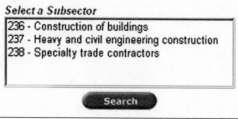

Select a Subsector

236 - Construction of buildings
237 - Heavy and civil engineering construction
238 - Specialty trade contractors

Search

Figure 4.2   Subsectors defined.

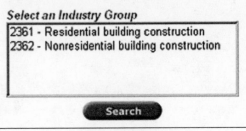

Figure 4.3   Industry group.

Selecting the "construction of buildings" option, we get the choices shown in Figure 4.3.

Selecting "Nonresidential building construction," our choices become those shown in Figure 4.4.

If you select "Commercial building construction," we get a summary screen that includes additional links to the following information:

➤ Employment guides on the industry

➤ An up-to-date report on industry trends

➤ Profile of an occupation in this industry

➤ Employment trends by industry and occupation

➤ Location of employers in this industry

If you select "Profile an occupation," the link will detail all the occupations that use your skills in the construction industry.

Selecting "Locate employers" takes you to another menu-driven series of screens that allows you to find qualifying jobs in any area of the United States.

To demonstrate the power of this tool, I performed a search on construction jobs in Anniston, Alabama. Figure 4.5 shows a screen shot of my search results.

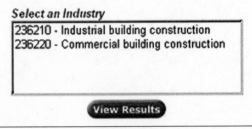

Figure 4.4   Industrial or commercial.

Below is a list of employers that match your criteria. Select an employer name for detailed information.

Your Search Criteria :

State - Alabama <u>Change State</u>
Region - Anniston, AL <u>Change Region</u>
City(ies) - Anniston <u>Change City(ies)</u>
Industry Sector - Construction <u>Change Industry Sector</u>
Industry Subsector - Construction of Buildings <u>Change Industry Subsector</u>
Industry Group - Residential Building Construction <u>Change Industry Group</u>
■ <u>Narrow Your Search By Firm Size</u>

Displaying Employers 1-25 of 36   **Jump to**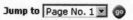

Figure 4.5   Select employer.

As you can see, I found 36 job openings that day. Clicking on a job link took me to detailed information on the company and the job.

Guerrilla, does it get much easier? I think not.

Here are 5 questions you should be asking yourself as you start to explore industries. Some of these questions are raised and answered in the available reports, but not all:

1. What are the general trends in the industry—by sector?
2. Where are the hot spots—those areas where growth will remain steady for several years? This can be represented by:

   a. A group of products or services

   b. A specific geographic area

   Construction may be slowing down in one section of the country and getting ready to boom in another, or residential construction may have peaked and commercial construction is rising. It is important to drill down to find details if you want to make an informed decision.

3. Which skills are in demand?

   a. Now and in the future

   b. By discipline: sales, marketing, finance, engineering, trades

4. What is the demographic profile of the workforce? These studies or reports are most often referred to as Labor Market Information (LMI) studies.

   You want to be able to assess whether there might be a continuing demand for your skills, and a good indicator of this may be the median age of the workforce. If the median age is, say 55, then there will be people retiring soon and this might increase demand for the profession.

5. Is the industry prone to outsourcing or offshoring?

Look into which businesses are starting up and getting funding from banks and venture capital firms and look at which companies the mutual fund companies are investing in. The easiest way to do this is to find the web sites of some of the mutual fund companies that are reported weekly in your local daily newspaper.

To see which industries are receiving start-up or additional funding, I recommend 3 sites:

1. The Money Tree Survey (www.pwcmoneytree.com/moneytree/index.jsp)
2. PE Week Wire (www.privateequityweek.com)
3. Just Sell (www.justsell.com)

If you can't find what you are looking for, you need to contact the industry associations. When you find the national association, visit its web site and see what free resources are available to help in your job search. This could include:

➤ Labor market information studies
➤ Membership lists
➤ Industry reports
➤ A job board

Also see if there is a local chapter that may have networking events. Some associations even have official discussion forums. Review all the industry information with a keen eye to what the industry leaders feel the challenges are for the future. For an up-to-the-moment view, read industry trade magazines. They are listed at www.specialissues.com/lol/.

➤ **Locating Companies of Interest**

Once you have identified an industry, you need to research companies. Your research may be broad and include all the companies in the industry because, frankly, you will move anywhere for the right opportunity—or it could be very local. Your first mission is to locate national directories that include lists of the companies. A guerrilla would start at CEO Express online at www.ceoexpress.com. CEO Express has links to nearly every source of information you need to get yourself started: news, stock quotes, and IPO filings, all in one place.

Privately Held Companies

These are the hardest to research cheaply because the companies don't have a strict requirement to report to anyone but their limited shareholders. If they have anything to hide, like pending litigation or poor financials, you really have to dig. Here's where to start:

➤ Dun & Bradstreet (www.dnb.com/us/ D&B) are masters of information, much of it a la carte or free.

➤ Thomas Register (www.thomasregister.com).

➤ Hoover's (www.hoovers.com).

➤ D&B Million Dollar Database (www.dnbmdd.com/mddi) has information on approximately 1,600,000 U.S. and Canadian leading public and private businesses.

➤ Forbes 500 Largest Private Companies (www.forbes.com/businesstech/) is always one of my favorites, but it is only useful for the largest companies.

➤ *BusinessWeek* works well, too (www.businessweek.com).

➤ Thomas Register (www4.thomasregister.com) provides information on most manufacturers.

Publicly Held Companies

Public companies are easier to research, especially with the increased reporting requirements that have been dictated by Sarbanes-Oxley compliance. However, it still requires work. Here are your best sources of information:

➤ Dun & Bradstreet (www.dnb.com/us/); always start here.

➤ Edgar Online People (people.edgar-online.com/people) searches Securities and Exchange filings by a person's name or displays all people associated with a specific company name. Very useful.

➤ Million Dollar Database (www.dnbmdd.com/mddi/) provides information on approximately 1,600,000 U.S. and Canadian leading public and private businesses.

➤ Lexis Nexis (www.lexisnexis.com) has legal, news, public records, and business information.

➤ Corporate Information (www.corporateinformation.com/home.asp) is a free site that requires registration.

➤ Financial Web (www.financialweb.com) lists stocks, SEC filings.

➤ Fortune 500 (500 largest U.S. companies).

➤ GrayMetalBox (www.graymetalbox.com) is the web site for Trade Scenarios Reports and Research Center.

➤ 123 Jump (www.financialweb.com); get SEC filings, company news, and links to home pages, current quotes and graphs, and so on.

➤ Wall Street Research Net (stocks.Internetnews.com) has the most comprehensive company news, EPS estimates, links to home pages, and so on.

Hardcore news sites you should monitor include:

➤ www.cnbc.com

➤ www.money.com

➤ finance.yahoo.com

➤ www.marketwatch.com

➤ www.foxbusiness.com

Next, visit those company web sites. If they are not available in this day and age, that will mean they are very, very small. The easiest way to research small businesses that don't have a web presence is your local Chamber of Commerce or the archives of the local newspaper.

Competitive Intelligence

Here are the questions you should ask about each company you are interested in.

Company Growth

➤ Is the company in growth mode? Why or why not?

➤ What external factors affect its growth?

➤ Where is this company in the cycle? At the end or just the beginning?

➤ Who are its Tier I and Tier II competitors?

➤ Is there turnover in senior management? Has it been forced by the board or did people reach retirement age? Was a successor being groomed in the wings?

Financial

➤ What do the numbers say? How are the company's balance sheet, income statement, earnings per share, dividend(s)? What do they indicate about the company's health?

➤ What is the debt-to-equity ratio? Remember, cash is king.

➤ How is the stock price doing? Why is it moving?

➤ How is the stock doing against its competitors? Against the market as a whole?

➤ Are there other companies where you should be interviewing?

➤ What do the analysts think?

Strategy

➤ What were last year's short-term and long-term strategies/objectives? Were they met?

Market Share

➤ Are they dominant players? Why? How big is the market? What percentage of the market do they own? What is the next market?

➤ Does the company have any new products/services/patents?

➤ Is the company strong or weak domestically versus overseas? Where does the company make most of its profit?

➤ What do each of the regions and products/divisions contribute to the whole?

Technology Issues

➤ Can cost efficiencies be driven through modernization?

➤ How does the Internet affect the company? If it is a threat, does the company have a strategy to address it?

Legal and Regulatory Issues

➤ Are there any pending bills or regulations that might have a significant impact?

➤ Are there any patent infringements?

People

➤ What do people say about the company publicly?

➤ Is the company being sued or has it been sued by former employees?

Assessing Fit

You don't want to waste your time and effort on companies that are not going to be a good fit. Guerrilla, use this information to get a picture of the organization. Do you think the company/organization has a future? Why or why not? What factors impede the company? It is critical that you understand this information thoroughly before you approach the company. Armed with this background information, you will be able to answer with confidence these typical interview questions:

➤ What do you know about our company?

➤ What are your thoughts on the challenges facing our industry and how can you help us?

➤ What would you do in your first 90 days if we hired you as a _____?

Imagine how surprised the interviewer will be when you can articulate what the company's issues are—how your experience fits with their needs and what you would do first. You'll blow them away. On the other hand, if you haven't done your homework before you go in for an interview, you're dead on arrival.

Librarians Are Your Allies

If you're having trouble finding lists of companies or information on specific companies, call your local library and talk to the research librarian. Treat these people like gold. Put them on your Christmas list. Bring them boxes of candy. Buy them flowers on their birthdays. They have forgotten more about how to retrieve information than you will ever know. They are the Sherlock Holmes of reference information. So make friends, ask lots of questions, and take notes, but only after you have at least tried to find some of the information on your own.

If your local library does not have anything on hand in the periodicals, business, or reference sections, then inquire about the interlibrary loan service. Chances are the information you need is available somewhere, just not there. Many people don't realize that libraries all over the world formally share books, CDs, and other reference materials with each other. The definitive source for any book published in the United States is the Library of Congress. If it is in print, the Library of Congress has it and your local librarian can get it.

The libraries may be able to help you access some of these market resource firms as well:

➤ Aberdeen Group (www.aberdeen.com)

➤ Forrester Research (www.forrester.com)

➤ Gartner Group (www.gartnergroup.com)

➤ IDG (www.idg.com)

➤ Business.com http (www.business.com)

Alternative Sites

The Internet allows you to search all types of alternate sources of information that may be of value to you as you narrow your list of companies:

➤ The Internet Public Library (www.ipl.org)

➤ The Digital Librarian: a librarian's choice of the best of the Web (www.digital-librarian.com)

➤ Vault (www.Vault.com)

➤ The Standard (www.thestandard.com)

Of particular interest if you're trying to get information on private companies is the Search Systems Free Public Records Directory at www.searchsystems.net. This is the largest directory of links to free public record databases on the Internet. What is of interest to guerrillas are the business information and corporate filings sections. Sometimes the best information is that which the company has no control over.

Then there is a very low-tech way—the Yellow Pages or sites that support business phone number listings on the web:

➤ Big Book (www.bigbook.com)

➤ GTE Superpages (www.superpages.com)

➤ How to Find the Hiring Managers

Now that you have a list of 10 to 20 companies, you need to find the people who can actually hire you.

Alternative 1

Guerrillas know the most direct way is often the easiest. Use your telephone. I always call first and ask who is responsible for "X." "X" is the title of the executive I want to speak with. Seven out of 10 times this will work. If it doesn't, call back at lunchtime and ask the noon hour receptionist; generally, they are not as guarded about the information they give out.

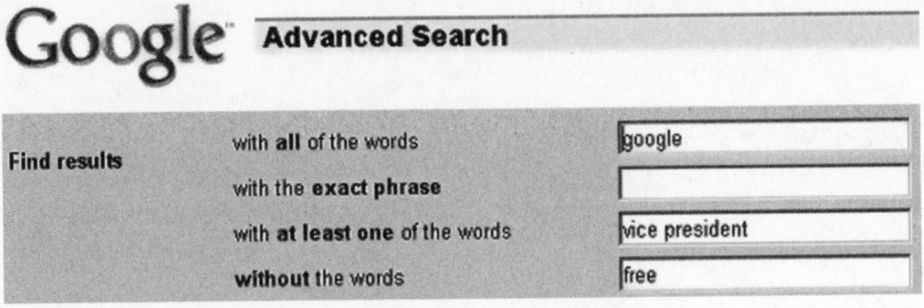

Figure 4.6 "Without the words."

Alternative 2
Go to each company's web site. If you are lucky, it will identify all their senior executives. Web information should be up-to-the-moment, but phone and verify.

Alternative 3
Google your way in. If you are having difficulty finding the name, go to Google's advanced search box. Type in the company name in the first box and the title of the person you think your future boss reports to in the third box. Try doing this with the company "Google" in the first box, "vice president" in the third, and "free" in the fourth box "without the words" (see Figure 4.6).

If you run the search, you will find a list of Google's executives at: www.google.com/corporate/execs.html. This is a simple way to find information fast.

Once you have the name, run a search on the individual through Google. This time you put the first and last name in the first box and the company name in the third box. This will produce a list of conferences the person has attended, speeches, press releases, news articles, clubs the executive belongs to, and so on.

■ A GUERRILLA RESEARCH ALTERNATIVE

What if you don't have time to do a full search because you need a job now or at least by tomorrow afternoon? Is there a faster way? Yes!

Here's a super-fast way to find nearly all the companies in your area that can use your skills:

➤ Decide what job you are going to look for. In our example, we are going to look for retail management jobs in New York City.

Google Advanced Search

Find results	with **all** of the words	retail manager resume submit
	with the **exact phrase**	212
	with **at least one** of the words	
	without the words	free

Figure 4.7   Advanced Google search.

➤   Choose key words that are specific to the type of job you are looking for. In Figure 4.7, we use Retail and Manager. You can use a job title if you wish, in which case you need to enclose the term in quotation marks: "retail manager."

➤   Add these 4 words: "job," "resume," "submit," and "free" as illustrated in Figure 4.7.

As constructed, this search string instructs Google to return web sites that have retail manager jobs but are not ads for resume-submitting businesses.

In the "without the words" option, we type the word "free." Why specifically ban the word free? Because the word free is not used on corporate web sites nor is it used in job descriptions. It is, however, used to sell resume-submitting services, and we don't want to waste time wading through those sites to find the real jobs.

You can see the number of hits that are returned by adding the words one at a time (see Table 4.1).

Table 4.1   Search Term Results

Words	Number of Hits	Relevance to Us
Retail manager	11,700,000	Low
Resume	1,670,000	Low, includes candidate resumes
Submit	302,000	Low, includes job boards
212	45,900	High, it restricts responses to just the area code 212
Not "free"	1,300	Very, very high, this excludes all the resume submittal sites and shows just the jobs available in area code 212 for New York

There are still too many hits, so we add the area code 212, which in turn reduces the hits to local retail manager jobs in the 212 area code only. This is a good list to start with.

Note: Your results may vary because Google changes minute by minute.

GUERRILLA MISSION

Now you try it. Fire up your PC and connect to the Internet. Go to www.google.com. Click the Advanced Search link and you should see a screen like the one shown in Figure 4.7. Replace the 2 words "retail" and "manager" with 2 words that are specific to your job search. Next, replace the 212 area code with your area code or the area code of the city you want to research. Click the "Google search" button and start reading. This research is fast and accurate. It won't uncover every opportunity, but it will enable you to find many more offerings than you would see using just the job boards or newspapers—and you will do it much faster, too.

■ FINDING LISTS OF PROSPECTS

Using the Internet is not the only way to gather information. Here are some easy ways to find lists of prospects for your job-hunting campaign.

➤ Chambers of Commerce

Nearly every city and town in the United States has a Chamber of Commerce whose sole job is to promote commerce. If you call their office, I guarantee you they will give you a list of their members. It may also appear on their web site. Chamber of Commerce members tend to be among the most civic minded in your community and are quite accessible. Finding them on Google is simple: just type in "Chamber of Commerce" with the name of your town or city and Google will find it for you.

➤ Industry Associations

If you are looking for information on a specific industry, business associations can be helpful. As noted, the American Society of Association Executives is a good place to start: www.asaenet.org.

➤ Industry Newsletters and Professional Journals

The targeted readership for these publications means that you can often pick up leads from the authors of the articles by calling them. These authors tend to be industry experts who know everyone.

Looking for start-ups? Then you have to check out startups.alltop.com/ run by none other than Guy Kawasaki of—you guessed it—Apples' first marketing guru and the author of many of the most useful books on management today.

➤ Web Sites for Conferences, Conventions, or Trade Shows

To find events that are specific to your chosen industry, do a Web search for an industry name and terms such as conference, trade show, or convention (see Figure 4.8).

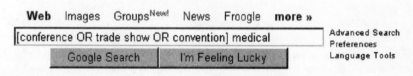

Figure 4.8   Google search industry.

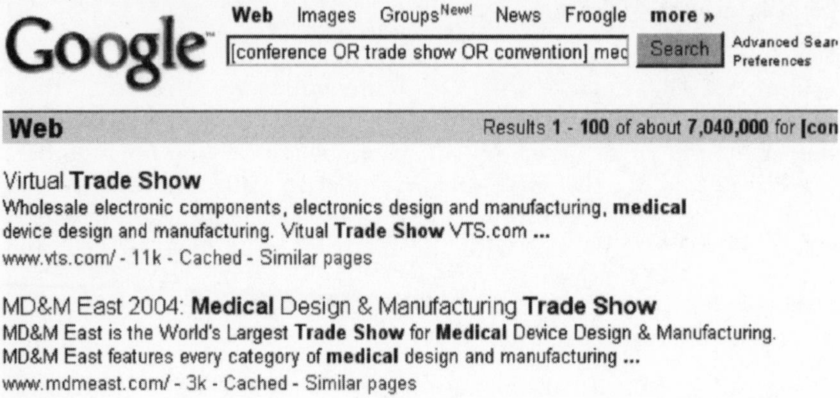

Google™ Web Images Groups^{New!} News Froogle **more »**

[conference OR trade show OR convention] med Search Advanced Sear
Preferences

Web Results **1 - 100** of about **7,040,000** for [con

Virtual **Trade Show**
Wholesale electronic components, electronics design and manufacturing, **medical**
device design and manufacturing. Vitual **Trade Show** VTS.com ...
www.vts.com/ - 11k - Cached - Similar pages

MD&M East 2004: **Medical** Design & Manufacturing **Trade Show**
MD&M East is the World's Largest **Trade Show** for **Medical** Device Design & Manufacturing.
MD&M East features every category of **medical** design and manufacturing ...
www.mdmeast.com/ - 3k - Cached - Similar pages

Figure 4.9   Google search industry links.

Google search industry shows the screen for a Google search for [conference or tradeshow or convention] and the industry, which for this example is medical.

Google's results reveal 2 large shows. Clicking on the links will bring you the site and a wealth of information (see Figure 4.9).

GUERRILLA INTELLIGENCE

Service Corp of Retired Executives (SCORE)

Mark Haluska

SCORE is comprised of both retired and working business executives. These people know decision makers! In many cases, they still work together, go golfing, belong to the same clubs, and mix at socials. So, they personally have a first degree contact with decision makers, many of which are current or past close colleagues.

Most people think of SCORE as a resource (which it in reality is) when you want to get advice to start up a new business venture. But with a little tact, a true guerrilla would turn that inside out to obtain solid leads.

Contact SCORE; ask to speak with an executive who (and this is important) has worked or (most preferably) is working in your profession/industry. They will assume you need business advice. Pleasantly greet them preferably on the phone and tell them you have a problem and thought they would be someone who could help. Then tell the counselor what you really need and do it in this order: tell them what you do then quickly (no more than 1 minute) hit them with quantifiable and truly impressive facts that you've outlined on your guerrilla resume. Next, ask how does my experience sound to you?

Then, go for the gusto and ask how you can obtain the specific decision makers' names and contact information (not human resources, unless you are in human resources) at a given company or companies who could use your expertise to help them solve a pressing problem(s).

This "back door" approach will probably take the counselor by surprise, but that is okay. They have volunteered to join SCORE because they want to help people. SCORE is a free resource that all guerrillas should attempt to use. This tactic can fast track you into a decision-maker's office and your competition won't even think about it until they've read this book. I highly recommend you find a SCORE representative near you (www.score.org/findscore/index.html).

Contributed by Mark J. Haluska, founder and executive director, Real Time NetWork, www.rtnetwork.net LinkedIn address: www.linkedin.com/in/MarkJ.Haluska.

GUERRILLA TIPS

An immediate way to find hot leads is to ask your friends, family, or business associates who have recently landed a job in the industry if you can see their lists of prospects. The research will be current and likely pretty detailed, too. They may even know of openings that were not suitable for them but might be ideal for you.

Here are a few other sources:

➤ Career centers and job clubs
➤ College and university career placement centers
➤ Internet career sites
➤ Job fairs and career days

➤ Local and federal government personnel offices
➤ Yellow Pages
➤ Your area business journal (www.bizjournals.com)

■ STUFF THE CIA WOULD RATHER YOU DIDN'T KNOW

The length of this book does not allow me to do a detailed exposé on the really advanced means for unearthing information. A lot of cloak-and-dagger work goes on behind the scenes of many search assignments. Your quest to find your dream job is unlikely to require that kind of search. Explaining those advanced strategies and tools is beyond the scope of this book and would require 200 or 300 additional pages, but I won't leave you hanging either.

The United States has 2 gurus on the application of competitive intelligence to recruiting and job hunting: Shally Steckerl and Dave Carpe. These 2 professionals are the absolute best when it comes to using the Internet. I highly recommend you visit their web sites if you want more information or a deeper understanding of how to use search engines and the Internet to maximize your job search.

Shally Steckerl's site Job Machine has more than 100 screens full of tips and techniques for finding your way around. A "Google Cheat-Sheet" and a "Tool-Bag CD" are available on Shally's site (JobMachine.net).

Dave Carpe's site Passing Notes at www.passingnotes.com is a virtual cornucopia of tools and tricks that will take you deep into the world of competitive intelligence. Check out the article, "Confessions of a Call Girl . . . or How to Give Good Phone."

GUERRILLA INTELLIGENCE

Become an Easy Target

Jim Stroud

If I wanted to hire you, could I find you? If I looked on Monster, CareerBuilder, and HotJobs, perhaps I could; but what if I did not look there, or on any other job board for that matter? Here is an ugly little truth that job seekers do not think about. When a company posts a job description on Monster or searches its database for resumes, it costs money. So, you know what happens? Large companies look for free resumes on the Web to save the money they would have spent on job boards, and smaller companies that do not have accounts with these job boards look on the Web to find free resumes. The bottom line is that if your resume is not online, you are doing yourself a disservice. If you search the Web for "free web hosting," I dare say that you will find plenty of resources for posting your resume (or any other content) online for free.

To be sure, positioning your resume where all recruiters will have free access to it is imperative, yet that is only part of a winning strategy. Recruiters look for resumes using a series of specialized searches called "searchstrings." Searchstrings are based on keywords that the recruiter thinks would be on your resume. For example, a recruiter looking for a programmer in Atlanta might visit Google and enter the following searchstring: intitle:resume programmer education atlanta | GA 678 | 770 | 404 -submit -apply ext:doc | ext:pdf.

To explain this searchstring, I am looking for documents formatted in Word or PDF that have "resume" as a title with the keywords "programmer" and "education" mentioned in the document. I am also looking for the words "Atlanta" or "GA" because that is the preferred location. Furthermore, I added area codes specific to the Atlanta area as well. Why? Candidates often list their phone numbers on their resumes. To see the results of this search, please visit: tinyurl.com/6b23h4 and you will be redirected to a Google search results page.

Now that you know how recruiters search the Web for resumes, why not make it easy for them to find you? I suggest that you create a resume profile page in lieu of a cover letter. What is that? A resume profile page is a keyword list a recruiter can scan to get a quick understanding of what you have to offer. When I was looking for work in 2002, I created an HTML version of my resume profile page and placed it online. Today, I am still being contacted by recruiters who have found my resume profile from a Google search. (See it for yourself: jimstroud.com/resume.htm.)

(continued)

The moral of the story is simply this: If you position yourself to be found, you will not have to look so much. (Smile.)

Jim Stroud is a social media development manager for *EnglishCafe*, the premier English learning community for global professionals. Prior to EnglishCafe, Jim Stroud amassed a decade of recruiting experience consulting for such companies as Microsoft, Google, MCI, and Siemens. He can be reached via his web site: www.JimStroud.com.

GUERRILLA TIPS

➤ Use free resources first: Yellow Pages, Internet, and the library.

➤ The more specific you can be about what you are looking for, the more relevant will be your results.

➤ Use free government services—you have already paid for them.

➤ Determine which companies are doing business in your field.

➤ Narrow your choices geographically if appropriate—look locally first.

➤ Read this year's annual report first and then compare it with last year's.

➤ Start with the company web site.

➤ Run a Google search.

➤ Review appropriate blogs.

➤ Google former employees.

➤ Always weigh information with a critical eye.

Part

II

Weapons That Make You a Guerrilla

Chapter 5

Resume Writing and Cover Letter Boot Camp

How to Overhaul Your Personal Marketing Materials

Common sense in an uncommon degree is what the world calls wisdom.

—SAMUEL TAYLOR COLERIDGE

Despite advances in technology and the ever-increasing sophistication of employers, job hunters have predictable habits. Most look for a job the same way they always have. They write a resume. Ask their friends. Respond to newspaper ads. Click and apply through job boards. And wait. And wait. And wait ... for something—anything—to happen. Not too terribly twenty-first century of them.

Guerrilla, your resume is a marketing tool. It must compel its reader to pick up the phone and call you. Job hunters who write conventional resumes can count on the competition to be fierce. Let me show you a more successful approach.

■ WHY YOUR RESUME MAY BE OVERLOOKED

My wife will periodically call me at the office and ask me to pass by the supermarket on my way home to pick up bread and milk to tide us over until her next trip to the store (we have 4 growing children). Like

95

most men, I enter the supermarket on autopilot with my list in hand and head straight for the items I need. The nice displays and weekly specials blur past me. The way I shop for groceries is not unlike how your resume gets screened when you apply for a job. Generally the people who do the first pass on a stack of resumes are working off a list someone handed them. Their instructions are, "just whittle down this pile by looking for these skills/competencies or technologies," so that's all they scan for.

There isn't really a lot of thinking beyond the exact list. If you have the right stuff, your resume goes into one pile if not ... well, you're out. If the checklist says "Oracle" or "project manager" and yours says "database" or "construction manager" you're out. There's no time, and generally little incentive, ability, or interest, from the people who do the initial scan to "read between the lines."

The one-size-fits-all mentality spills over into their cover letters, too. Many job hunters respond to the specifics of an ad in their cover letter and then cross their fingers and hope the reader connects the dots. In reality, though, cover letters are rarely read with interest because most are so vague or poorly written they add little value. It's likely that only the opening line has been customized and the rest of it is as generic as the accompanying resume. People who spend even a minimum of time scanning resumes can spot these fakes quickly—with typical results.

Candidates often stuff their resumes with laundry lists of the functions and responsibilities they've had in past jobs in a desperate attempt to cover all their bases. This approach rarely pays off, however, because the amount of information you would have to put into a general, all-purpose resume is so enormous that you'd need to write a book—which of course no one would read.

Length is not an issue. Content is. People will read any length of resume *if* the content is of interest to them, and that's the secret. Ideally, a resume should contain no more and no less than the exact information an employer is looking for. After all, every employer expects that you are so interested in their company that you have written a resume just for them. Realistic? No. Reality? Yes, I'm afraid so.

Never assume that just because you had a particular responsibility, performed a particular function, or accomplished miracles that required super-human effort, the person reading your resume can automatically link that to the challenges faced by their company. The onus is on you to guide them to the conclusion you want them to draw. You have to motivate them to pick up the phone and schedule an interview with you.

The content of your resume has to be relevant to your reader. It must address their specific needs clearly—instantly. It's a laser-guided missile, not a dumb bomb. If your resume is in response to an advertised opening, it reflects the exact needs profiled in the ad. If it's sent to a targeted group of companies, it demonstrates how you can make them money, save them money, and increase their efficiencies. If it's a networking resume, it addresses the type of problem your contact's peers are likely to be facing. It's never vague or wishy-washy. It's always direct and specific.

Guerrillas know this. They understand that people are motivated by their own selfish interests. They know they need to guide, cajole, and dare interviewers with a snapshot of what you can bring to the table. A hint of the results you can accomplish.

Most people have many great accomplishments they can leverage for their next career move. Yet for many of these same people their resumes are bland replicas of the generic all-purpose resume in vogue these days. A document that merely mimics what a resume writer thought was important. In reality, only you understand what you've accomplished that would be of interest to a potential employer.

Ask yourself. No—better yet—cut your name off the top of your resume and give it to a couple of your best friends. Tell them it's the resume of one of your mutual contacts and ask them if they can guess who it is. If they can't tell it's you or, worse, if they think it's someone else you have a problem—the description of your accomplishments and your jobs are too generic. If it makes you look like a hundred other applicants who are also "project managers," "teachers," "accountants" or whatever, how do you expect an employer to select you for an interview? Yes, you could get lucky, but luck is so unpredictable!

So, your first objective is to make sure your resume is read. One of the biggest mistakes candidates make is assuming that just because they send a resume to a prospective employer or recruiter, it will be read. Ain't so!

■ ALL RESUMES ARE NOT CREATED EQUAL

If you want to be seen, you have to have a competitive resume to stand out. It's rarely the most qualified that land interviews; it's normally the ones who are the most impressive on paper. The best resumes "speak" to employers, providing quick insight into your personality and drive to succeed.

A resume can serve you in a variety of ways, but it is primarily used in making contacts with prospective employers so that you can:

➤ Respond to a job opening.
➤ Create unsolicited demand for your skills.

➤ Cut and paste to fill out an online application form.

➤ Supplement (not replace) a company's standard job application.

➤ Rehearse before interviews.

➤ Draw the interviewer's attention to a particular accomplishment during interviews.

➤ Tailor a person-specific thank you letter after an interview.

➤ Send an aid to your references so they'll remember what you did, especially if you were one of many on a team.

➤ Refer to it during telephone interviews as a reminder because, after all, the interviewer has a copy.

➤ Prompt a recipient for the purposes of networking.

A guerrilla resume is a multidimensional, multipurpose document. It is:

➤ Your introduction to a prospective employer,

➤ The first impression recruiters will have of you,

➤ The key to positioning your seniority, and

➤ A bargaining chip for your salary negotiations

In other words, it is a significant document in the advancement of your career.

■ STANDARD AND EXTREME GUERRILLA RESUMES

A Standard Guerrilla Resume is a cross between a chronological resume and a functional resume ... on steroids.

Like a functional resume, it highlights your best skills and achievements. Like a chronological resume, it presents your experience and education in order, from most recent to earliest.

You can use a Standard Guerrilla Resume if you:

➤ Are just leaving school and lack experience,

➤ Have extensive experience,

➤ Are making a career change, or

➤ Need to explain time away from work due to illness or other matters.

In short, the Standard Guerrilla Resume will work for most people in most situations.

This resume has all the information that we, as experienced employment professionals, are looking for in a candidate. Every Standard Guerrilla Resume includes the following 5 parts:

1. *Objective* or *Summary*, focused on either one job title or a narrow skill set.

2. *Select Accomplishments* and/or *Special Skills* list as a kind of executive summary of the best, most relevant 4 or 5 points about you, which map to the requirements for the position you want or would be most relevant to the employer[s] you're targeting. If you have a strong mix of specific achievements and skills, you can include both sections.

3. *Experience* or *Employment History*, detailing your relevant paid and unpaid work history, as well as internships. This section should go back only about 10 to 15 years in detail and summarize earlier work.

4. *Education/Training* section, where you list your degrees, relevant training, certification, and so on.

5. *Additional Information*, as needed, at the end. Here you can include your computer skills, relevant hobbies, volunteer work, and so on.

In Appendix 2, take a look at a Standard Guerrilla Resume that won its author a job.

A WAR STORY

Steve Duncan

I remember when I first saw David's Extreme Resume example, and I thought it was pretty cool. I had some endorsements on Linkedin.com, which I quoted in the margin, added accomplishments and skills, and got it together over a few days. I remember at the time that it seemed like such a bold way to do a resume. I was just sure the first time I sent it to anyone I'd get clobbered. My earlier efforts at nontraditional resume styles resulted in surly calls demanding a rewrite. I just didn't get the point. I'd rewrite it, resend it, and never hear anything again.

I sent my Extreme Resume to the first opportunity, and immediately got a call. The person was very interested in me, but then asked if I could send a "real" resume. At first I was frustrated. After all, isn't a resume supposed to be the silver bullet? First date, courtship, and marriage proposal all in one document? Nope. Part of David's advice was that the only purpose of a resume is to *get a call*. And it did. It took me a while to understand this and really leverage it.

"Real resume?" I learned to ask, innocently. "What do you mean?" The ensuing conversation was a great chance to learn what was important to the caller and was always decisive and effective, even if the opportunity wasn't a good fit. It helped me better understand what I was really looking for, and also helped me tweak the resume to better represent myself. Usually the person would ask about something that was already on the resume. "Where's your work history?" they'd ask. I'd point it out to them, and they'd soften. It's about getting enough foot in the door so you can start a conversation and real communication.

I used my Extreme Resume to get my current position, and the human resources director made no bones about telling me she loved it. Others, including headhunters, have said the same. I've had a few who apologetically asked for it in word format, or in strict chronological format, to satisfy the computer-based resume systems. That's okay, I don't mind because by then it's done the job—the rest is just satisfying the bureaucracy.

I've also had a few who just didn't get it. I've learned to not chase after them because if they don't understand the resume, then I'm not going to be a good fit. It's good to remember that the goal isn't just a position, it's the *right* position.

Compliments of Steve Duncan at www.linkedin.com/in/steveduncan/.

The *Extreme* version takes the Standard Guerrilla Resume to a whole new level. Like a triple espresso or a Ferrari Testarossa, it's not for everyone.

CAUTION

If you use an Extreme Guerrilla Resume, be prepared to back it up with facts and figures in the interview. You will be asked! So be sure to document your claims meticulously ahead of time.

Use an Extreme Guerrilla Resume if you:

➤ Face enormous competition for a limited number of jobs and need to crush your competition

➤ Want to "test the waters" before launching a comprehensive job hunt

➤ Want to create a job in a company that has no openings

This version has all the parts of a Standard Guerrilla Resume, plus one or more of the following (the more of these you include, the more powerful your finished product will be):

➤ *Proof section (mandatory):* This column goes on the left side of the resume, below your name. Here you can insert logos of past/current employers or clients, to take advantage of the halo effect of prestigious company names. Also, you can include quotes from people familiar with your work; these function like mini-testimonials and are *extremely* powerful.

➤ *"Grabber" statement at the top (optional):* This can be a dictionary definition ("rainmaker" or "catalyst," for example) or a brief quote from someone familiar with your work. The grabber functions as a hook to literally grab a reader's attention.

➤ *Career Driver section (optional):* This aggressively worded statement comes right before your experience section. Here is where you tell employers—in no uncertain terms—how much better you will make their lives after you are hired.

Done correctly, an Extreme Guerrilla Resume will get you an interview almost every time. It's that powerful.

In Appendix 2 take a look at an Extreme Guerrilla Resume that won the author a job.

➤ The Standard Guerrilla Resume

In Chapter 2 you assembled the necessary facts, figures, and results. It's time to start putting them all together. It's time to start writing.

Create a Standard Guerrilla Resume. Even if you plan to do an Extreme version later, you'll still need to include the parts found in this chapter.

To recap, your Standard Guerrilla Resume is made up of the following 5 components:

1. Objective or Summary

2. Select Accomplishments and/or Special Skills

3. Experience

4. Education/Training

5. Additional Information

And, it bears repeating that your Guerrilla Resume, whether it's a Standard or Extreme version, will be one page in length—no more. You may be asked to bring a longer, 2-page resume, but don't worry, just do a 1-page Guerrilla Resume aimed directly at their needs.

Objective or Summary

The first and most important part of your Guerrilla Resume is the Objective or Summary statement at the beginning. It should be focused on either one job title or one narrow skill set.

A narrow focus is essential, because you don't have 10 or 15 seconds for your resume to impress readers, as you may have thought. You have only about 3 seconds to impress today's harried, hurried, frenetic, time-starved readers. That is, employers must find something compelling in the first 3 seconds of reading your resume for them to want to keep reading. Otherwise, it goes in the trash.

So let's make the most of this all-important real estate at the top of your Guerrilla Resume—the part they'll see in those first 3 seconds—by leading with an eye-catching opening.

If you don't know the title of the job you're applying for, you should at least know what skills you can use. So, start your resume with 1 of 2 headings: Objective or Summary.

An Objective including a job title is a great way to start your resume. It shows that you know exactly what job the employer is trying to fill. Examples:

OBJECTIVE

Restaurant Management where more than 10 years of food service and management experience will contribute to efficient operations.

OBJECTIVE

Network Administrator where 3 years of successful experience and training will add value.

OBJECTIVE

Pharmaceutical Sales Rep where 8 years of training and experience in health care and sales will add to profitability.

Notice the language and format here. By starting off with the title of the job you know the employer is trying to fill, it's like calling them by their first name. It shows you know something about their company and their situation. It creates immediate rapport with your reader and gives you an immediate advantage. It's so simple, yet so powerful!

Plus, not only does the wording of this Objective tell the hiring manager exactly what job you want to fill, it also tells him that you want to "add" or "contribute" something that will make his life easier. Again, this is simple, subtle, and ... effective!

But what if you don't know the exact job title the employer wants to fill? (Well, you should, from your research of the company and its job postings. So don't give up that easily.)

But let's say you don't have one specific job in mind. Then what?

Start your Guerrilla Resume with a Summary. This will focus the reader on the skills you've used while giving you a bit more flexibility to apply for different jobs. *Bonus:* you can include a second "killer" sentence that compels the reader to keep going. Examples:

SUMMARY

Seeking a position where **network engineering/administration** and **software development** skills and experience will add value. Accustomed to long hours in pursuit of company goals.

SUMMARY

Experienced **quality management** professional with 10+ years of proven results. Turned around quality and operations for 2 business units, increasing efficiency 100 percent (2005–2006).

SUMMARY

Accomplished **customer relations management** professional with 5 years of award-winning experience. Quadrupled client satisfaction ratings, from 1.0 to 4.0 average (2003–present).

Again, note the language here, especially those killer second sentences.

The way I see it, why wait to fire off your big guns? You already have the reader's attention, so why not include a compelling fact about you in this first section? Doing so will force her to read the next section of your Guerrilla Resume. And the next section. Line by line you build and stoke the fires of her desire to meet you. Then, she calls you!

Whether to use an Objective or Summary can be a sticking point for some people. Some folks even leave them off the resume, because they want to be considered for all jobs.

No, no, no—Never Do This!

A focused resume is a powerful resume. A resume that tries to be all things to all people ends up being nothing at all. You can always write a second or third resume to give you more options.

Spend as much time on this section as necessary to create a powerful opening for your Guerrilla Resume. Your Objective or Summary should be 2 or 3 lines long at most.

Your goal is to start your resume with a focus on the employer and his or her needs. Tell readers what you can do for them. Then, force them to read further.

Select Accomplishments and/or Special Skills

Think of this second part of your Guerrilla Resume as an executive summary of the best, most relevant points about you. It should be so powerful and relevant that employers should not need to read any further to determine that you are the right person for the job.

In fact, according to many hiring managers I've talked to over the past 20 years, this section summarizing your key qualifications is the most important part of your resume. Employers who have to read hundreds of resumes are looking for shortcuts—and this section gives them one.

To make this section effective, it's vital that you target your reader. You need to understand who your reader is because different people read resumes looking for different things. For example:

➤ *Recruiters* look for "hot" marketable skills because they want to make money marketing you. If your skill set is not in high demand, they won't call unless you are an exact fit for a job order they have.

➤ *Human resources folks* look for an exact skill fit with a job first, then your stability, then your personality type.

➤ *Hiring managers* look for skill sets first, then how flexible you are, and finally what they think your ability to learn on the job is.

How long should this section be? About 3 to 5 bullet points in length—not much more. If you need a dozen bullet points to "summarize" your experience, you're not really summarizing, are you? And it's always an odd number—3 or 5 are best. (Why? Go ask an advertising copywriter.)

What title should you give this section, Select Accomplishments or Special Skills?

In general, people who produce revenue, such as sales or marketing folks, will have an easier time talking about *accomplishments*. Other folks, such as people in IT, customer service, accounting, and so on, have *skills* to highlight.

There are exceptions, of course, so feel free to break this rule. In fact, if you have a strong mix of specific achievements and skills, you can include *both* a *Select Accomplishments* and a *Special Skills* section in your Guerrilla Resume.

Here are 3 rules to help focus your accomplishments:

1. The accomplishment must be important to someone, ideally the organization itself, or its customers.
2. The result should have had a favorable impact, that is, enhanced their bottom line or increased their visibility/viability and ideally both.

3. The accomplishment must specifically illustrate your competence as it relates to the position for which you are applying,
highlighting your skills, experience, and personal qualities.

Now let's take a look at your current resume from an employer's
perspective. Here are examples of both kinds of sections:

SPECIAL SKILLS

Operating Systems: Windows NT/XP/Vista, UNIX on Sun SPARC
and MS-DOS.

Programming Languages: C, C++, HTML, and Java.

Software: Microsoft FrontPage, Image Composer and Word; Lotus
1-2-3 and mSQL.

SPECIAL SKILLS

Execution: regularly delivering to fixed time schedules against
all odds.

Experimentation: relentless probing for new R&D and product
approaches.

Management: optimizing people and finances to meet objectives
with customers.

SELECT ACCOMPLISHMENTS

Developed a **Global Strike Team** to rapidly engage customers in
the FP1000.

Delivered **triple digit growth** numbers 5 times since 2000.

Ignited sales for a U.S. multinational, closing **$6 million** in year
one.

SELECT ACCOMPLISHMENTS

Sold a 2-year global software contract to XYZ Company valued at
over $10,000,000.

Developed a Global Strike Team to engage senior level management at 17 Level 1 financial institutions, including Client A,
Client B, and Client C.

Initiated leveraged worldwide partnership/relationships with
Client (London), Client (Geneva), and Client (Hamburg) Client
(OPQ) in 2006.

Have a look at the example below, from a resume that won a job for one new graduate. It combines university and off-campus work experience:

Select Accomplishments

Helped improve company performance by surveying customers, then analyzing results with coworkers. Used data and staff discussions to increase service levels (Applebee's).

Experienced writer. Led research project to study how expectations determine outcomes. Required superior skills in communication and analysis. Surveyed more than 230 students, then conducted telephone follow-up to interpret data (University of NY).

Proven training skills. Experience orienting, supervising, and clarifying goals for up to 25 employees (Applebee's).

Experience Section
You can also call this Employment History, if you'd like. Again, the name you choose is not as important as the details that follow.

The purpose of this third section of your Guerrilla Resume is to show employers what you have been doing since school. They will have already been intrigued by your opening Objective/Summary and the Skills/Accomplishments section that follows, so by the time they get to this Experience section, their mind will largely be made up.

Here you should follow a consistent, easy-to-read format. You can present a description of each job you've held in 1 of 2 ways, depending on what information is more relevant. Choose only one of the following formats and use it consistently. Don't alternate between the two, as you'll simply confuse the reader.

If your past job titles are more relevant to the job you seek next, lead with them, like this:

Lan/Wan Administrator: U.S. Marine Corps, Camp Lejeune, NC (1993–1999).

However, if you've worked for impressive companies and want to lead with those names, you can do so like this:

IBM, Vice President of Research and Development, San Jose, CA (2006–2007).

For each job you've had, include your title, company name, city, state, and the years you worked there. There's really no need to include the months because this takes up valuable space and may highlight any gaps in your employment.

GUERRILLA TIP

Attention Recent Graduates

If you lack experience since graduation, you can include a brief explanation of what you've been doing since then. You can also include any jobs you had while in school in your Experience section, so long as you make them relevant by stressing desirable working traits that can't be taught, such as reliability, attention to detail, work ethic, and so on.

Look at the example wording that follows from a resume that won a job for one new graduate:

EXPERIENCE

Following graduation, began extensive online research of information technology job market and leading firms. Also created Web pages; samples available upon request (2006-present).

Detail Specialist: University Car Wash, Huntsville, AL (2004–2005).

Provided detailing services and superior customer service. Employed while full-time student.

Followed up with commercial and individual customers to ensure high levels of satisfaction.

Proactively sought out new tasks to make best use of available time.

Maintained good working relationship with all 5 managers and 17 colleagues.

While there are exceptions to these rules, this format gives you a lot of flexibility to describe your experience in an effective manner.

GUERRILLA TIP

You will notice that the Experience section of a Guerrilla Resume is limited to listing your job titles, company names, places of employment, and dates. Nothing more. And this is done for a reason—your Guerrilla Resume is designed to make the phone ring, not tell your whole life story. You can do this in the job interview.

In the advertising industry they call this a "teaser"—it gets you the initial invitation to interview. You can expand on your work history once you are face-to-face with the interviewer.

(Another way to think of this is that your Guerrilla Resume works like a classified ad. The job of a classified ad is not to tell every detail about the car or refrigerator you're trying to sell—you just want to grab the attention of an interested party and get them to call you on the phone.)

In fact, you may be asked to bring a longer resume and provide more information about what you did on each job. This is a good thing. In Chapter 8, we will show you what to add to your resume and how to do it, if you are asked by a hiring manager or someone in the HR Department.

Education/Training
Every employer is looking for this section, so you must include one.

GUERRILLA TIP

If your degree is more relevant to the job you seek than your recent experience, put this section ahead of your experience. Otherwise, it should come later in the resume.

Follow this format when describing your education:

EDUCATION

Master of Arts: Communications, University of Florida (2004)
Bachelor of Arts: Art History, San Diego State University (2002)

Now, what if you don't have a degree or an extensive formal education?

Well, here's an insider secret. You can call this section Education/Training and list all the relevant courses, certificates, and training you've received after high school. This is a *great* way to give more substance to an otherwise skimpy Education section. It shows initiative and employers like that—A LOT!

Your combination section could look like this:

EDUCATION/TRAINING

Professional training includes courses in sales, problem solving, leadership, management, quality, market research, and presentation skills (2005–present).
Associate of Arts Degree, City College, Chicago, IL (2004).

If you went to college but didn't graduate, you can describe your course of study, adding to it anything else you did that was notable, such as working full time or a GPA above 3.0, like this:

EDUCATION

BS: Finance course work, Ohio State University, Columbus, OH (2 years). GPA: 3.2.

Worked full-time throughout to self-finance 100 percent of education.

Finally, if you're currently in school for something, include your expected year of graduation, like this:

EDUCATION

MBA program: Finance, Michigan State University (in progress; due in 2008).

Additional Information

If space allows, you can include an Additional Information section to combine good things about you that don't fit in other parts of your Guerrilla Resume. If it's a hobby or volunteer position and you think it's relevant to the job you seek—and room allows—put it in.

Example: you can mention golf and marathon running if you want a sales job, since these interests portray you as active and energetic (plus more sales deals get done on the golf course than anywhere else on earth). But including such interests may not be relevant if you're applying for a position as a copy editor.

I recommend you put this catchall, Additional Information section last, to finish the Guerrilla Resume with a bang. Follow this format, and list items from most relevant to least:

ADDITIONAL INFORMATION

Languages: Arabic, French, and English (fluent).

Computer skills include Windows, Excel, Word, PowerPoint, Oracle, HTML, and search engine optimization (SEO).

Interests include marathon running, golf, softball, and international travel.

Volunteer experience includes Habitat for Humanity (2001-present), adult literacy tutoring (2002-present), and fund-raising for diabetes (1999-present).

Note: I once got an e-mail from a reader, who wrote: "Why do your resumes have hobbies listed? I have interviewed many candidates for jobs in the past and at no time was I concerned if a person was a black belt in karate unless I was."

Everyone's entitled to his or her opinion. In this case, that opinion is wrong. If one hiring manager isn't interested in hobbies, that doesn't mean all hiring managers aren't. After all, if it's cloudy in Chicago, that doesn't mean it's also cloudy in New York.

Many hiring managers will start talking about your hobbies or interests as a way to break the ice and ease into the interview. They do this to put you at ease and, in some cases, to see if you have a life outside work, or if you're a workaholic who might be prone to burn out.

Because you're dealing with humans here and humans are unpredictable, you never know what part of your resume will make a hiring manager want to call you. So if you think your hobbies, interests, volunteer work, and so on are relevant and may give you an edge, include them.

Please refer to Appendix 1 for examples of Standard Guerrilla Resumes that won jobs.

In a hurry? Need to send a resume to an employer today? Refer to the resume examples in the downloadable Word file available through www.gm4jh.com. Pick one that appeals to you, customize it with your own information, and voila, you have an "instant" Guerrilla Resume.

➤ The Extreme Guerrilla Resume

Now that you've assembled a Standard Guerrilla Resume, you're ready to take it to a much higher level by creating an Extreme Guerrilla Resume.

Remember! This format is very aggressive. You should send it only to senior executives who can either hire you for an existing job or who can create a new position just for you.

Do NOT send an Extreme Guerrilla Resume to anyone in the human resources (aka "Hiring Resistance") department or anyone else but a person with the authority to hire you. Why?

Human resources types, administrative assistants, and other "gate-keepers" simply won't know what to do with this style of resume—it breaks too many rules. While every company "claims" to want to hire bold, courageous leaders (that's really just the president speaking), rank-and-file staff rarely want to hire people better than themselves.

To recap, your Extreme Guerrilla Resume has all the components of the Standard Guerrilla Resume, *plus* one or more of the following (the more you include, the more powerful your finished product will be):

1. Proof section (*mandatory*),
2. Grabber statement at the top (*optional*), and
3. Career driver section (*optional*).

Ready? Let's start with the . . .

Proof Section (Mandatory)

This part runs down the left-hand side of your paper, below your name. It should be about 1 inch wide and it will include third-party information to "prove" you are a candidate every sane employer would want for his or her team.

What goes in here? The 2 best things you can include are:

1. *Logos* of past/current employers or clients. Doing so lets you piggyback on the value of company brand names. It's called the *halo effect* and it sets your resume apart.

   Essentially, you're borrowing the credibility associated with that company. The opposite is also true, so be careful how quickly you claim Enron as a customer, for example. You know who the most-respected companies in your industry are, so try to find a valid reason to insert their logo in your resume. You can often download logos from company web sites—that's the easiest way to do it. Simply save them to your computer and insert them in your resume.

2. *Quotes* from people familiar with your work. These serve as mini-testimonials and are very powerful. You can get them from past/current managers, clients, suppliers, college professors, newspaper or magazine articles about you—anyone who's seen you doing what you want to do in your target job. You can also lift quotes from personnel/annual reviews of letters of reference. *Obvious warning:* don't ask anyone for a quote whom you don't want to know about your job search.

GUERRILLA TIP

If you need help setting up your page so that you can include this "proof" section, refer to the Extreme Guerrilla Resume Master Template in the downloadable Word file available at www.gm4jh.com. Open the Master Template and simply paste your quotes and/or logos down the left side of the document.

When it comes to quotes, you *must* have written versions of any material that you quote from to back up your claims. Never, ever include a quote that you cannot verify in an e-mail, performance review, letter of recommendation, or other written format.

Refer to the Extreme Guerrilla Resume example for Mark Smith, or the other examples in Appendix 2 to see how these logos and quotes can be used.

Grabber Statement (Optional)

This section at the top of your resume is supposed to—yes, you guessed it—grab a reader's attention from the get-go and compel him or her to keep reading.

Your grabber can be a dictionary definition (*rainmaker* for a sales pro or *catalyst* for a manager, for example) or a brief testimonial from someone familiar with your work.

Example: Mark Smith's grabber from his Extreme Guerrilla Resume in Chapter 3 has this dictionary definition at the top:

---

rain·mak·er—One whose influence can initiate progress or ensure success

---

Did this get attention? You better believe it.

Was Mark able to back up this rather bold claim? You better believe it. And you had better be able to back up any claims you make, too, whether it's in your Grabber section or elsewhere.

Here's another example Grabber statement, from a sales operations manager who used his Extreme Guerrilla Resume to get hired:

En*tel′e*chy—Becoming actual what was only potential.

And here's the Grabber successfully used by a president/CEO:

---

cat·a·lyst—An agent that provokes or speeds significant change or action

---

Keep in mind that, unlike the Proof section, this Grabber section is optional. If you can come up with something that suits you and that you're comfortable using, go for it. If not, leave it out. You won't lose points with the employer for leaving it out. You will lose if it's dorky!

Career Driver Section (Optional)
This third and final Extreme Guerrilla Resume component is also optional.

Your *Career Driver* is an aggressively worded statement that comes right before your Experience section. It's the part of your personality and skill set that literally drives your career forward.

Think of it like this: what one thing about you will make employers ecstatic about their decision to hire you? In other words, why should they hire you? The answer to that question is your Career Driver.

Here's an example:

Career Driver

Taking the surety of success, the passion to succeed, and the deft handling of economic drivers to build great organizations.

Here's another:

Career Driver

Inspiring and leading teams to develop breakthrough products, which solve customer demands and have real commercial value in the global market.

It's easier to show you how all these elements fit together than it is to describe it. So please take a moment now to view the example Extreme Guerrilla Resumes you'll find in Appendix 2.

After you've reviewed the examples, decide which formats and wording are most attractive to you. Then, consider including those in your own Extreme Guerrilla Resume.

And, as we'll explain in Chapter 8, be ready to bring a longer version of this resume to the job interview, if asked. Some managers or human resource types may ask to see more information to flesh out your Experience section, and this is a simple matter to provide, once you have the Extreme Resume framework in place.

As with the Standard Guerrilla Resume, if you need to send a resume to an employer today, refer to the resume examples in the downloadable Word file available through www.gm4jh.com. Pick one that appeals to you, customize it with your own information, and you have an "instant" Guerrilla Resume.

■ GRAPHICS THAT ADD PUNCH TO YOUR RESUME

Advertisers use their knowledge of human nature to evoke emotional responses from you like cool, sophisticated, comfortable, and secure—that's what prompts your buying decision. You don't buy a car because it's made of metal and glass. You buy it because of the way it makes you feel. You can motivate a hiring manager to action through the clever use of 3 types of graphics:

1. *Logos:* The advertising industry knows all too well that a picture is worth a thousand words. Today we buy the value implied by our favorite brands, and employers do the same! Do you buy generic beer—clothes—cars? Not likely. Put your employer's logo on your resume if the company has a good reputation.

2. *Symbols:* One million dollars is less likely to be noticed than $1,000,000. Numbers and symbols jump off the page so use $, %, not dollars or percent.

3. *Charts:* A graph adds visual appeal and is ideal for demonstrating any type of quantitative improvement.

GUERRILLA TIP

➤ The purpose of graphics is to draw the reader's attention and lend credibility.

➤ They need to be in line with your accomplishments.

➤ Use logos and product pictures sparingly.

■ GUERRILLA PROOFREADING CHECKLIST

Print this page for easy reference. Then, proofread your resume for each section below. Check the box after completing each task, just like a pilot does before takeoff:

- ☐ *Contact information:* Verify that your name, address, ZIP code, and phone are correct.

- ☐ *E-mail address:* Use a personal e-mail on your resume, not one from work. Besides looking unprofessional (readers will assume you'll use company time to look for a job again after they hire you), it's dangerous to get e-mail at work about career opportunities. Employers often have the right to read any e-mail that comes to your work address. Furthermore, make sure your personal e-mail address is *not* something like hotstuff@aol.com or gameboy111@msn. If you need to get a new e-mail that looks professional, do so. And put some thought into it. Best yet, put in your LinkedIn personalized URL so they will check out your online portfolio.

- ☐ *Facts and figures:* Check all years and numbers in the resume and cover letter. Do they add up? Are they consistent?

- ☐ *Clarity and content:* Read the resume aloud for awkward, missing, or extra words.

- ☐ *Spacing:* Make sure the space between each sentence and section is the same.

- ☐ *Spelling:* Use your word processor's spell checker and then read it yourself. Most misspelled words occur in the headings and in the names of software and companies.

- ☐ *Punctuation:* Read the resume backward, looking for missing or incorrect punctuation, such as commas, dashes between dates, apostrophes, and so on.

- ☐ *Layout:* Are the upper and lower margins even and pleasing to the eye? Is there white space throughout the document, or is the text too dense? Print the resume and show it to friends for their comments.

■ SELLING YOUR VALUE-ADDED ADVANTAGES

What's your personal 2-for-1 strategy? Why should an employer hire you over the next equally qualified person? You can bet that in the United States today there are thousands of people who have skills similar to yours.

Don't get me wrong. I'm sure you're well qualified, and I really am on your side, but you have to know that you'll have competition for every job you go after. Your competition will come in 3 forms: internal candidates, external candidates, and the status quo. You will need to convince interviewers that hiring you will get them to their desired future result better than any other option. Doing nothing is a very viable option, especially for people in middle management who are risk averse.

So, back to my question—why you?

As a job hunter, if you understand that you are likely to have competition for a coveted position, you can leverage other skills to appear more qualified. You do this by selling your personal value-added qualities, and everybody has one or more.

The *American Heritage Dictionary* of the English Language defines value-added as: adjective—"Of or relating to the estimated value that is added to a product or material at each stage of its manufacture or distribution." In short, it is something added to a product to increase its value. In this case, the product is you.

Your value-added is a skill, life experience, or attitude that when added to your basic qualifications gives you an advantage over the next candidate because you exceed the employer's expectations for the position. For example:

➤ Nurses who have had active combat training could have an edge on other candidates applying for an emergency room job at a hospital because they're already acclimatized to the environment.

➤ An engineer who has graduated from Toastmasters, or a similar public speaking program, could have an edge because he or she can also be a spokesperson for the company.

The preceding job hunters added an unexpected but welcome dimension to the job because they highlighted their value-added in their cover letter and later in the interview. In essence, they shifted the interviewer's focus to areas they knew others were not likely to have.

On a more personal note, my wife was selected for a job as a drug and alcohol education supervisor by focusing her cover letter, resume, and interview around her military experience. The fact that she has a degree in psychology and ran several addiction centers qualified her for the job. But I'm convinced she was chosen because the selection committee knew she had the self-discipline to create the course material and the presence to deliver it.

Your value-added can come in the guise of:

- ➤ Complementary skills
- ➤ Alumni
- ➤ Attitude
- ➤ Industry contacts
- ➤ Domain expertise

➤ Complementary Skills

For example, a nurse who becomes a doctor could leverage her bond with nursing staff when managing a medical team.

➤ Alumni

I can't count the number of people who have specifically asked me to recruit Wharton or Harvard grads because they would have experienced the discipline needed to graduate from those institutions.

Microsoft recruits engineers from the University of Waterloo because many employees are alumni. Want to know what happened to all those high achievers you went to school with? Surf over to www.classmates.com and start networking.

➤ Attitude

Employers understand that passionate employees outperform normal employees 10-to-1. Passion is a simple cost/benefit equation and qualities like drive, ambition, and vision tend to come as part of the package. Here's an example:

Fresh from Teachers College and two thousand miles from home, my younger sister Monica decided to apply for a coveted position as a kindergarten teacher. She did her homework. She briefed me on the highlights of the six-hour interview, and I asked what questions they asked her. She replied, "Well not many really.... I asked most of them.... I started by saying I was not very experienced at interviewing so did they mind if I asked a few questions ... and the time just flew ... we talked about best practices, educational philosophy, and the work ahead of us." I roared with laughter. Monica's passion was evident by her preparation. Monica is the most passionate teacher I've ever met—it shows in the eyes of her students' parents and the hearts of her students.

➤ Industry Contacts

Time is money, and if you can leverage your industry contacts to get up and running in a new job faster than the next candidate, all things being equal, you will be hired. Your contact list is very valuable. Are you leveraging it correctly?

➤ Domain Expertise

For a job hunter, domain expertise is knowledge and experience that has been acquired through a track record that represents a core competency in a specific technical area or marketplace (e.g., you could be a property manager who understands everything there is to know about HVAC systems, which in the building facilities industry makes you worth your weight in platinum).

Domain expertise is a hot commodity for headhunters. Someone in banking could be a success in insurance or financial services. Sales professionals in the technology industry often have both domain experience and specific industry contacts, making them more valuable than the next candidate.

GUERRILLA TIP

This "new economy" and relentless cost-cutting place great strains on the ability of managers to pick those few candidates who can provide them with the value they need to stay alive. Since top people knock on the door daily, you need to:

➤ Differentiate yourself by demonstrating you bring more to the job.

➤ Highlight your complementary experience in your cover letter.

➤ Exploit alumni points of reference.

➤ Leverage your domain expertise.

If you did something like the following, say it:

Proposed and presented in-house training so that shippers would avoid mixing heavy and delicate items. Reduced product damage and customer complaints by 95 percent.

This shipping clerk is thinking, acting, and communicating like a manager and will be on top of any good hiring manager's resume file.

■ THE ONLY COVER LETTER YOU WILL EVER NEED

What does your cover letter tell employers about you? The one-size-fits-all form letter addressed to "Dear Sir/Madam," tells employers that you're too lazy to do a little digging to find out who should receive it and that you're not the type of person who is willing to go the extra mile when necessary. Think I am a little harsh? I'm not. If you remember nothing else, remember this—a cover letter with a proper salutation is essential—always!

A cover letter is a personal sales letter, and all good sales letters keep the reader's interests foremost. Correctly researched and written, your cover letter is your best opportunity to tap into an employer's hopes and fears. Your cover letter is your opportunity to go beyond the resume and its focus on the past and target what employers care most about—themselves.

Put yourself in the employer's shoes. Your resume may be one of several dozen or even several hundred they have to read. Most employers will quickly separate those resumes that deserve a full read by reading the cover letter first. The cover letter is a screening device, but beyond that there are more important reasons employers like a cover letter:

➤ It tells them why you are interested in "them"—remember it's not about you, it's about them.

➤ It demonstrates to them whether you can write succinctly and express yourself—a vital skill for modern managers.

➤ It provides a snapshot of your accomplishments as they pertain to their needs, thereby answering their biggest question—can you fix my problem?

The goal of your cover letter is to convince that initial reader to select you for an interview. Your letter and resume may travel through many hands before they reach a hiring manager's desk, so put your best foot forward right from the start. This is your last opportunity to stand out from the crowd. Make sure you tell employers what's in it for them right up front. Make it clear and compelling that not interviewing you is an opportunity lost.

Initially, hiring managers don't know who you are, nor do they care for that matter; they have a problem to solve or an opportunity to exploit—and you are either the solution or you aren't. You can be the most competent person in your field, but if you can't connect your skills to their needs, you will go undiscovered. Make them believe that you can help them achieve their goals and they will interview you.

Here is an example of a Guerrilla Cover Letter for you to read:

EXAMPLE GUERRILLA COVER LETTER

① Dear Mr. Smith,

② You have great technology and a great market opportunity. Now it's time to build a great company. That's why we should meet. I could tell you that I am an exceptional executive and leader, but why not let the facts speak for themselves?

③ Here are a few of the successes I have achieved before and can achieve again for you:

ABC Corp.—From $0 to $40 million in 5 years. As co-founder and then eventually president, I was instrumental in growing ABC Corp. from 3 employees to more than 350 in 10 locations, with revenues of more than $40 million.

EFG Mega Corp.—From $0.69 USD per share to $7.10 USD in 2 years. I joined as vice-president, North American Operations, just as 7 consecutive quarters of losses had driven the share price down to $0.69. I delivered 8 consecutive quarters of profit and increased earnings, helping take the stock to a high of $7.10 before the company was acquired.

XYZ, Inc.—From start-up to strategic acquisition in 4 years. Starting as chairman and then as CEO, I successfully packaged and promoted XYZ Inc., resulting in the company's acquisition by Bigger Systems.

④ I think you get the idea: I have repeatedly outperformed in the face of startup, turnaround, and growth challenges. I have done this in diverse markets and tough economic conditions, generating hundreds of millions of dollars in sales. I have developed a rare combination of experience, vision, and leadership—and that's exactly the combination your company needs to achieve its full potential.

⑤ I will call you Tuesday, June 10, at 8:30 AM to arrange a time for the two of us to talk. If this is not a convenient time, please ask Ms. Jones to call me and suggest an alternative.

Thank you,

⑥ Bob Smith
www.bobsmith.com
bobsmith@bobsmith.com
212-555-1212

Now, here's that Guerrilla Cover Letter dissected, for you to analyze and emulate:

1. Salutation—Addressed to the hiring manager, by name. Do whatever it takes to get the name of the person with the authority to hire you.

   Great grabber. He's got my attention.

2.–4. The "Here's What I Can Do for You" part. The 3 bullets here demonstrate that he can do a startup, a turnaround, and successfully position a company for sale. He has prioritized his most important points and done the thinking for the reader.

   Here he implies that there is more and hints that you should read the resume.

5. Just in case you don't call him first, he tells you when he is going to call.

6. His contact info is readily available.

Is this letter too bold? No way. As an executive search professional, I would call straight away.

Keep this distinction in mind: if you talk about how you took a company from $0 to $40 million in 5 years at a neighborhood barbeque, you are bragging. But if you do it in your cover letter and resume, you are smart—and perfectly justified.

Employers respect take-charge, get-it-done, self-assured individuals. And this cover letter is all of that.

You can modify this Guerrilla Cover Letter for different uses, too, usually by slightly changing the first and last paragraphs.

For example, this paragraph:

You have great technology and a great market opportunity. Now it's time to build a great company. That's why we should meet. I could tell you that I am an exceptional executive and leader, but why not let the facts speak for themselves?

Can become:

Does one of your clients [clients can be changed to colleagues for networking purposes] *have great technology or a tremendous market and need to get traction quickly? If so, then perhaps you and I should meet. I could tell you that I am an exceptional executive and leader, but why not let the facts speak for themselves?*

I guarantee you this opener will elicit a return call from a recruiter or a colleague if they know of an opportunity.

➤ Other Ways to Open Your Guerrilla Cover Letter

Here are 3 other ways to open your Guerrilla Cover Letter, listed in order of effectiveness:

1. *Personal reference:* "Bill Smith from [ABC Corp.] suggested I contact you because ..."

   This is one time that it is okay to drop a name, especially if the hiring manager thinks highly of Bill. Be sure to let Bill know that you're doing this, of course, and ask him for any insider information he may have about the hiring manager. This can help you make a great first impression if you get the call to interview.

2. *Reference to an article or speech:* "Your article on customer service in the February 27, 2009, *Business Journal* was excellent. As a matter of fact, I have used 3 of your techniques to increase revenues 65 percent in my 5 years managing client relations for National Widget Corporation. In addition, I have found 2 other methods to be helpful, including one that rescued a $3.4-million account.

   "Perhaps we should meet? I could tell you that I am an exceptional executive and leader, but why not let the facts speak for themselves?"

   I usually do this when I can't find a personal connection any other way. In the end, no one really cares about what you've read, but if you quickly segue into discussing how this news made you think that you can contribute to the organization, then you've got a strong opening.

   Also, if the person mentioned in the article didn't write it, I try to connect with the writer first to get background info. I usually search Google or Elyion.com. Either way it's surprising what you can discover. On several occasions, I've even called the author of an article when the person appeared in an interview in the business section of the newspaper. Reporters are great resources.

3. *Question or headline:* "How often have breakdowns in information technology cost your business time and money? I can help."

   I love this approach and use it when all else fails because it's still a strong opener. I adopted it from Tony Peranello's book, *Selling to VITO* (VITO stands for Very Important Top Officer). The book is a brilliant primer on booking appointments. It masterfully explains how to draw attention to your accomplishments in a manner that screams, YOU WANT TO MEET ME!

As a Guerrilla, you know that you may only have a hiring manager's attention for a few seconds, so get to the point. Once you have a reader's attention, you must supply him with information that stokes his desire to read more and more until he has to call you.

Every sentence matters. Every paragraph must connect. Your thoughts must be crystal clear and written to benefit the reader—not you—so that when you ask for a meeting, he understands it's in his best interest.

■ HOW TO ASK FOR THE INTERVIEW IN YOUR LETTER

For years I've told friends and colleagues to close their cover letters this way, and it's worked very well for them. Here's that example closing again:

> *I will call you Tuesday, June 10, at 8:30* AM *to arrange a time for the two of us to talk. If this is not a convenient time, please ask Ms. Smith to call me and suggest an alternative.*

Note: You need to get the name of the hiring manager's assistant or the person who opens their mail, then put that "gatekeeper's" name in the letter. The effect of this is extremely powerful. It tells the reader, "Hey, this person was motivated enough to find out who sets my schedule. If they're doing clever things like this now, before we've even met, I wonder what kind of creative solutions this person might deliver when he [or she] is on my team?"

How will the hiring manager respond to this "ask for the interview" tactic?

Like the Sex Pistols, asking for the interview in your cover letter might be loved, it might be hated, but it will *always* get a reaction. Specifically, the hiring manager who reads it might:

➤ Throw it out.

➤ Call you right away.

➤ Ask his assistant to call you and tell you when he's available.

➤ Make a note on his schedule and wait for your call at the appointed time.

More often than not, he or she will call you right away or wait to see if you call at the appointed day and time. People who have used this closing in their letters have reported that the hiring managers have picked up the call on the first ring and said, "I was sitting here waiting to see if you would call." As you can see, it's vital that you follow through on this.

If the person isn't there when you call, leave a message stating, "Sorry I missed you. I will be waiting for your call back between [give a specific time span] today." If this doesn't work, call his assistant and ask to schedule a call or meeting. If he is at all interested in you—and he should be because you researched his needs ahead of time—he will call.

■ BONUS! ONE UNUSUAL WAY TO END YOUR GUERRILLA COVER LETTER

Here's a quirky, unusual and, for true Guerrilla Job Hunters, excellent way to end your cover letter—include a P.S. at the end, after your name and signature.

Let me explain.

Go open your junk mail right now (or fish it out of the trash). By junk mail, I mean all those letters that try to sell you credit cards, magazine subscriptions, 10 CDs for a penny, and so on. Look at the bottom of each sales letter. What do you see? Ninety-eight out of 100 times, you'll find a P.S. at the end.

Why? Because over the past 100 years, direct-mail copywriters have found that a P.S. almost always gets read. So they put a compelling sales message where they know it will be seen—in the P.S. at the end of the letter.

You can increase the number of calls you get from employers—by including a provocative P.S. at the end of your Guerrilla Cover Letter.

All you have to do is think of the one statement you absolutely, positively want hiring managers to read. Then stick it in your P.S.

Here are 3 examples to get you started:

1. P.S. If you do not have a current need, please pass my resume on to someone who wants to turn a $400,000 loss into $800,000 profit in 2 years, as I did for my current employer.
2. P.S. Please call me at (612) 555-0000 to find out why my supervisor recently said: "I have absolutely nothing but great things to say about Dan. His strengths are troubleshooting problems,

taking care of situations in a timely manner, and always being willing to go the extra mile.... Dan is a great team player."

3. **P.S.** If you don't see a fit at this time, please pass my resume on to someone who needs to increase qualified deal flow by more than 300 percent and sales closing ratios by more than 25 percent, as I have repeatedly done.

Take advantage of the fact that people are trained to look for and read the P.S. in a letter. You will gain an immediate advantage over ordinary job seekers.

A WAR STORY

Mark J. Haluska

In November 2008 I received a phone call from Anthony, who is at the Director Level in the fast-food (QSR) industry. He asked if he could send me his resume. I said, "sure." The resume was like 99 percent of all the resumes I get. BORING!

It just so happened that the timing could not have been better because I just received a heads-up from an industry insider regarding a restaurant organization that is well funded and has an aggressive growth plan of becoming a $100 million dollar company within the next 2 to 3 years. I was told they needed someone at the Director or VP level that could lead the operations side of the company.

As a favor to Anthony, but more realistically in my own $elf-$erving interests, I asked if I could help him do an Extreme Guerrilla Resume. He had no idea what that was, but he said, "Sure, you're the expert." Under my guidance, within 2 days we had the perfect marketing piece.

Now, I've never met, much less ever had spoken to, the CFO or the COO of the company, but with a little networking and research I did obtain their e-mail addresses. Uninvited, I sent both the COO and the CFO Anthony's Extreme Guerrilla Resume. I did blind his contact information to ensure the company had to call me if there was an interest.

Two days later a call comes into my office from the CFO of that company. She introduced herself, and said, "How soon can we see this candidate?" I asked her what she liked about Anthony's credentials and she replied, "the company officers looked at his (Extreme Guerrilla) resume and were simply blown away!" The *first* Guerrilla Lesson here is that Anthony's resume looked like everyone else's. Although he is impressive in every respect, his resume certainly did not reflect it and it certainly did not scream, "Hire ME!" The *second* lesson is that Anthony was also doing what everyone else does. He was going directly to HR rather than to decision makers. No wonder he had yet to get any interviews!

We broke all the so-called "rules" and within 1 week of my first contact with Tony, he was invited to interview with this company that neither of us had ever spoken with, and as I write, these talk's are ongoing between Tony and the company.

Contributed by Mark J. Haluska, founder and executive director, Real Time NetWork, www.rtnetwork.net LinkedIn: www.linkedin.com/in/Mark J.Haluska.

Chapter 6

Twenty-First Century Digital Weapons

If You Build It, They Will Come for You...

Do not go where the path may lead, go instead where there is no path and leave a trail.

—Ralph Waldo Emerson

So, your resume is done. Your cover letter is complete and you're feeling pretty good about yourself. Any employer that reads it will immediately know that you've got the right stuff. Great! Now what? Resumes, cover letters, and job boards are passive tools for job hunting and require your continuous involvement.

The million-dollar question is, *How* can you make employers knock on your door and ask you to interview for a job? How can you make it easier for employers to find you?

British battlefield strategist Liddell Hart summed it up years ago when he coined the term the *indirect approach*. It means you don't keep banging headfirst into the problem—that just makes it worse. Attacking the trenches head-on in World War I is a tragic example of the direct approach. Instead, you do something surprising that maneuvers around the blockage. In World War II, the Nazi army used an indirect approach when it attacked through the supposedly impassable Ardennes Forest and swept around the Maginot Line

129

behind the French Army. Today, going around human resources (HR) and straight to the hiring managers also requires an indirect approach using the Web.

■ DIGITAL BREAD CRUMBS: THE MAGIC OF SEARCH ENGINE TECHNOLOGY

How do you apply the indirect approach to job hunting? You start by leveraging the changes in candidate recruiting to your benefit, and make it easier for people to find you. Reading the following brief history on the evolution of Internet recruiting will be worth your while.

Despite the softening of the economy in 2009, many employers reported they were finding it harder to find the right candidates. Many people reasoned—and the billion-dollar staffing industry heavily promoted the idea—that the best candidates were already employed. Right or wrong, passive job candidates became the most prized by employers. As profit margins were squeezed and sales dropped, the "war for talent" quickly morphed into the "war for the best talent." Search engines and social media sites became the vehicle of choice for finding passive candidates.

Today, you are far more likely to be Googled by a recruiter than found on a job board. That, or recruiters will track you down through Facebook, MySpace, or LinkedIn. Keyword searches in "communities of interest" have replaced the tedious telephone spadework that recruiters have long used.

That's great for you as a candidate because having your phone ring is much better and easier than trying to make someone else's phone ring. One of the secrets to long-term full employment is constantly being on the radar of potential employers and headhunters.

■ BEING EASY TO FIND

In this section, we describe how to use Internet tools that recruiters rely on, and explain how to use the same tools to bypass gatekeepers and contact hiring managers.

You should manage your Web presence, or online identity, the same way you monitor and manage your financial credit statement. Make sure you can be found on the Internet and that what's out there reflects you at your best. Consider the Internet as today's venue for a first interview—it is where you make your first impression. You never get a second chance to make a first impression, so make sure your Internet presence will get you to the second step.

Admit it, you've Googled yourself. Well, keep on doing it, and do it often, so that you can see what others see if they search for your name. On Google, you can buy your own name as a keyword, directing searchers to your blog or web site.

Go to sites like ZoomInfo at www.zoominfo.com where information about you is summarized and optimize your summary. Many of the top recruiting firms—including myself—and 100s of the Fortune 500 use ZoomInfo to search for candidates. On ZoomInfo you can actually go in and edit the information, adding missing information and correcting inaccuracies. STOP—do this now. If you are not "Zoomable," you do not exist for 100s of thousands of recruiters who are looking for people like you every day. These are easy digital bread crumbs to leave that will bring job offers knocking.

➤ **Beyond Job Boards and Networking—When Being Passive Can Be a Good Thing**

You know about job boards and you know about networking, but how much do you know about recruiting for passive candidates? Some recruiters think that the best candidates are the ones who aren't out there looking, so they use clever tools to find people who fit their search criteria, but who are likely still in a job. How do you make sure that they can find you when they're looking for someone to fill a job for which you would be a perfect fit? Make yourself known in the places they search.

Recruiters hunting for the perfect passive candidate use search tools like Google and ZoomInfo to locate candidates at competitors' companies who have the skills and experience they seek. Again, you need to make sure you can be found, and that might include actually building a web site and marketing it. Web summaries on sites like ZoomInfo, as well as blogs, provide personalized URLS that can be used as crawlable homepages on the Web and are good opportunities to showcase your work and interests (more about this later in this chapter).

■ DIGGING INTO THE WEB TO GET TO
HIRING MANAGERS

When you've struck gold and actually see a perfect job advertised, or you've found the perfect company and no jobs are listed, the HR department isn't the only avenue in. ZoomInfo allows you to click on its advanced search link and search by company. To refine the search, they offer an on-demand product where you pay per search to refine the target list by company, job title, location, and other areas of specialization. Make sure you open your search process to include all the tools available to you and take advantage of those that have already been used by leading employers; which of course means going to Facebook, MySpace, and LinkedIn to see:

➤ If the company has a corporate page and who's connected that you may know
➤ What jobs they have listed there
➤ If they have an alumni page

Don't forget virtual sites like SecondLife.com and the virtual job fairs like those held through the *Wall Street Journal.* You don't have to get dressed up and you can visit the site on your own schedule.

WARNING

Only read the following section if you want employers and head-hunters to find you and offer you the best jobs before anyone else. I am serious. You will always be one of the first people that they call when they have an opportunity. If you're naturally shy and can't handle being popular, don't read any further. Here are 3 unconventional weapons to heighten your visibility. Building them is easy and there are lots of shortcuts for smart guerrillas:

1. Your personal web site
2. Your blog
3. MySpace and Facebook

I put them in this order because of their usefulness, ease of construction, and control. You can control the first three. MySpace and Facebook accounts, while free, are subject to each site's particular terms and conditions, which, if you violate, can have your site taken down. I also find there are a lot of people who cannot stay off their MySpace and Facebook account once they're on it, which will reduce the effectiveness of your job search.

Employment 2.0

James Durbin

As the wave of information unleashed by the Internet continues to overwhelm recruiters, your ability to stand out in the online crowd adds a new dimension to job seeking. It's no longer good enough to be a good or great employee. Broadcasting your abilities in search engines and social media sites, even when you're not ready to switch jobs, is something you'll need to learn.

The good news is that small actions you take now can help insulate you from the turmoil of the job market. Building a comprehensive online presence now gives you the advantage in both current and future searches.

Here is your Must Do List for Employment 2.0:

1. *Sign up for LinkedIn.* LinkedIn is a social networking service that allows recruiters to search for you by title, school, company, and geographic location. Take the time to fully complete a winning profile, reach out to a few friends, and accept invitations when they are offered. Also make sure your LinkedIn URL is attached to your e-mail signature. Having a LinkedIn profile is like wearing a Rolex in a hotel bar: it says you're looking without having to be obvious about it.

2. *Update your online directory info at ZoomInfo, Naymz, and JigSaw.*

3. *If you have a blog, post on it frequently with your name and title.* Add descriptors like your current projects, technical expertise, and examples of anything you have done that shows up in the public record. Add conferences, meetings, user groups, and leadership positions in the community. Be specific with your expertise—try to imagine what a recruiter might type into a search engine. Put in niche software you have used, complex projects you have run, and descriptions of your certifications. The goal is to be obvious, but not too obvious.

(continued)

4. *If you don't have a blog, offer to guest post at blogs that discuss your industry and your metro area.* Take advantage of their search engine ranking to put your name within easy reach of a Google Search for your industry.

5. *Write articles for trade publications, newspapers, and the local company newsletter.* Recruiters seek out expertise, and someone who is published is going to have a better chance of getting noticed than someone who keeps his or her expertise confined to the company e-mail.

6. *Sponsor or start a networking event for your specialty in your local area.* The truth about networking groups is the most benefit goes to the people who start the group. Why not make that you?

7. *Go to Ning.com and search for industry sites in your area.* Even if the group isn't active, a complete profile with contact information will be a big fat target for a researcher.

8. *Get involved in online discussions about your industry.* This is the single best way to showcase what you know without actively asking recruiters to call you. If you aren't currently looking, take an hour a month to look for discussions where you can answer questions and demonstrate your expertise. If you are looking, make it an hour a day. LinkedIn Answers, Yahoo Answers, industry forums, and Google Groups are all good places to start.

These suggestions are all good, but the most important piece of advice I can give you is to set aside your fear and your pride and start immediately. You spend most of your time doing your job, and the danger is that you'll find yourself siloed within your organization at the worst possible time. The truth about networking is you need to do it before you want to see results. Trying to jump-start a job search is a lot harder when no one knows your name. Following these steps will make you easy to find online, and they'll also sharpen your abilities and reputation in your current position. If your corporate recruiter keeps finding you when looking for that next executive position, the call you get might be from the inside.

James Durbin, The Social Media Headhunter www.socialmediaheadhunter.com, LinkedIn: www.linkedin.com/in/jimdurbin/.

➤ Your Web Site

Building your web site is simple. You already have most of the content. Nontechies (us normal people) shrink at the thought of creating a web site because it's complicated. That doesn't have to be the case. For years, I have been referring people to 3 great sites where you can buy a ready-made template that you can customize to fit your own needs.

The first is Templatemonster.com at www.templatemonster.com. Historically, the advantage of using a template has been that you save time by not needing to master the technology first, but you do it at the cost of good looks. Frankly, looks matter. If a web site doesn't look good, people will not bother with it. CEO David Braun has assembled a top-notch team of graphic artists who build and release up to a dozen new templates every day. These sites are pure eye-candy and cost as little as $25. Guerrilla, you can't beat that.

Two other options include 1and1.com and Godaddy.com These are superb resources. In both case you can choose a template and publish it to the Internet in minutes through their online, menu-driven, self-serve web site. The content is all you need to provide.

However you choose to get your site up and running, here are the major sections you need to include:

➤ Home page

➤ Contact page

➤ Resume or experience page with all your resumes on it: Guerrilla, Extreme, ASCII, and so on

➤ Interests or links page

➤ Any optional pages you deem appropriate

The content of those pages must do the following:

➤ It should engage the reader.

➤ It must present a clean professional image.

➤ Be consistent. It should present the same brand you are trying to achieve with your resumes and cover letter.

➤ It should have a call to action—you need to tell readers what to do next or, at the very least, make it easy for them to contact you.

➤ If you write a blog, there should be a link to it.

If you want to be seen in the best possible light as a potential employee, then your web site *should not:*

➤ Appear folksy or cute

➤ Link to any questionable web sites of a religious, political, or sexual nature

➤ Have pictures of you and your family—especially young children—because you don't know who is looking at the site and for what reason

➤ Have your home address

➤ Make mention or hint of your marital status

➤ Your home phone number (get a second line or make them use e-mail)

➤ Any personal information of any kind that could lead to identity theft such as your Social Security number or driver's license number

Recruiters (whether they be the employer's or a headhunter) search the Internet for keywords. If you have a "Projects" section, you need to have hyperlinks that connect as described in the e-resume section, with links to:

➤ Your current and past employers

➤ Associations you belong to

➤ Articles in which you or your project are mentioned

➤ University and colleges you have attended

➤ Special certifications you have received

➤ Anything else that would prompt a call or inquiry from a curious recruiter

Most of the content for your web site will come straight from your resume. Keep your writing short and tight. The site's purpose is to prompt the reader to call you, not to answer all questions.

Darryl Praill's site is a great example (see Figure 6.1). It's engaging, informative, and bold like the man himself. See what he's done that you might incorporate in yours.

➤ **Your Blog**

A blog is a powerful addition to your web site.

A *blog* is an electronic journal that has been made available on the web for others to read. The activity of updating a blog is *blogging,*

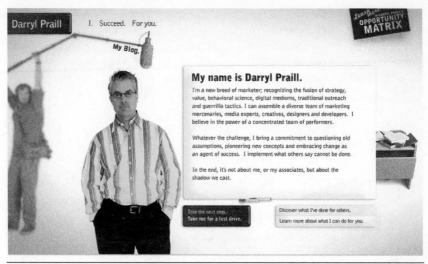

Figure 6.1   Darryl Praill.

and someone who keeps a blog is a *blogger*. Blogs are typically up-dated using software designed for people with little or no technical background.

Your strategic use of a blog can make you a prime target for em-ployers and headhunters. Why? Because you're making it easier for people to find you on the Web. Just think of it: no more waiting for your blue-haired Web designer to update your site. You can post to your blog yourself. Having your own blog gives you credibility and a forum to demonstrate your expertise. If you're not an expert, you can become the oracle by linking to other bloggers, articles, news sources, and web sites. You build your credibility by highlighting what others are doing. For example, if your goal is to be hired as a teacher, you can talk about the latest developments in K-12 or ADHD.

Best of all, blogging can be done for free. Check out these sites to start your guerrilla job-hunting blog:

➤ www.typepad.com

➤ www.wordpress.com

➤ www.blogger.com

If you are not certain what to write about, then go to www.blogsearch.google.com and look at what other bloggers are do-ing. BlogSearchGoogle.com will allow you to keyword search any sub-ject. (There's that term again—You should get used to hearing it because finding things on the Web—and being found on the

Web—relies on understanding how to exploit keywords.) Fire up your Web browser, surf over to www.blogsearch.google.com, and enter the keywords that are relevant to your area of expertise. In fact, while you're there, create a Blog Alert [on the left-hand side of the screen]. Now, read what other people are writing about. It is that easy.

From a personal branding perspective, your blog is a billboard on the Internet. Use it to get people to stop at your web site, read your resume, and call you for an interview. Blogging can help you find a job in the following ways:

➤ Increase your visibility because search engines love blogs.

➤ Demonstrate your critical thinking and communication skills, which employers look for.

➤ Establish and legitimize you as an expert in the field/function you want to be recruited into.

➤ Brand you as informed and savvy.

➤ Invite discussions and inquiries.

Being easy to find is the first step in securing your career future. If you do it correctly, you may never need to go looking for a job again because you're making yourself easy to find. Being found is what you want; it enables you to market yourself 24 hours a day at little or no cost. Make certain to link your blog post to your web site, LinkedIn account, Facebook, and/or MySpace account. Type pad will do this automatically for you with the widgets (mini applications) available on its site.

Does this work? Adam Swift started a blog on mixed martial arts in his spare time while completing his law degree. Mark Cuban found him, bought the blog www.mmapayout.com, and acquired Adam in the process.

A WAR STORY

Adam Swift

During my second year of law school, I realized I didn't want to be a lawyer. I had always had a passion for sports business, particularly for the promotional aspects of professional wrestling as a child, and later mixed martial arts (MMA). Since I had entered law school, MMA had exploded into one of the fastest growing sports in the world. I decided to give it a shot and began mailing resumes and making phone calls to the leading companies in the industry. After months of frustrating cold calling, I realized that if I was going to land my dream job, it was going to take a more nonconventional approach.

I read *Guerrilla Marketing for Job Hunters* over the summer before my final year of law school. One of the strategies discussed was the use of blogging in order to demonstrate expertise and become more accessible to headhunters. I decided to implement this strategy by starting a blog dedicated to the business of MMA. I've always enjoyed writing and figured that at worst I would find a fun hobby.

MMAPayout.com was born in September of 2007. It didn't take long for the blog to develop a following and start to produce networking opportunities. My timing couldn't have been better because almost simultaneously a contract dispute broke out in the UFC, allowing me the chance to put my legal education to work. The exposure I gained covering that story generated some professional writing opportunities with magazines. I was able to parlay that into more networking opportunities and even a little side cash.

By the spring of 2008, I was being sought out by the *New York Times* and *Washington Post* for my expert opinion. I had also begun receiving feelers from various employers about potential job opportunities. The site even produced a fairly lucrative part-time consulting practice and I counted among my clients a billion-dollar public corporation.

Shortly before graduation, about 9 months after I started blogging, I accepted a position with Mark Cuban's HDNet Fights as manager of Marketing Alliances. Mark and Andrew Simon, the CEO of the company, had become familiar with me by reading my blog.

Adam Swift is the manager of Marketing Alliances of HDNet Fights (www.hdnetfights.com), one of the leading MMA organizations in the country, founded by Mark Cuban.

➤ MySpace and Facebook

MySpace has more than 200 million users. If MySpace was a country it would be the fifth largest in the world. More than 25 percent of all Americans are on MySpace. On average, 300,000 people sign up to MySpace every day. Do you think recruiters are using it to find passive job hunters? You bet. They use MySpace and Facebook with equal regularity.

I can hear you saying, "Geez, Dave, this is a lot of work," and you are right, but there are a few tricks you can use to decrease the time it takes to be found and it is still a lot faster than looking for a job the old fashioned way. Remember, thousands of recruiters and employers may be looking for you right now and, if they can't find you, your next job may go to a lesser qualified, more Internet savvy individual. It doesn't have to be. First, you already have most of the information you need to start a Facebook or MySpace account. Just recycle it from your resume, blog, and web site. Make sure that each Web presence you create links to all the others because this increases your ranking in Google and moves you to the top of the list. Invite your friends and colleagues, current and past. Join groups that are in line with your professional interests.

Last, check out the employers you are targeting by searching for their corporate profile on MySpace and Facebook. If you go to Alexa.com, you can see who has the most traffic of MySpace, Facebook, Monster, and CareerBuilder. Can you guess? Try it!

GUERRILLA INTELLIGENCE

Targeted Advertising with Facebook

Willy Franzen

Traditional career experts will tell you that "job wanted ads" never work. "It's been done a million times, and it never delivers results." If you asked about Facebook as a job search tool, they would probably tell you that your embarrassing pictures from college can only cause trouble. "It's a good way to lose your job or never get hired in the first place. Stay away from it." This well-meaning advice is dead wrong.

As a business owner, I've used Facebook's targeted advertising platform to bring college grads and internship seekers to my web sites. Since Facebook allows advertisers to target their ads to individuals at a given workplace, I've also dabbled in using the advertising to reach employers who might be interested in advertising jobs on my web site. I quickly realized that job seekers can also use Facebook to target employers. To test my idea, I organized an experiment with 5 recent college grads. I encouraged each to design a Facebook ad and target specific companies they would like to work for. Their ads included a picture, a quick note about why they wanted to work for the company, and a link to an online version of their resume. The results were almost immediate—all enjoyed some level of response. One received dozens of e-mails from people willing to help her land a job at their company.

Facebook ads won't instantly land you a job but they will open the door to new opportunities and get your resume to the top of the pile. By using creativity to stand out, you can make a positive initial impression.

To get started with your ad campaign, all you need is a Facebook account, a credit card, and some sort of publicly accessible online resume (a solid advertising campaign can be done for under $20). Once you have those, head over to www.facebook.com/ads/, and use their simple interface. You can have a campaign running in under 10 minutes.

The most important thing that you must do is write your ad copy specifically for each employer you target—it's amazing how changing a few words can drastically change the number of people who click on your ad. Once your ads are running, monitor them. Try different variations.

If you do it right, employers will be knocking on your door to talk about their job. From there, it's up to you to impress them and seal the deal.

(continued)

For a step-by-step guide on how to manage your own Facebook job-wanted advertising campaign, type the following into Google's search box, "Use Facebook Ads to make employers hunt you down."

Willy Franzen is the founder of One Day, One Job—www.onedayonejob.com—and One Day, One Internship—www.onedayoneinternship.com—2 sites that help college students find entry level jobs and internships. He can be reached at Willy@onedayonejob.com.

■ YOUR PUBLIC RELATIONS STRATEGY—PUBLIC RELATIONS IS NOT JUST FOR PRODUCTS

After the invention of blogging, it didn't take long to attach voice capabilities to an RSS feed. Next came the software to allow people to organize and automatically download posted mp3s from podcasting web sites. Enter Peter Clayton, an award winning writer-director of corporate image, marketing, and documentary films and founder of TotalPictureRadio.com. TotalPictureRadio.com was the first-ever podcast for job hunters and career strategists. Now some 50,000 people download his show and listen to it whenever and wherever they want.

GUERRILLA INTELLIGENCE

Working with the Press

Peter Clayton

Working with the press can be a good thing. In fact, it can be a very good thing. It can help build your personal brand (a term I'm not all that keen on, but I can't think of a better one), expand your network, and add credibility and exposure to your professional credentials. Here's a framework you can use to successfully develop relationships with traditional and new media/online reporters.

First, a word of caution: if you work for a company (especially a publicly traded company) and are contacted by a reporter, blogger, podcaster, public relations (PR) firm—whatever—who wants to interview you; using your name, title, and employer in their article, you must get clearance from your internal public relations/communications department before you agree to an "on the record" interview. You'll need to get as much information about the reporter, publication, and topic as you can, along with the reporter's contact information. What is the subject of the article? Who else is being interviewed? When/where will it be published? What's the deadline? Will you have an opportunity to review, and approve, the article (video, podcast, blog) before publication?

Is the reporter a freelance journalist or staff writer? When you hang up the phone, Google the individual: read some of what they've written to make sure they're someone you would want to write about you. I've produced a number of webcasts for the American Management Association that required recording interviews with executives of large organizations. Even in these situations, with a very well known and respected brand, there is always a PR or communications person involved. I provide information about the webcast, an overview of the topic, who else will be interviewed, and a list of questions I'll be asking.

Sometimes, you may be contacted for "off-the-record background information" regarding an idea a journalist is researching. Once again, you need to find out who he or she is writing for and something about the reporter. Why are they calling you? Helping a journalist can be a smart investment of your time. Developing these relationships can prove to be extremely useful as your career and reputation progresses. That said, I would avoid negative comments regarding a current or past employer. If they're doing something unethical or illegal that's a different story, but just to dump on an employer will do nothing to advance your career.

It's pretty much of a no-brainer if you are contacted by the *Wall Street Journal, Fortune, Newsweek,* the *New York Times:* you'll want to try and cooperate with the reporter. Sites like ZoomInfo (popular with recruiters), spider online editions of publications, so the chances are very good that your ZoomInfo profile will contain the article. But what about podcasts and blogs? You're probably familiar with Chris Anderson's book, *The Long Tail.* I think this concept is very powerful. You'll still want to approach

(continued)

anyone who contacts you with caution. Google is a beautiful thing. My podcast is focused on career and leadership development. That's it.

Many, many of the professionals I've interviewed have generated useful contacts and business from our podcasts. People are still downloading interviews recorded 2 years ago from Total Picture Radio.

So. . . . Here's your handy-dandy press checklist:

➤ Who's calling and why?

➤ Are you freelance or staff? (Are you writing on spec or for an actual assignment?)

➤ What is your deadline?

➤ What is the subject, the lead? (opening lines of the article).

➤ Can you e-mail me questions you'll be asking ahead of time? (frequently called talking points).

➤ If it's a podcast, is it live or recorded? If recorded will it be edited? (If you are being recorded, you'll need to be on a landline phone in a quiet environment. Cell phones and speakerphones don't work.)

➤ If it's a published article, can you get reprints? If it's a blog or a podcast, will you be able to link to your web site?

➤ Avoid talking off the top of your head when a reporter calls. Get the details and schedule a call after you've had time to prepare.

Build your reputation through blogging, writing white papers, submitting articles to your local newspaper or trade journals with an interesting twist on your profession. Newspaper editors love to receive timely, valuable advice from subject matter experts in their communities. Join a local Toastmasters group and hone your public speaking skills. Invest in a webcam and create YouTube videos that showcase your expertise.

Get actively involved in professional associations; volunteer to work with nonprofits that are able to take advantage of your professional skills. Participate in your community. If you're knowledgeable in an area of interest to a general audience, meet with your librarian and offer to give a free lecture at the library. To quote Woody Allen, "80 percent of success is just showing up."

Peter Clayton is producer and host of Total Picture Radio—The Voice of Career Leadership™—www.totalpicture.com LinkedIn: www.linkedin.com/in/peterclayton/ Twitter: twitter.com/petertpm/.

■ NINE WAYS TO GET OTHERS TO SPREAD THE WORD

Here are a few ideas to increase your visibility, credibility, marketability, and value. You can get other people to start talking about you without having to ask or buy a round of drinks. These ideas cost little or no money. In all cases, go out of your way to invite the appropriate media:

1. *Conduct a seminar.* Become a strong public speaker and learn how to educate people on your industry. Simple "how-to" seminars are best. Keep it to under an hour. You can use other speakers but be sure you are seen as the primary idea person. Make sure you video- and audiotape the session. Inform the media and provide a press release. Videoblog and podcast it as well.

2. *Organize a seminar.* Find a need in your community and bring in speakers to fill it. If your topic is of general interest, present a version of your seminar to the public, perhaps under the sponsorship of a civic or business organization. Hook up with local media people to sponsor and promote the event. If you charge admittance (and you should, to ensure you attract serious participants only), then consider teaming with a local charity and donating a portion of the proceeds—you'll get twice the publicity and have a willing partner if you want to do it again or take it on the road and tour the country.

3. *Write.* Compose a thought-provoking piece connected to your seminars. Podcast it.

4. *Host a TV show.* Public television stations must fill a certain amount of time with homegrown programs. Why not offer to host a biweekly half-hour segment? Invite guests and run simple question-and-answer segments. You can also distribute

the tapes later or put them on your web site as videos. See www.perrymartel.com/video/janice/ for an example.

5. *Host a radio show.* Find a local morning news station and offer to be a guest, or better yet, guest host. Answer callers' questions. I know people in dentistry, home renovation, journalism, sex therapy, and so on, who have received huge boosts to their careers by doing this. If you can tie in sponsors, all the better.

6. *Develop a video series for distribution.* Remember the seminars you gave or organized? If you can get waivers signed, you may be able to distribute them free or for profit. Moderate each segment.

7. *Record and distribute CDs.* You can easily make a compilation CD of your radio or TV interviews.

8. *Become an editor.* If you are the "salt of the earth" type and prefer to play solid supporting roles, consider editing a magazine or e-zine. About.com has a cadre of more than 475 people who edit 50,000 topics.

9. *Volunteer.* Join a civic organization like the Shriners or Rotary Club and give back to your local community. This selfless act will provide many networking opportunities and make you feel great while you're doing good. Be aware, though, shameless self-promotion will get you a ticket to the exit door. Make certain that your fellow volunteers view you as a "giver" to the community and not as a "taker," or you're wasting your time.

GUERRILLA TIPS

➤ Be humble. In calling attention to your deeds and achievements, take care not to become an obnoxious braggart.

➤ Encourage other people in your industry to participate. You can build your credibility and goodwill while building an indirect support network.

➤ Make all pertinent articles, seminar brochures, and newspaper clippings available to your boss and coworkers, and anyone else who may help advance your career.

➤ Involve other members of your company as you see fit, if their contribution will make the TV program, radio show, or written article more interesting.

➤ Whenever you perform any kind of public service, take a backseat to your employer. It reflects well on you as a loyal team player, which ironically is just the thing to attract job offers from other employers.

The secret to self-promotion lies in letting others do your talking for you. Once others see what you're doing, get out of the way and let them do the bragging. Doing this makes you easy to find whenever a recruiter or employer is looking for someone in your industry. Job offers will fly your way.

■ HOW TO INTRODUCE YOURSELF WITH A SOUND BITE

You don't need to be a public figure to introduce yourself to the media. Contact local newspaper, radio, and television reporters—particularly those who cover business topics—and describe your professional expertise. Offer to comment on topics and questions in your field of work through interviews or written articles. Be friendly, not pushy. Become recognized as an expert.

Keep in contact with reporters; chances are good that they'll call you when a story breaks. When you do get a chance to comment, be clear and concise. Particularly for radio and television, you'll be edited into sound bites (segments lasting only seconds) that are inserted into the story. Your prospects for being aired are greater when you reach the point quickly and quotably. Subscribe (free) to Peter Shankman's HelpaReporter.com web site that helps reporters connect to new sources for articles through his daily e-mail of reporters' article queries.

■ WRITE AND PUBLISH

Getting published gives you an important, added credential. Writing articles for trade, professional, business, or specialty magazines is a good way to get exposure. And it is easier than you think. Most editors are hungry for writers with a good technical grasp of their field. If you demonstrate expertise, an editor will often polish your writing for you.

➤ Become an Author and Authority

Start small with your local paper or business journal, writing articles about what you know. Give it a personal spin and take a side. Write how-to articles that are relevant to your industry. Editors often need them for filler. Try writing a couple and have your friends read them and tell you if they are interesting. Then take a course, or borrow or buy a book on writing short information pieces.

Editors at magazines like *Fortune, Time,* or *Newsweek* will not take a chance on a first-time writer, so don't waste your time trying. You need to build a portfolio first. Just get the first few articles published anywhere and then start to target specific publications. That includes posting it on your blog first because many journalists cruise the blogs to find ideas and the unique opinions of people just like you whom they then interview and write about. You may very well be discovered on your blog.

➤ Some Ways to Get Published and Get Hired

Write and distribute your company's newsletter. Make sure you send copies to the magazines you want to write for, indicating they have the right to republish the article if they do so in its entirety. Make sure they either give you a byline or a pull box at the end of the article where you can put your name, profession, and e-mail address—just like all the contributors in this book do.

Write your own newsletter and distribute it to the people in your industry for whom you would like to work. If you're courageous enough, you might try writing a "roundup article." This is an article where you round up and interview experts on a subject. There's nothing quite as exhilarating as getting to see a half dozen of your industry's best people and asking their opinion on the state of the industry. You can interview them about such things as:

➤ Trends in the industry,

➤ Greatest contributions of the past few years, or

➤ The effects of new technology.

Your options are endless. Senior execs know it's important to be visible, so they'll cooperate if the project is appealing. You can even phone your industry trade magazine and pitch your idea to them, mentioning the names of some of the people you plan to interview. Then ask if they're interested in running the piece when you're finished. When you call your list of interviewees, you can tell them you are doing a piece for their industry publication.

Sound overwhelming? Well, you don't have to do all the work yourself; you can call your local college or university's journalism department to ask for help. Most professors will take the time to meet and explain how to frame your idea and prepare your questions. They may even agree to assign a student to look over your work for extra credit. Easier yet, hire a professional from sites like: elance.com, guru.com ifreelance.com, or odesk.com. Come to think of it, these are great groups to flog your own skills on in between gigs.

When the piece is finally published, you need to ensure your interviewees get 2 copies. One has a handwritten thank-you note on the front page. They'll keep the autographed one and distribute the other. Suddenly, everyone in the company knows who you are. They are reading your article because it's important to their boss and therefore their career. Even those people whom you didn't interview for the piece will read it, and many will call to let you know they are available for comment if the need arises.

Write white papers on your industry and have them published by your marketing people. They are always looking for free publicity and your piece may be just what they need for the company web site.

GUERRILLA INTELLIGENCE

How to Find Your Next Job for Free Using Social Networks, Blogs, and Other Underutilized Web 2.0 Methods and Tools

Glenn Gutmacher

I'm a veteran recruiting researcher, aka sourcer: the online detective who finds talent (that's what we in the industry call job seekers) that regular recruiters can't, in ways they don't know exist. I'm going to flip that around and show you how to use those ways to FIND a job.

Today, It's More than Resumes
I'll assume (a big "if") that you have an easily findable resume—so congrats on a great start! But some recruiters have a bias against job boards' resume banks and other easily found resumes. They label you as an "active job seeker" and you aren't

(continued)

as desirable as someone who's gainfully employed or otherwise perceived to be a busy consultant-expert. (I'm about to show you how to become the latter, regardless of your status.) These "passive job seekers" are found in other ways—and you can be there, too. Even among the majority of recruiters and hiring managers who happily review "active" resumes, they are more comfortable selecting people to interview if the person is a somewhat "known quantity."

In either case, how do you make that leap? Other parts of this book discuss LinkedIn, personal networking, and some other proven methods for getting an edge when you don't have connections into an employer. However, if that's all you do, you're shooting yourself in the foot.

Do Professional Networking on Social Networks
Today's Internet sites and tools, dubbed "Web 2.0," can help you greatly, and they're almost always free (typically advertising-supported). Let's start with larger virtual communities like Yahoo 360 (360.yahoo.com), Blogspot.com, LiveJournal.com, and so on, where you can post content. When you join one of those communities, you're not obligated to post family photos or accept dates from everyone you connect to. Instead, use it as a professional networking platform.

These sites typically host interest groups by topic and geography, so you can join all the relevant ones free, which lets you browse and search your fellow members' profiles. Look for interesting people (i.e., those working at companies of interest and holding job titles 1 to 2 levels above you in the corporate hierarchy, since they're in the best position to employ you). A second job title preference (but not to be ignored) is recruiter—also known as Talent Acquisition Specialist (or Manager), sourcer (executive) search consultant, and staffing professional (among others—remember the value of keyword synonyms when searching!).

Focus on the Big Social Networks
Two good places to look for professional interest groups are Ning.com and LinkedIn's Groups Directory. Also find specific contact information for any of 10 million people at over 1 million companies with the business card trading service, Jigsaw.com.

You can't ignore the 2 largest social networks nowadays: Facebook.com and MySpace.com, each with over 100 million profiles. Even if you're not yet a member, here is a quick way to search MySpace profiles to find interesting people using Google.com's main search box (type this exactly, including punctuation and spaces): site:www.myspace.com ("occupation * CPA" OR "occupation * accounting manager") (intitle:Atlanta OR intitle:Georgia).

The only things you have to change are what job titles and locations to use for the kind of person you want to find. If you do not have a MySpace account, you may need to start one in order to contact people who do not list public contact information on their profiles. It's also good to create a MySpace profile (need not include any compromising photos of yourself!) to give potential employers another way to find you.

On Facebook, the regular search (www.facebook.com/srch. php) lets you type a job title and/or company name and find people with that in their profile across the entire Facebook network. The profile search (www.facebook.com/advanced. php?ref=search/) has many more search criteria to narrow your results, but only searches within your Facebook networks (i.e., your school/alma mater, your geographic area, and your current employer) and your directly connected friends (equivalent to first-degree connections on LinkedIn).

You can change your location under Facebook Settings up to twice every 60 days. This is great if you desire to relocate: now you can see and search for people in your target metro area. To jumpstart your network, use Facebook's Friend finder (www.facebook.com/findfriends.php) to upload your e-mail address book or IM list file, or search Facebook using a name or e-mail for a particular person. (Most social networks offer this functionality.)

There's a lot of buzz nowadays about Twitter (www. twitter.com). With over 10 million members, this may be the most popular way to communicate over mobile devices. However, you don't need a cell phone to use it. The web site's advanced search (search.twitter.com) lets you search for people by keywords and/or geographically. Note the syntax: SQL near:Boston within:50mi.

(continued)

Replace SQL with your keyword/phrase and Boston with your target metro area, and you will find everyone who has ever made a post containing your keywords and lives near that city. This works internationally (e.g., type SQL near:Amsterdam within:50km), too. It's beyond the scope of this article to explain other ways to use it, but start with their help/FAQs.

So what if you have someone's name and want to learn more about them? Try using a social network aggregator: these are sites that gather profiles from many social networks and let you search all of them from one place. Examples are 123People. com, Wieowie.nl, Pipl.com, Spock.com, Wink.com and—a nice twist for network monitoring—Spokeo.com lets you aggregate all your friends' (personal and/or professional) sites into one location so you can stay up to date with all their events.

It's Time to Reach Out

Now that you've found lots of interesting people, reach out to them—at first, with a short message, and not with a desperate plea for job help. Focus on reciprocally beneficial networking. Say you found them on "X" site, they seem knowledgeable/ interesting in your professional area of interest, and ask how you can help THEM. Yes, you heard me right: instead of being like every other job seeker who wants something, you're offering something instead. Like honey, this refreshing approach attracts more bees.

Use whatever tools the community offers to communicate: sometimes e-mails or instant messaging (IM) addresses are displayed, or you may have to use their internal message system. Don't send your resume, but it's fine to include the Web address as a link at the end of your message.

Share Your Expertise, Build Your Personal Brand

Don't stop there. These communities also give you the opportunity to convey your expertise. This is the "personal branding" concept that career consultants advocate nowadays. You can put that on steroids using Web 2.0: answer questions posed by others in your industry that show you're knowledgeable, and append your auto-signature to each post (include that resume link again!) so it's easy for the reader to reach you. LinkedIn Answers (www.linkedin.com/answers/) lets you search through questions and answers and automatically links your responses to your profile.

The 2 largest sources of these niche discussion groups by industry subtopic where people are asking questions and (relative) experts are answering are Google Groups (groups.google.com) and Yahoo Groups (groups.yahoo.com). At these sites, type unique keywords/phrases to find people talking about your subject matter. For example, if I were a quantitative investment guru, I might type "equity derivatives." This will lead you to posts within particular groups. Join relevant groups, see what people are saying in their posts, contact the interesting/knowledgeable ones (they can help you find a job, too), and reply to a discussion thread when you have something useful to say. Another way to find free discussion lists by topic keywords is Catalist (www.lsoft.com/lists/listref.html).

Blogging Enhanced by Web 2.0

Also start a blog—a type of online diary—most social networks have blogging tools built in. To see what others are doing, use a blog search tool like Technorati.com, IceRocket.com, or Google blog search (blogsearch.google.com) to find relevant posts and people. Some blog search sites are even industry-specific (e.g., legal blogs via Blawgsearch.com), but with the right keywords you can narrow your results on any of them.

A good way to stick your toe in the water is to respond to others' blog posts by typing a comment: under each post, click the comments link or type in the box provided. Say something complimentary and/or semi-intelligent (constructive contrasting opinions are also fine), and you can't go wrong.

When you're ready to start posting to your own blog, don't waste your posts talking about restaurants or what you cooked for dinner (unless you seek a job as a chef!). Focus your opinions on what's happening in your industry (positive or negative) or simply share a few links to interesting tools or articles you've seen, with brief commentary on why they may be valuable. Again, make sure your blog links to your resume, just as all your discussion list posts should link to your blog and resume.

You never know who's going to find one of your comments interesting and now can follow the links to learn more about

(continued)

you. This process effectively presells you to your target audience without having to set up interviews. Some may ask you to contribute a post on their blogs (do accept, if it is a reputable resource) and you should offer likewise. Don't wait to volunteer a guest post if you respect others' blogs and have started to build rapport with them by commenting on their posts, and so on. This typically results in the blogger initiating direct communication with you. Before you know it, people will start linking to your posts and forwarding links about you to others looking for an expert like you—did you realize you are one at this point?—without your even knowing!

Ready for the Next Level and Scale Up Efficiently?

Now you're making my job of finding you easier. Here's how you can make it a lot easier for all the recruiters out there: get your thoughts distributed even more widely by using more social networks. When you register with sites like MySpace, Twitter, LinkedIn, Facebook, and others that let you blog and share content in other ways, you increase your exposure—and thus the chance of being noticed by the right people.

What are those other ways to share content? Audio, video, and social bookmarking are 3 hot ones nowadays. Social bookmarking is sharing your favorite links with others. Sites like ClipIt (www.clipit.com), Digg (www.digg.com), and Delicious (www.del.icio.us/) facilitate this. If you discover neat resources, post them. You'll get more fans.

With simple free tools and a $20 webcam on your end, you can produce short audio and/or video segments called *podcasts* that can include whatever you'd type in a blogpost, plus open other content possibilities thanks to these dynamic media. Why not interview experts in your field and post those on your blog? Or do a short how-to video yourself. When you go to an event, blog about what you see—and let them see it, too. For great examples of online video and podcasts that will give you ideas, go to Blinkx (www.blinkx.com) and Everyzing (search.everyzing.com) and type a unique phrase to find relevant content. These search YouTube.com and many other sites all at once.

Now you're saying, "Glenn, wait, I don't have time to post on all these sites and do all this multimedia!" Time to leverage Web 2.0: tools like Hellotxt (www.hellotxt.com) and Ping (www.ping.fm) allow you to post once and that message is auto-posted to your accounts on all of those sites. If a site doesn't let you cross-post multimedia, you can at least enter a text link to your podcasts.

Also, many of the tools to add multimedia and all kinds of other functionality to your blog/web site are available free. Usually called widgets, you can add them with little technical knowledge, especially if you use a popular blogging platform like Typepad.com or Wordpress.org. Some great sources of widgets are Widgetbox.com, Sixapart.com, and Widgetoko.com. These will make your blog more interesting and further grow your audience.

All this may strike you as overwhelming. But remember, you don't have to do everything discussed above to succeed—though the impact of each is synergistic with the others. Try a couple of the techniques that resonate with you, at first. As you start to see success with positive response from interesting professional contacts, that will motivate you to try other things. Even after you land that next job, you'll still be using social networks because their career value continues even while you're working!

Glenn Gutmacher is founder of www.recruiting-online.com and vice president of www.JobMachine.net He shows corporate employers and staffing firms how to find job seekers of any skill set, industry, location, using the Internet, whether they have a resume floating around or not. He can be reached at glenn@jobmachine.net / Arbit.net or glenn@recruiting-online.com.

Chapter 7

Recruiternomics 2.0

How to Work Your Job Search Commandos

Strategy without tactics is the slowest route to victory. Tactics without strategy is the noise before defeat.

—SUN TZU

FIRST LAW OF RECRUITERNOMICS

In a knowledge-based economy and society, the employers with the best talent win.

More than ever in our history, huge value is being leveraged from smart ideas—and the winning technology and business models they create: the people who can deliver on them are becoming invaluable, and the methods of employing and managing them are being transformed. Today, demographics on a broader scale are radically altering the recruiting landscape. An aging workforce of 65 million baby boomers was poised to retire by the end of this decade. The "market correction" in 2008 caused many to rethink their plans. No one yet knows how this will affect the supply of people, but it will make it more difficult to locate and keep the best talent.

Do not mistake today's, "War for *Talent*" with, the "War for *Any Talent*" prevalent in the late 1990s. People and talent are mutually exclusive. While everyone has some talent, TV shows like *American Idol* have proven that some should not yet quit their day jobs.

SECOND LAW OF RECRUITER*NOMICS*

Regardless of the unemployment rate, the market for talent is always strong and extremely competitive. Employers will pay to hire the best of the best.

For those with talent, the fast track inside the hidden job market is through recruiters—in any economic climate.

■ RECRUITER*NOMICS* 101

I'm going to give you an overview of the recruiting industry and a framework to guide you in working with the industry by explaining:

➤ The third-party recruiting industry
➤ Four major categories of recruiters
➤ Behind-the-scenes of the recruiting process
➤ Rules of engagement
➤ Frequently asked questions (and their answers)

If you know the game ahead of time, you're odds of winning are greatly increased.

➤ The Third-Party Recruiting Industry

Human resources people use the generic term *third-party recruiter* to describe individuals or companies that help them fill their recruiting needs. You are probably more familiar with the term *recruiter,* also a generic term that encompasses the many flavors of recruiters including executive search professionals, headhunters, and temporary staffing agencies.

The industry is characterized by both huge revenues and enormous fragmentation. Estimates show revenues of more than $410 billion globally, with nearly half coming from the United States with more than 20,000 staffing firms and 174,532 professional recruiters. Here's what you need to know to incorporate recruiters into your Force Multiplier:

➤ The industry is completely fragmented.
➤ Recruiters rarely talk to each other (professional paranoia).

➤ Recruiters are in business for themselves—not you.

➤ There are no educational or training prerequisites.

➤ There is no official code of conduct governing the industry.

➤ Licensing is nearly nonexistent.

➤ Little training is required to make a lot of money.

Business maturity is what differentiates recruiters. There are 2 broad camps: the highly educated inexperienced recruiters who tend to cluster in the large firms or franchises and the seasoned business executives entering their second career—most often found in boutique firms. Each has their place. This explains why some recruiters understand the fine points of your industry or profession and others need to be educated. Understanding how to distinguish between the two is the key to your success. Recruiters can be the single biggest asset to your career.

➤ Four Major Categories of Recruiters

Companies have come to recognize that, when a position requires a somewhat unique set of skills and experience, or is surrounded by specific political or cultural circumstances, passively advertising a position makes a good hire difficult, if not impossible. More and more companies are turning to professional recruiters outside their company to deliver talent because successful people don't voluntarily raise their hand and say, "Here I am!"

There are 4 broad categories, and you lever each for a different outcome. By understanding the differences, you will know which ones can help you and which ones you shouldn't hold your breath waiting for a return call. The 4 major categories are:

1. Executive search firms
2. Headhunters
3. Temporary employment agencies
4. Contract placement recruiters

Executive Search Firms

It's not unusual for job hunters to mistakenly regard the "don't call us, we'll call you" mentality of most executive search firms with contempt. Rule 1: It's not about you. Employers retain Executive Search Professionals (ESPs for short) to find candidates to fit a specific role the company has identified. This is common with executive level hires, especially where the position is highly visible and critical to the organization's mission. As a rule of thumb, the greater the need and the more complex the search, the more likely an executive search firm will be retained. The ESP is paid handsomely regardless of the outcome.

When the position to be filled is a CEO, president, vice president, or board member, an ESP will be working with an employer's search committee and a target list of potential candidates who were identified by a researcher. A candidate must meet rigid requirements to receive consideration. The job of the ESP is to convince the targeted candidates to look at the opportunity and to then assess their fit. Search firms are not really interested in job seekers, other than to fatten their databases. There is little to be gained by stalking them when you're already knee-deep in your job search. You are better off to wait for them to discover you. If you excel at your job, they will find you—without prompting.

You can accelerate the process by increasing your visibility in the community through board memberships and civic organizations. In the meantime, send them your resume electronically and mail them a hard copy. Do not call them to see if they received it—it brands you as light and desperate. If they have a suitable opening, they will call you. That's how they make money. Do send a resume to every *executive search firm* in your vicinity or niche that deals with your skill set and/or industry. Research your niche through Kennedy Information (kennedyinfo.com).

➤ *Tools of their trade:* In-house databases, ZoomInfo.com, LinkedIn.com, ExecuNet.com, association directories, Who's Who, bizjournals.com, and a fulltime researcher. Make sure you can be found. Read more about this in Chapters 4 and 5.

➤ *How to reach them:* Ask for a referral from a college, kennedy info.com, or ExecuNet.com.

Headhunters
Headhunters come in 2 basic flavors: retained and contingency. Both offer you benefits:

1. *Retained:* The firm has a financial relationship with the client company much like that of an executive search firm. Retained recruiters are paid an up-front fee and a further success fee for completing the assignment. Completing an assignment requires the recruiter to match a candidate to a job specification.

Retained recruiters usually have an exclusive relationship with the employer and may even be their unofficial talent scout.

2. *Contingency:* The recruiter can present candidates but is only paid if the company likes and hires that candidate. Often many contingency recruiters compete to fill the same position. Time is of the essence, so if you want to be considered, you have to be available for interviews on a moment's notice.

Sometimes a headhunter is also a good "promoter" and will play both sides of the employer/job hunter equation. Find a recruiter who specializes in your industry or the industry you want to enter. If possible, find a recruiter at least 6 months before you need to because it will take the recruiter a while to hunt through the market for possible opportunities. Do not work with more than one recruiter at a time in the same city without discussing this up front with the recruiter. Do not try to circumvent recruiters who already have a relationship with a firm. Money is at stake. They don't get paid if you approach the company without them, and they will have no incentive to ever talk to you again.

While you may be trying to save the employer a few dollars, circumventing the recruiter shows that neither the recruiter nor the employer can trust you. The employer understands that using the newspaper or job boards will not necessarily deliver the results they want. The recruiter's fees are part of the hiring cost, which has been budgeted for already. It is not coming out of your paycheck. I have heard about several candidates who tried this, only to have the recruiter blow up the bridge to ensure that the candidate was definitely not considered. Headhunters have a "one-strike-and-you're-out" mentality. You don't write the headhunter's paycheck directly: the client company does.

Headhunters don't work for you; they work for themselves. You are just the product. They assume all the risk and costs in marketing you. Make sure you know what you are looking for before you contact them. Make sure they understand what you are looking for and keep them informed about your progress on the interviews they arrange for you. If you are looking for a good recruiter because your job search is stalled, ask your friends to refer one. Treat them with respect and don't bother them unnecessarily for frequent updates.

➤ *Tools of their trade:* In-house databases, ZoomInfo, Linked In.com, referrals, split networks, national and regional niche job boards, bizjournals.com, and a contract Sourcer. Make sure you can be found. Read more about this in Chapters 4 and 5.

➤ *How to reach them:* Ask for a referral from a college, kennedy-info.com, ExecuNet.com, the recruitinganimal.com blog, RecruitingBlogers.com, The Fordyce Letter, LinkedIn, TheLadders.com.

Temporary Employment Agencies

Temp agencies do exactly what their name suggests. They provide employers with temporary help on a day-by-day temporary or contract basis. The industry is huge—upward of $100 billion per year in the United States.

Because human capital is now easily expensed away or treated as a variable cost, there is a built-in incentive for an employer to hire people on a project basis for only as long as the company needs them. In most cases, the temp agency will pay you and invoice the company separately. Many agencies supply benefits that are equal to those provided to full-time employees by major corporations.

Temp agencies are a great place to get your foot in the door of an industry or a particular company. Starting as a temp can mean you are the first in line when a permanent position opens up. Temp agencies normally work with hourly employees or those earning less than $30,000 per year. The exceptions are specialty agencies for techies or senior executives, for example, where salaries can run from $15 to $400 per hour, or more.

Each agency will have different corporate clients. Register with as many as you can that are specific to your skill set or represent the industry you want to work in. Then keep in touch with them on a biweekly basis. Every time you go out on a project, take pains to overperform and build a reputation for being reliable and honest. By doing this, you will ensure that the agencies are fighting to represent you and keep you busy. It is not unusual for a temp agency to have 100 or more clients. By registering with the top 10 agencies, you will have your finger on the pulse of more than 1,000 employers. Little if any effort is required on your part—beyond doing a great job.

➤ *Tools they use:* In-house database, bizjournals.com, LinkedIn for specialized skills, referrals, networking, regional and/or niche job boards, newspaper classifieds.

Contract Placement Recruiters

This type of recruiter places people into companies to carry out special projects or to staff a department and to get around corporate (salary/benefits) budget constraints. Simply stated, full-time employees of a company are paid out of a separate pot of money from contract employees. It is not unusual for a company to freeze hiring yet still bring on contract employees. A contract employee is actually an employee of the contract placement firm.

Just like any other employer, these firms can offer the employee a full menu of benefits, a highly competitive hourly rate, and sometimes employment for many years at one location. You'll find contract employees in almost every conceivable profession. A contract employee may be anything from an information technology professional to a human resource manager, to an engineer or a nurse, an interim CEO or teacher, and just about everything in between where *specialized* skills are required. Due to the critical shortage of some skill-challenged organizations, some contract placement firms may even handle visa and immigration sponsorship matters to help ease these employee shortages.

Although many younger workers are contract employees, expect to see many baby boomers who "thought" they would be able to retire end up at the same company working in the same department and at the same desk that they did prior to retirement. This time around, however, they will be contract employees.

➤ *Tools they use:* In-house database, bizjournals.com, LinkedIn for specialized skills, referrals, networking, regional and/or niche job boards, newspaper classifieds.

➤ **Behind the Scenes of the Recruiting Process**

Recruiters are matchmakers. Their role in the hiring process is to bring together strangers in an economic marriage that is good for both parties. If you understand the mechanics of the process, you will be in a better position to work the outcome to your advantage.

Most recruiters have created a logical process for finding and attracting top candidates that looks something like the following:

1. *Needs analysis:* Every search begins with understanding what is required by the client in the role to be filled. The depth of understanding at this stage will determine the search's success.

   ➤ *What you need to know:* This is where most searches die. Understanding why will save you a load of grief during your job search. It often happens that clients *do not* have a clear understanding of exactly what they expect from the person they are hiring, so they don't give precise direction to the recruiter. You may have experienced this yourself if you have ever been on an interview where it was clear the interviewer wasn't certain of what he or she was looking for. All too often hiring managers will give recruiters only the vaguest of ideas about what they want, saying to the recruiter "I'll know them when I see them." That's a fact and often it's enough for most recruiters to begin. This happens less frequently when a recruiter is on retainer but it still happens. You need to be able to ask enough intelligent questions to gather the information yourself about the opportunity before the interview *without* alienating the recruiter.

2. *Research:* Here the firm will make a long list comprised of the names of individuals they want to contact from companies and organizations that directly relate to this search. In the "old days" (5 years ago), this was a 3- to 4-week process for a researcher/project manager whose sole purpose was to gather names and up-to-date contact data of potential candidates. Research is an ancillary function of the recruiting process. Tools like ZoomInfo, LinkedIn, and Google have streamlined the process considerably.

➤ *What you need to know:* Today if you're not on the long list, you won't get the call. In the old days, recruiters had to ask, "Who do you know?"—now they already know. The search will be over before they know you even exist. Take me, for example. I have a paid subscription to ZoomInfo and I consult it before I start any search. I'll take the top 100 people from ZoomInfo and cross-reference it with my search of LinkedIn. If you're in both databases, I know you want to be found. At the very least, I know you're managing your career smartly. If you have uploaded your picture to ZoomInfo, I know you want to talk to me. I'll also check ZoomInfo to see when you last updated or changed your profile. If you did that in the past 60 days, you move to the top of my list. (Do you really need any more reason to claim your ZoomInfo profile or create one at LinkedIn?)

3. *Short list, recruit, and interview:* The recruiter's goal is to ensure his or her time and that of the clients is spent interviewing only exceptional candidates. The key interviewing determinants are

personal chemistry and fit. The recruiter will condense the long list of 100 to 200 or more profiles down to a manageable 2 dozen suspects. They then reach out to that group and try to cull it down to 10 prospects. Often this is done with an initial phone call. Their assessment of each potential candidate begins with that call. From the first conversation, they begin analyzing the candidate's knowledge base, experience, and attitude. In-depth interviews provide an opportunity to conduct a thorough assessment of each viable candidate. From here, one or more candidates will be selected for interviews with the client. As you can see, a lot of work goes on behind the scenes and the assessment continues throughout the process.

➤ *What you need to know:* If you get a call from a recruiter, you have been prequalified for an opportunity 60 percent of the time—even more if they have found you on ZoomInfo or LinkedIn. (*Too subtle again?*) Be on your best behavior when you interview with a recruiter. Be yourself but better. Be together. Know what you want out of life and how the recruiter's opportunity fits into your career path. The recruiter will make the first assessment of your suitability for the employer's role. You will pass or fail at this stage. If you treat them like a confidant or marriage counselor you are DOA (dead on arrival). Respect their time and ask questions that are appropriate to the level of the position you are being considered for—be that an executive position or entry-level.

4. *Reference checks:* Most recruiters informally reference candidates before they are presented to their client. (LinkedIn is an ideal way to do this, by the way.) Recruiters often discover things employers can't, and many times they are things the candidate wished they hadn't. They will tell the client, because most professionals would rather admit they were pursuing the wrong candidate than make a costly mistake. (More on this in a moment.)

➤ *What you need to know:* If there is something you do not want the recruiter to know that will affect your candidacy for the position, rest assured they will find it. Tell the recruiter ahead of time if you are expecting a bad reference from a former employer and explain the circumstances. No one's perfect—as I'm constantly reminded by my children. If the recruiter finds out on his own, you may never have an opportunity to discuss or dispute the reference.

You will be deselected and you will never know why. Instead, call your references and tell them who to expect a call from. At the same time, tell them why you are interested in the position, why you are ideally qualified, and why the employer is interested in you. Send the reference a copy of your resume. Highlight the achievements that the employer will be looking to confirm. Take a moment to remind them about the role you played in those projects. Take credit for your accomplishments without prompting the reference.

Reference checks are *not* a license for the employer or recruiter to invade your privacy. Under no circumstances should you reveal your social security number or any banking or credit information.

If you'd like a better understanding of the reference process from the employer's viewpoint, download a copy of the guide, "Don't Hire a Liar," from our web site at www.perrymartel.com. (On a personal note, I have replaced just 2 people since 1985. Perry-Martel's standard reference check covers the 10 need-to-know areas of a candidate's background, including leadership attributes, managerial skill, character, and more.)

5. *Psychological assessments:* Personality assessments and evaluations have become commonplace in the interview process both at the senior executive level and below. Many firms including Perry-Martel have gone beyond the simple Myers-Briggs to include more sophisticated measures like the BAROn-EQ, which measures Emotion Intelligence. For many organizations, a personality profile will be administered in addition to thorough reference checks. It is designed to give the employer an extra bit of reassurance by assessing your "fit" with the rest of the team.

➤ *What you need to know:* Answer the questions truthfully. Do not try to outsmart the test. You will lose. The tests are set up to flush out cheaters. You will fail and destroy your chances to go further in the process. Fortunately, most employers only administer these tests when they are very interested in your candidacy. That is a good thing. Ask what the test is being used to measure and then answer the questions in that context. Read carefully any permission form you are asked to sign. Understand what they have the right to do with the information. Ask to have the original returned to you or destroyed.

6. *Offer negotiation:* Most recruiters will help negotiate the terms of an offer. Their job is to come to an agreement that is satisfactory to both you and the employer.

➤ *What you need to know:* Let the recruiter negotiate your package. It's a whole lot easier for both sides to deal with the money issues through an intermediary. It's easier for a third party to take their ego out of the equation.

7. *On-boarding and guarantee:* Most recruiters will provide a guarantee in the form of an insurance policy for the candidate's performance. Guarantees run the spectrum from none to 6 months, or more. The norm is 30 to 45 days. This period acts as a buffer for the employer to determine your competency on the job and decide if you are indeed qualified. The recruiter may be required to replace you during that period or in some cases even refund their well-earned fee.

➤ *What you need to know:* The way recruiters are paid is often reflected in how much upfront work they do to understand the project, which is directly related to how long they will "guarantee" a candidate. In short, a firm that provides a *yearlong* guarantee, for example, is more likely to go to great pains to understand an employer's needs and to make an exact match. Anything less is shortsighted. Understanding this will tell you how much "due diligence" you must do personally to ensure the opportunity is a good one for you versus a quick buck for the recruiter.

Note: Obviously, the longer the guarantee, the more risk the recruiter assumes for your performance and thus the greater their incentive to thoroughly appreciate the need for an exact fit. That means you can expect the process to take several months to conclude.

GUERRILLA INTELLIGENCE

Recruiters and Research

Donato Diorio

Most recruiters do what is called the full life-cycle recruitment. Finding a client is the sales portion of the process. With "job

(continued)

order" in hand, they do the initial name sourcing and then they recruit the best prospects. Next, they screen the prospects and present the best candidates to their clients. On top of all this, they must prepare both candidate and employer for the interview, debrief them afterward, and eventually negotiate a job offer.

Recruiters Who Are Successful Are Extremely Busy People

Recruitment and all its complexities tends to foster a level of impatience that is required to succeed. Whether recruiters came into the field impatient (and thus succeeded) or became that way due to the demands of the job is debatable. So prevalent is this trait among top recruiters, recruiting managers have put a positive spin on this trait, calling it a "sense of urgency."

Help for the Recruiters

In the past few years, there has been a growing trend in the recruiting world. Emerging are the new assistants to the recruiters, armed with the latest technology and killer research skills. They are known as the "sourcers." So new is the term, that as of this writing, Microsoft Word spell checker did not recognize the term. It will.

Sourcers Are Polar Opposites of Recruiters

The term *sourcer* in the recruiting world describes the person who is doing pure research and name generation. Sourcers use the Internet, job boards, internal databases, and corporate phone directories to gather names and then turn them over to a recruiter. They almost never talk to anyone, and if they do, it is very brief. Usually, they are more introverted and prefer to work behind the scenes. If you are working with a recruiter, you may never talk with this person, nor know that he or she even exists.

Most Recruiters Don't Have Sourcers Working for Them

Think. This impatient force of nature recruiter that you are dealing with ... do you think he has time to do thorough research? Usually not; ... most successful recruiters have good instincts, but they don't have the time to do thorough research.

If you can provide valuable information to a recruiter, he will go out of his way to help you and give you attention above and beyond that which the typical candidate receives.

Here are several tips for working with a recruiter as a source of information:

➤ Find out if the recruiter works full life-cycle or if they work with sourcers and researchers. If he or she has a team, get to know the players on the team.

➤ Ask what he needs. Don't make assumptions. It may be insight on additional job openings (new business for him) or candidates for positions he is trying to fill. Learn about all the positions he is working on; keep notes during your job search.

➤ Always call to give something. Every time you ever pick up the phone to talk to him, have something of value in hand: insight on a new position, candidate referral, news of a layoff at a competitor of his client. Train that recruiter. Teach him that your name is synonymous with valuable information.

➤ Keep him in the loop. If you are sending information to one of the recruiters' team members, sourcers, or assistants, copy the recruiter on the communication. Don't assume that if you are sending leads to the sourcer, that you will get attributed as the source.

➤ Maintain the relationship even after you get a job. If you've spent the time to understand and work with a recruiter, you will continue to have great value to each other. Many recruiters pay referral fees; don't be shy to ask. A trusted referral source is well worth a $500, $1000, or greater referral fee.

Some of the best client-recruiter relationships are developed with a person that is first placed by the recruiter and then uses that recruiter to fill positions at his new company. Whether he places you at the position or not, you will use his services in the future. Remind the recruiter of this.

Bringing information to your recruiter will separate you from the mass number of connections that are simply reaching out to the recruiter to get something. Taking this approach of being a purveyor of insight and information will open the doors

(continued)

to creating a strong professional relationship that will endure throughout your career.

———————

Donato Diorio is the founder and CEO of www.broadlook.com. Broadlook Technologies develops research tools for executive and corporate recruiters. Donato is a former top billing recruiter and is now a speaker and thought leader in the field of Internet research. Donato's blog is www.iDonato.com.

➤ **Rules of Engagement**

Here's what to do if a recruiter calls you at work:

➤ Be flattered. If a recruiter calls you, in most cases the recruiter's team has prequalified you. Don't ask him where he got your name right away. There's time enough for that later.

➤ Take the call only if you can speak without whispering. If you can't talk freely, ask for a phone number and a convenient time to call back. Better you say nothing than blow the call. This also gives you an opportunity to look up the recruiter's firm to make sure the call is legit. Take a minute to first read the firm's web site to see if they normally recruit people like you. Can't find their site? That's an early warning sign. Check if they are using a Yahoo, Hotmail, Gmail, or other generic account. Yes? Be careful. It may be a ruse from your employer trying to cull the ranks for deserters ahead of an upcoming layoff. If they send an unsolicited e-mail to your work address, respond that you're not interested because employers can legally monitor your e-mail. Then send a follow-up e-mail from your hotmail account.

Ask the recruiter the following 4 questions. Do not deviate from this exact sequence:

1. Are you on retainer or contingency?
   ➤ *What you should understand:* You want to know how the recruiter is being compensated—retainer or contingency. Learning this can tell you if the project is real or if he's fishing. It may also tell you how quickly you have to decide whether you are interested in being considered. If the recruiter is on retainer, the project is real. Go forward. You have time to consider your options.

If the firm is on contingency, the recruiter is likely under the gun to close the project before another firm does. Time is of the essence. You must move quickly if you are interested.

2. Do you have an exclusive?

➤ *What you should understand:* If they have an exclusive, it means that they are the only firm working on the assignment. Listen to the recruiter describe the opportunity and decide if you want to go forward. If they don't have an exclusive, they are competing with other firms and possibly even the employer's own internal human resource people.

3. Have you successfully placed people with this hiring manager before?

➤ *What you should understand:* It pays to be cautious. You need to decide if the recruiter has the capacity to represent you and get you an interview. From the moment they forward your resume to the employer, the recruiter is entitled to be paid his full fee (for a period as long as a year or more) should that employer hire you, regardless. Understand, even if you were to land an interview on your own during that period, the employer would need to pay the recruiter's fee, even if the interview was for a different job in a different department or division. "Hold on," you say, "I don't even know who the employer is!" Too bad. That's the Catch-22. It's your responsibility to get as much information as you can and make an informed decision to forward your resume to the recruiter.

4. Have you vetted the job description with the client, and may I have a copy?

➤ *What you should understand:* If they haven't met with the client or vetted the job description with the client, it's not ideal for you, but it's not necessarily the end either. Ask for a written copy of the job description. Read it carefully and ask the recruiter as many questions as he'll allow. And make an informed decision to proceed. Should the recruiter refuse (rare), I advise my closest friends to terminate the call. The recruiter is just looking to fill his database of candidates. He may be performing business development and wants some new resumes to introduce himself to prospective companies.

➤ Frequently Asked Questions (and Their Answers)

Q: The recruiter only had a limited job description. What should I do?

A: A lot of research. Quickly. Employers expect you to be well prepared to discuss their needs versus your fit, whether or not the recruiter has prepared you. So you must do it yourself. Focus on what their 5 top competitors are doing that keeps the employer up at night. Start by reviewing their competitors' latest products or service offerings, then reach out to your network. Consider using LinkedIn's "Ask a Question" feature to gather covert intelligence. It's a fast free way to poll 29 million people.

Q: I did the interview and the recruiter hasn't called me.

A: First off, you should have agreed ahead of time with the recruiter to call them back right after you finished the interview. So did you? Or did you have a cigarette and go for lunch? Time is of the essence. Call and leave an upbeat message with your impressions. Save any concerns for when you connect. You don't want to leave them with the wrong impression. If you don't hear back immediately, it's likely the recruiter is busy. They may be with the client already reviewing the interviews. Normally, though, the recruiter will want to talk to you before talking with the client—but not always. Be brave. Wait five more days and then call back. DO NOT—under any circumstances—call the client directly.

Q: Should I rewrite my resume for the recruiter's client?

A: Yes! The resume you sent has done its job—the recruiter called you. Structural changes to the resume will likely help present you in your best light to his client. Ask if the recruiter has a specific template to follow and complete it promptly. Ask the recruiter what he saw in your background that you should emphasize for the client.

Q: Is there anything I should do when I meet the recruiter's client for the first time?

A: If the recruiter is present [I always am], he will introduce you and frame your background with the employer before you start. If the recruiter is not there, then you need to take the initiative to frame the discussion by telling them what you understand the role to be. Ask if your understanding is correct *and* ask if anything has changed since the employer last spoke with the recruiter. This provides both you and the employer a subtle opportunity to get on the same page. Fail to do this and you run the risk of answering the employer's questions out of context. Do it and the interview transforms into a conversation. This free flowing exchange of information relaxes both parties and is the first sign your interview is going well.

Q: The recruiter said I am the benchmark candidate. Is that good?

A: Depends. Naturally if you are first to be interviewed then you set the bar for the candidates who follow. You are the equivalent of the pace car at the Dayton a 500. If the recruiter has worked with the client before, he is putting his best foot forward—you. Now, if the recruiter has never worked with this client *and* if he sits in on the interview—you're cannon fodder. After your interview, the recruiter and client will spend time discussing what you did or did not have which makes you a perfect fit—hence the term benchmark—and then the recruiter starts the real search. On the other hand, if the recruiter has 20 years' experience, you will likely be at least a 90 percent fit, which means you will still be considered as the rest of the slate of candidates are tabled. So always be on your A-game.

THIRD LAW OF RECRUITER*NOMICS*

If you want to be found, you need to be visible. If you want to be considered, you need to cooperate. If you want to be successful, you need to be proactive.

■ RESOURCES

Podcasts

➤   *Totalpictureradio.com:* The voice of Career Leadership, the podcasts you need to keep your career on track

➤   *JobRadio.fm:* Career advice and jobcasts founded by renegade podcast veterans Chris Russell and Peter Clayton.

Mashups

➤   *RecruitingAnimal.com:* The King of Recruiting Media. Home to *The Animal Show*. Intelligent irreverence for insiders (Michael Kelemen).

➤ *RecruitingBlogs.com:* The central nervous system for recruiters. Blogs, videos, events, chat, and cool people (Jason Davis).

➤ *TheRecruitersLounge.com:* Explores the wacky world of employment. Includes the latest Web search hacks (Jimmy Stroud).

Forums

➤ *Electronic Recruiters Exchange (ERE.net):* Featuring opinions and perspectives from leaders in the recruiting and human resources fields. Blogs from Shally Steckerl, Maureen Sharib, Glenn Gutmacher, Kevin Wheeler, John Sullivan, and the rest of the best.

➤ *OnRec.com:* The magazine for online recruitment around the world.

➤ *FordyceLetter.com:* The oracle for headhunters.

➤ *Xtremerecruiting.tv:* Home of legendary recruiter Bill Vick. A Trojan Horse for you.

Part

III

Tactics That Make You a Guerrilla

Chapter 8

Guerrilla Networking

A Radical Approach

It's more important to reach the people who count, than to count the people you reach. Networking is not a numbers game.

—DAVID PERRY

At the core of every job search lies one individual who will determine your success—*You*. You are at the core of everything that goes on in your life, no exceptions.

You and you alone are responsible for the failure or victory of your job-hunting mission. Nobody cares more about you than you—not even your mother. Job hunting is all about you and what you do for yourself. You can count on other people, but you're the one that counts. Too subtle?

■ GUERRILLA NETWORKING

The world of work has changed dramatically over the past 5 years. Isn't it ironic, then, that most job hunters still depend on the same old tired ways to find a job? Traditional networking ultimately relies on having a fundamental belief in the kindness of strangers. At its core, it preaches that job hunters must have faith that they'll find a job through a friend of a friend of a friend. This is largely a myth.

Although I've heard that this strategy yielded great results in the past, it's not enough today. With the constantly changing marketplace, there is more competition for fewer leads. Traditional

177

networking is much like casting your fate to the wind. It is too passive to rely on. Moreover, there are 3 flaws in traditional networking:

1. You need to have a network at hand when you find yourself out of work (by the way, being out of work is not the best time to start building a network).

2. It requires you to be at least a little outgoing because you need to talk to strangers.

3. There's no way to guarantee the jobs people refer will be ones you'll excel at, much less be interested in.

Today, networking can either be the shortest route to your dream job or to a lengthy series of unsatisfying lunches—the difference lies in how you approach it. Let me show you how a guerrilla networks.

Focus all your networking at the tip of the spear; the companies you have already identified as being the Tier 1 buyers of your product—you. Anything else is a waste of your time, energy, and money. Target those companies where you know you can help solve a problem. We've been preaching target, target, target, for a reason—it works. Target with laser precision.

■ HOW TO NETWORK LIKE A HEADHUNTER

Headhunters network every day out of pure necessity. More often than not, they will have an assignment for "X," whatever "X" may be today, even when they've never recruited an "X" before. That doesn't stop them from completing the mission. Instead, there are tried-and-true methods for locating, identifying, and recruiting candidates. The following 4 steps show you how to do that for yourself.

➤ Step 1: Locate Your Target Companies

Determine which companies you want to work for, how you can add value, and why they should hire you. If you've read up to this point in the book, you've already done this work.

➤ Step 2: Identify Who Runs the Department

Find out who is in charge of the area you want to work in. This generally means identifying a vice president or general manager.

For companies with less than 50 people, it may mean the owner or president. You can get this information by calling the company and asking, "Who's responsible for X" or by looking on the firm's web site to find the person in that position. Several methods for doing this are outlined in Chapter 4.

➤ Step 3: Research Referrals

Find people who worked at this company in the past. Call them on the telephone and get information about:

- ➤ The person you are targeting
- ➤ The department the person runs
- ➤ The company

Be sociable and ask these people how they liked working there. Watch for any hesitation before they answer. The pause may be a clue that they don't want to answer negatively and are framing a safe answer.

The reasons for asking most of the following questions should be obvious. Having said that, keep the following select questions in mind even though it may not be immediately clear why you need to ask them. This exercise will help you prepare for an interview at a later date.

You should ask the following questions in the order they are presented here:

About the Potential Boss

1. Did you work directly for [insert name of potential boss]?
   - ➤ If the people you question did not work directly for the person, they may not be able to answer the questions 100 percent accurately, but their feedback may still be of value.
2. How long did you work for [insert name]?
   - ➤ Longer is better.
3. What is [insert name] like?
   - ➤ What they mention first will be a dominant characteristic. You may need to push a bit to get the response.
4. What kind of person is [insert name]?
5. What kind of manager is [insert name]?

6. What does [insert name] look for in an employee?
   - ➤ How does your experience compare to that of the people they normally hire?
7. How is [insert name] positioned in the company?
   - ➤ This is a crucial question to confirm that you are targeting the right person.
8. Is [insert name] on the way up or down?
9. Does [insert name] have the ear of the president or owner?
   - ➤ You need to know whether this person has the capability to hire you and can get the president to sign off.
10. Is [insert name] political or a straight shooter?
11. What is his temperament?
12. Where does he get his good people from?
13. What type of people does he hire?
14. Is [insert name] forward thinking or reactive?
15. Is he aggressive or laid back?
16. How's his ability to pick winners?
    - ➤ You need to know now if this manager can easily recognize talent. This will dictate the amount of effort you may need to put into your approach.
17. Will [insert name] go to bat for his staff?
18. What was his biggest accomplishment?
19. Does he seek professional growth for himself? (If not, it will be difficult for you to grow on the job.)

About the Department
1. Is it growing or shrinking?
   - ➤ Either way, the information will influence which of your skills you emphasize.
2. Is the department under pressure from competitors?
   - ➤ How is it handling this?
3. What are the department's biggest issues?
   - ➤ Can you solve their problems?
4. Is the department respected by the rest of the company?
   - ➤ This determines whether it can get another hire in the budget.

5. Is the department seen as adding value to the company or is it viewed as just another cost center?

6. How's the department doing compared with other departments in the company?

7. What's the biggest thing the department needs to do to be successful?

About the Company

1. What new products or services are they looking to build or offer in the near future?

   ➤ How can my experience apply?

2. How are they doing financially?

3. If there's one thing they need to do better than their competitors, what is it?

4. What do they do better than their competitors?

5. Who are their best customers?

6. Who would they like to have as customers?

7. What do their customers think of the company?

8. How's the turnover?

9. Can you think of anyone else I should talk to?

   ➤ Get referrals, if you can, to people who currently work there to help cement your position even before you come in for the first interview.

10. Would you work there again?

11. Why did you leave?

    ➤ Asking this directly is a good idea, especially if the person has made negative comments about the individual, department, or company. A person who won't or can't return to a former job may have a beef with the company that makes any opinion of doubtful value.

12. Does the company have a clearly stated vision? Do people in the company know what it is?

Your All-Important Last Question

13. "If I decide to talk with them, can I say I was speaking with you?"

    ➤ You ask that question for 2 reasons: (1) If your questions with the former employee result in positive answers, that employee's name may help you later in securing a meeting with the hiring manager; (2) the former employee may decide to phone his old boss and tell him about all the background due diligence you're doing on the company. That's a great thing.

Your Icebreaker Question

Here's your opening line—pick up the phone, dial the number, and say:

Hi, my name is _____. I'm doing some research on XYZ Corporation and I know that you used to work there because [explain how you found the person's name]. I'm thinking of applying for a job there. Can I ask you a couple of quick questions to see if it's worth my time and effort? I know this is an unusual way to do a job-search but . . .

Now be quiet and let the person answer yes or no. In my experience, most times they'll say, "Sure, what do you want to know?"

If they say "No," ask: "Do you know anyone who I can talk to about the company because I'm really interested in finding out as much as I can before I approach them?"

Either you will get a referral with your second attempt, or the person may decide to answer your questions after all. Someone who had a good experience at the company will answer your questions without hesitation. If it was a bad experience, the person may tell you as well, but it's unlikely. If you don't get anywhere, move on to the next person on your list.

Expect results! With a few minor variations, this is exactly how headhunters network to find candidates.

Ask whatever you think is important for you to know before contacting the next person. You will be amazed by how much you will learn. Further, you may be stunned by what people will disclose about former employers—if you just take the initiative to ask.

The competitive intelligence you gather is valuable. Now you can assess how your accomplishments fit with the employer's needs. After doing 3 to 4 of these interviews, you'll have the inside track. You will be able to assess which of your accomplishments might be of most interest to the employer.

When you approach the company, you will know far more than any other job hunter before you've even had your first interview. You might be able to decide if it's even worth working there. How powerful is that? That's how a guerrilla job-hunter networks.

➤ **Step 4: Refer Yourself**

Instead of relying on someone to refer you, take the initiative and refer yourself. The rejection rate will be very low if you use the following script exactly as I have written it. There is powerful sales psychology at work here—too much to explain in this book—just do it. Trust my 20 years of experience.

The following words are what you should say. The text below each statement briefly explains why you are saying what you are saying and what the employer's response is likely to be.

Telephone the person you identified as running the department. Keep calling until you connect with the person and say:

You: My name is _____. I've been researching your company and have talked to [name 2 of the people you spoke with if you have their permission] and they think that we should talk. Do you have time for coffee next week?

This opener is designed to build curiosity and establish your right to talk to this manager. Using the names of the people who have worked for the person in the past gives you credibility.

Employer: What's this about?

The tone of voice could be curious or annoyed because you still haven't said what you want. Stay with the script.

You: I've been examining the way you [market your product—sell to people—manage inventory—develop new products—(fill in the blank with the problems you know they have that your experience can address)], and I have a few ideas I'd like to share with you. Do you have time for coffee next week?

The manager may think you're a consultant—which could be good or bad and there's no way to know in advance—or could sound grateful that the former employees were thoughtful enough to refer you because the department does have a big problem to solve. The person may invite you in right now or continue to cross-examine you.

Note: Make sure you're hitting the company's problem areas.

Employer: Are you trying to sell me something?

You may sound like a bit of a classic salesperson, but don't panic. Follow the script.

You: No. In the course of doing my market research on the [name the industry] industry, I've learned that your company might be a good fit for my [project management skills] but frankly you're the only one who knows that for sure. In the interests of time, I thought I would see if you had time for coffee so I can see if the types of results I achieved for [name the company] could be replicated for your company.

Now you're talking about how you solved a similar problem elsewhere and that will build your credibility and his interest in seeing you. But it still may not be enough.

Employer: Thanks, but we're not hiring anyone right now.

If you hear this, you need to verbally pull back to maintain control. Here are the 2 rebuttals you should use, one after the other if necessary.

Rebuttal A
You: "That's good because I'm not saying I'm interested in working there—at least not yet—but we both know the time to identify talent is long before you need it—would you agree [you want him to say something at this point to keep him in the conversation]?

"[Name 2 more people you spoke with if you have their permission] said it might interest you to know how [throw out your biggest accomplishment at your current or last company that matches this company's need] for XYZ Corporation. Do you have 15 minutes for coffee next week?"

Often one accomplishment that addresses their problem will be enough to secure a meeting, but maybe not.

Rebuttal B
You: "You know XYZ Corporation had the same concern—Here is what I did for them [throw out your next biggest accomplishment].

"I have no idea if that's important to you or if you're the type of company I can do this for, but [name a few of the people you talked to] thought it might be of interest. Do you have 15 minutes for coffee next week?"

A second accomplishment that addresses their problem should be enough to secure a meeting, but again it may not be.

Employer: No, we're not hiring, but you can send me a resume.

Don't be fooled. The employer just wants you off the phone. Finish with this statement.

You: I don't have an up-to-date one. I'm not your typical [name your position]. I'm being smart about this. I've researched a few companies I want to know more about, and yours is one of them. After we meet, if you think my experience can benefit your company, then I'd be happy to do a formal resume and wait until you have an opening. Can we meet next week for coffee?

If you get the appointment, you need to pick the place and time and confirm it 2 days prior.

If the manager still doesn't bite, there's not much more you can do with the situation. Frankly, there's probably something wrong with the person and, in my experience, that may actually be the company's problem. So there's only one thing you can do—move up the chain of command to this person's boss. If you get the same reaction from the boss, move on to the next company.

GUERRILLA TIP

➤ Follow the script but practice until you don't sound like you're reading it. You need to sound relaxed and natural.

➤ Practice on a blind lead—approach companies where, for whatever reason, you specifically do not want to work. In the headhunting business, we call these throwaways; companies we try new marketing material on before approaching a real employment lead.

➤ Throwaways don't matter, so be as bold as you like. Practicing will build your guerrilla confidence.

■ USING GOOGLE FOR LEADS

Right about now, you're probably saying: "Great idea, Dave, but where do I get the names of the people to call?" Thanks for asking. Remember Google? Go to www.google.com and type in the name of the company you're interested in with the words "resume," "work experience," and "apply," exactly as shown in Figure 8.1.

Google™ **Advanced Search**   Advanced Search Tips | About Google

Find results	with **all** of the words	peoplesoft resume	100 results ▼
	with the **exact phrase**	work experience	Google Search
	with **at least one** of the words		
	without the words	apply	

Figure 8.1   Google advanced exact word search.

For illustrative purposes, we're using PeopleSoft as the company. This will bring back results that will include people who have worked for PeopleSoft in the past. The preceding example resulted in 127,000 hits at the time—your results will vary because Google changes by the minute.

Substitute the name of the company in this example for the company you want to research. Find a contact name among the returned links, get a phone number, and call that person. Using Google in this way should provide a handful of leads to former employees.

There are other ways to do this. One of the largest databases of professionals in the United States is Zoominfo.com (www.zoominfo .com). This search engine allows you to do a keyword search by title, company, location, and a host of other criteria. The free version of the product allows users to search for a specific person by name with or without a company name. The lists include former employees. They are ideal because it's a universal truth that if approached correctly, they will most often discuss previous employers quite openly. This is a tactic that successful headhunters use and so should you. After the first couple of awkward calls, it'll become as easy and matter-of-fact as pouring a cup of coffee. The good news is you can always hang up if you get nervous. Of course, there is an easier—if somewhat slower—way to do this.

■ TARGETING REFERRALS USING SOCIAL NETWORKS

The key to networking is to find people you can network with. For those of us who are terminally shy, the Internet has made it possible to network from our computer keyboard and avoid those awkward mixers most people associate with networking events.

➤ Social Networking for Success

There are many online sites that facilitate networking. Most are based on the "six degrees of separation" principle that recognizes actor Kevin Bacon as the center of humanity. Each site has slight variations on how you build and grow your network.

First you join a site and create a personal profile. Your profile can include anything you want but generally it's your business profile that is of interest. Before you get too excited, let me tell you right now that the sites are designed to protect your privacy and that of the other members.

Second, you invite all your friends and business associates to join. Many sites have technology to facilitate inviting your entire Outlook database. When these people join, they are "1 degree" away from you. Their network of contacts then would be "2 degrees" away.

Your network will grow as quickly as you recruit members who recruit members. Your ability to e-Network your way to a new job grows exponentially as your network develops.

➤ Link In and Connect

LinkedIn (www.linkedin.com) is my favorite. A basic account is free and you can upgrade to premium accounts for less than one night out on the town.

LinkedIn works by first requiring that you set up your online profile and then invite your friends to join your network. After people join, they ask their friends and colleagues to join. For job hunters, this is a treasure trove of leads.

There are several ways to use the site to find people you're looking for quickly. This site recommends doing a search on the company you want to be referred to and see whom you find. You then send a note to the person who is directly linked to the person whom you want to connect to. With our PeopleSoft example it would look like Figure 8.2.

The Results Show 13,653 Contacts

You can experiment with the technology to get more or fewer results. In my case, 13,653 people (via my network) is far too many to start to network with. I want fewer people but at a higher level in the organization. By putting in the title vice president, I narrow the number of contacts down. In our example, this amounts to 1,263. I can narrow this further by location if I want to, so I select to narrow it down by zip code 10001 in New York. The 68 hits is a manageable number for me.

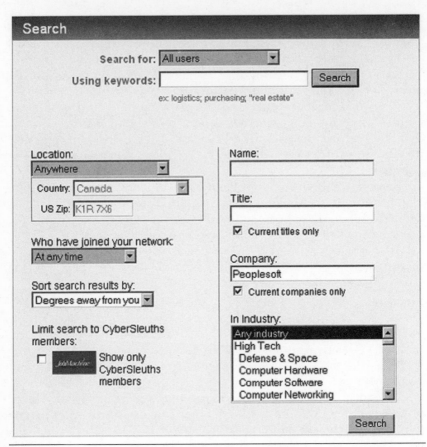

Figure 8.2   Networking example.

The basic idea is to then request, via the technology, for someone to connect you to the person you want to network with. The technology is set up to facilitate the introductions electronically.

LinkedIn also lets people who have linked with you leave testimonials on how you were to work with. As a headhunter, I can view the testimonials, click to see if the testimonial writer is someone I should believe, and then decide if I want to contact the person. Not having testimonials doesn't mean someone is a dud, but having 10 or more that are consistently good will make me want to connect with that person.

From a headhunter's standpoint, LinkedIn has it all. From a job hunter's standpoint, LinkedIn represents an opportunity of a lifetime to establish a powerful network of influential colleagues and friends.

Here's a dirty little secret: recruiters can and will use your LinkedIn profile as a screening tool. In fact, recruiters use LinkedIn every day to find candidates for positions. A recruiter may be looking at your profile even as you read this. This is not how LinkedIn was intended to function when it was built, by the way, but this is how the site has developed. Many consider it your first interview. They'll read your profile and assess your previous employers and your accomplishments. They'll look to see if the resume you sent is consistent. If you said you accomplished "x" at your last employer, it would be in your best interest to have a quote saying so from your previous boss as part of your profile.

LinkedIn gives you all the tools you need to create and maintain your online identity. It is not a toy. Unlike many other social networking sites, LinkedIn is for serious career-minded professionals. Like ZoomInfo.com, LinkedIn is currently used by 252,285 third-party recruiters. Often it's the first site they visit in the morning—even before opening their e-mails. It's that powerful. There are several great books on LinkedIn, so what I'm about to tell you will help you get up on LinkedIn quickly and "supersize" your exposure quickly.

➤ Super-Sizing Your Online Career Portfolio—FREE with LinkedIn

Guerrillas are not slaves to technology. They leverage it for their advantage. Here's what you should do right after you have created your LinkedIn profile:

1. *Send a request to link to me.* You'll get access to my second-level network of more than 700,000. They will become your third-level contacts instantly (www.linkedin.com/in/davidperry/).

2. *Get a personalized e-mail signature (like mine just above).* It's free and you'll have it for life, so no matter where you are 5 years from now your clients, friends, and favorite headhunters will be able to find you. Follow the instructions.

3. *Download and install all of LinkedIn's productivity tools.* LinkedIn has made it so easy to search, build your network, and manage your contacts, all from the applications you use everyday like Outlook, Internet Explorer, and Firefox.

4. *Download the Jobs Insider applet.* This applet displays the personal connections you already have in your LinkedIn account that are tied to the hiring managers and companies

for any job listed online at Monster, CareerBuilder, HotJobs, Craigslist, Dice, Vault, and many more. It's a Trojan Horse (the good kind, i.e., clever Odysseus's wooden horse in the battle for Troy).

5. *If you have a blog, web site, Facebook, or MySpace account that will add value to your job search, then link to it through the "web sites" section of your profile.* Go to the widgets section and download—at a minimum—the Company Insider and Share On LinkedIn applications.

6. *Go to www.toplinked.com and follow the instructions to Link to the largest "connectors" in LinkedIn.* These people, known as LinkedIn LIONS are "open networkers" who will accept your invitation to connect with them without question. This will instantly grow your contact base overnight. You can always uninvite people later…but why you would want to is beyond me.

7. *Become a groupie.* Go to the Companies Tab at the top of your page. Select company search. Scroll to the bottom of the page and select "Browse All Industries." Now select the industry(s) you want to search for a job in. Choose a company you want to work for. Find anyone in sales or marketing or the company's recruiter and look at their profile. Got it open? Now scroll down the page until you find the "Groups and Associations" section. Now, look at the groups this person belongs to. Remember the expression, "birds of a feather flock together"? It's important in networking. If appropriate, join the group. At last count there were more than 2,600 different groups. Make sure you join the Guerrilla Job Search group (www.linkedin.com/e/vgh/1189487/). Or, go to the "Groups" link on your home page right now and join.

8. *Show and tell.* Just like when we asked you to prove your claims with your Guerrilla Resume (reread Chapter 5 if need be), you'll want to show people that you're the real deal. To do this, you need to ask your colleagues, customers, and so on for recommendations. LinkedIn steps you through this on the site. Get the ones that back up your accomplishments first.

9. *From the "Applications" link on your home page choose which of the applications you'd like to install.* Are you a sales or marketing person? How about uploading a PowerPoint that you use to sell your company's product/service (you may need

permission from your employer). Are you an accountant who can make a spreadsheet sing and dance? Upload an example. Remember, everyone says they're smart, creative, driven, and so on. With LinkedIn, you can also prove it.

10. *Install the "Polls" function.* When you have 150 or more of your own first-level contacts, create a poll related to your job search. Send it to them. It's faster than a networking letter or the phone.

11. *Connect to your other social networking sites.* Just as you can connect your blog or web site and so on to LinkedIn, you should link your Facebook and other social networking accounts to your LinkedIn profile. Many sites automate the process for you. For example, my Guerrilla Job Search blog hosted on Type Pad automatically updates my Facebook and LinkedIn account. This way I only need to enter my data once—in this case on my blog—and it appears in LinkedIn and Facebook auto-magically.

GUERRILLA MISSION

Stop reading! What you have just learned is so powerful that, before you do anything else, I want you to establish your LinkedIn profile and invite your network of friends and colleagues to join you—right now! I'm serious. Joining LinkedIn is free and not something you want to "get around to." It's very likely that your next job won't be your last. You must do it now. Read the online tutorials and learn how to maximize your network.

Be Found

Jason Alba

If recruiters, hiring managers, human resource managers, owners of companies, executives, and other professionals are searching for you, don't you think you should be findable? There are plenty of opportunities for you to optimize your LinkedIn account and proactively find contacts and information to help you in your job search and career management. Let's explore what you can do.

To be found on LinkedIn, make sure your profile has the right stuff in it. Make sure when people come across your profile they find it to be credible. Make sure you look like you are a part of the social environment there and not just poking around. None of these take much time, but they all help you become more approachable by those who really need your services.

If you are a project manager, what terms might someone search for? Project Manager, of course. How about PMP or PMI? What about any other associations, professional designations, or even conferences? Make sure you put all of this in your profile—ensuring you put acronyms as well as the entire spelled-out name.

In addition to putting these special key words and phrases in, write your profile so people can read it easily. Put in compelling information about you as a professional. A LinkedIn profile is not a resume, so it doesn't have to read as stiff as a resume might read, but it should show you in a professional light.

There are things I look for on your profile that tell me whether you are just playing around, or that you see value in this awesome tool. Is your picture there? Did you claim a "vanity URL"? These are very easy and quick to do, and makes it look more "on purpose." Additionally, I'll look to see how many contacts you have (three is not enough), how many recommendations you have, and what relationships the recommenders have with you, and whether you participate in Answers. None of these are deal-breakers, but I'm going to know you take networking and professional development seriously.

When we talk about finding on LinkedIn, think about finding 2 different things: network contacts and information. The most basic search you should do is with the search box at the top of every page. If you want to get into Acme Widget, Inc., do a search for "Acme Widget." You may find current or past employees, as well as possibly partners, vendors, or customers (depending on what people have put in their profiles). Any of these professionals could be network contacts for you, to help you learn more about the company and issues.

LinkedIn's original value proposition is that you can tap into your contacts' connections. Think about it—the value you get from using LinkedIn is not that you can track your professional connections, rather, that you can find out who they know. You should ask, "Who do you know." LinkedIn automates that step of the process for you.

Jason Alba is CEO of JibberJobber.com and author of "I'm on LinkedIn—Now What???" and "I'm on Facebook—Now What???" Reach Jason at www.linkedin. com/in/jasonalba/.

■ MY PERSONAL EXPERIENCE WITH THE POWER OF NETWORKING

Mark J. Haluska is the executive director of Real Time Network, www.rtnetwork.net, in Pittsburgh, Pennsylvania. He and I first met online at RECNET, an international online forum for recruiters and headhunters.

Mark and I have worked as colleagues for 9 years now. I think we initially clicked because of our similar military backgrounds and because Mark has an offbeat sardonic sense of humor not unlike my own. He has a real ability to cut to the chase. In fact, we first got to know each other by trading barbs on recruiting for the first 2 years over the Internet.

Mark was one of the first headhunters to read my initial book, *Career Guide for the High-Tech Professional: Where the Jobs Are Now and How to Land Them* (Franklin Lakes, NJ: Career Press, 2004), and he was pretty blunt. He liked the book all right, but he thought it had wider appeal than just the technology industry. When I was approached to write this book, I asked Mark if he would mind proofing some of the chapters. I wanted another industry insider to review the material to ensure my strategies and tactics were state-of-the-moment, accurate, and coming across correctly.

Well, let me tell you, face-to-face we've become great friends, and the working relationship has been outstanding. Not only has Mark read every word in the book, he has challenged my assumptions and encouraged me every step of the way. You would think our desks were right next to each other. We are colleagues in every sense of the word. We talk on a regular basis and e-mail each other daily about more than just the book and headhunting. That is the real power of networking.

Kevin Donlin, my partner in the Guerrilla Job Search Boot Camp project, found me online after reading my book and a few of my articles. He just called me up for a chat. I talked to him, as I had talked to so many other people who had read the first edition of *Guerrilla Marketing for Job Hunters* and wanted to "partner" with me, and I casually said, "The next time you're in town call." Given the chance to follow through on a big idea, most people will do nothing. Not Kevin. That was the only opening he needed. He called me back a few days later to tell me he was going to be traveling through Montreal on his way back to Minneapolis and he was "wondering if that was very far from my house?" I got in my car and drove.

We met, talked about our similar vision for job hunters, and started working together, first on our e–book *Guerrilla Resumes* and then speaking presentations, and now on the rollout of our Boot Camp. One of the reasons the relationship has worked out so well, despite his obvious talent, is that Kevin delivers on his promises—always. Nothing is more important in business than doing what you promise. When you're making a new acquaintance networking, it's 10 times more important because the other person will scrutinize the relationship looking for inconsistencies and a reason to break it off. The secret is to pay it forward.

Personal networking aside, the monetary value of these relationships can easily run into the hundreds of thousands of dollars.

A WAR STORY

Stephen Forsyth

Linkedin.com is one of the most useful networking sites for job seekers. In fact, it was the vehicle that gained me my position at CML Emergency Services. After submitting my CV to David Perry, I decided to research the company. I decided to utilize the "search by company" function on the "people" tab on Linkedin.com. In the results, I recognized Allan Zander's name, since we had attended engineering at University of Western Ontario together. Ironically enough, he was the hiring manager at CML and had also worked in the same group with me at Nortel. I sent a connection request to him through LinkedIn and a few days later I was being interviewed by him and subsequently hired. It was quite apparent that without LinkedIn, I would not have made the connection with Allan and may not have been selected for an interview. Since then, I have used LinkedIn to power my business network.

Stephen Forsyth's connection request to Allan Zander through Linkedin.com:

Allan,

I recognize your name and it appears that we have crossed paths in Nortel and at Western Engineering, so I'm sure that we must have some common contacts and interests.

I am currently searching for opportunities in product management in the Ottawa area and came across your name through LinkedIn.

I am a senior manager with expertise in product management, strategic planning, relationship management, product development and change management within the telecommunications industry. I also recently completed the executive MBA program at the University of Ottawa, and I have eight years experience at Nortel, including a 2-year expat. assignment in Germany.

I noticed that you are looking for some PLMs at CML Emergency Services and I would appreciate it if we could connect to discuss opportunities.

Please contact me at your convenience.

Regards,
Steve

Stephen Forsyth, Director Product and Strategic Management Link: www.linkedin.com/in/stephenforsyth/.

■ WHERE ELSE TO NETWORK ONLINE

Chat rooms, networking web sites, and other community forums exist all over the Internet. Many industries have specific sites they use for sharing knowledge and discussing trends. Yahoo! has the largest assortment at groups.yahoo.com. Some other accessible ones include:

➤ Vault.com (www.vault.com)

➤ Lycos Communities (www.lycos.com)

➤ America Online (www.aol.com)

There are hundreds of networking sites on the Internet. The easiest way to find one that may be useful for you is to enter this phrase into Google: "List of social networking web sites." It will bring you links to web sites that have indexed all the major social networking sites.

The biggest challenge with social networks is that you're still relying on the kindness of others to send your request for a referral forward to the intended recipient. Of course, nothing stops you from finding the name of someone you want to talk to and contacting the person directly. If you do this, bear in mind that there's no guarantee the person will be receptive to hearing from you. They may report the violation of the terms of agreement for using the site and that may cause your account to be suspended. I suggest you obey the rules posted on each site. It's been my experience that most people respond to my request for a referral within 24 hours. I know other recruiters who will simply pick up the phone and call, saying "Hi _____ you and I are connected on _____ and I was wondering..."

■ SELECT TWISTS ON TRADITIONAL NETWORKING

Okay, so maybe you want to network in person. If that's the case, here's how to find the venues you need and what to do when you get there.

➤ Networking Venues

Every town and city in the United States has a "hot spot"; a place where all the "heavy hitters" congregate. Find it and join. The easiest way to locate these business or professional alliances is to ask professional people such as your banker, insurance agent, or investment consultant what groups they belong to. The main job of bank managers is to solicit new business, and to do that they go where the influential people in town congregate. It will probably be a civic organization, golf club, or industry association. It really depends on where you live.

Your contact network should always be growing, and the best way to expand it is to seek out new people and build relationships. It doesn't really matter whom you choose, as long as you like them, they like you, and you can help each other. And when you get a job, let them know they helped with a quick note of thanks.

➤ Classmates.com

The granddaddy online community-based networking is Class-mates.com. The basic version is free. Using Classmates is closer to traditional networking because it's based on your alumni. At Class-mates, you can join a network of people you went to school with (high school, college, or university) as well as military, industry, or company alumni. The challenge with using it to source contacts is that you need to search by state. I did a search for PeopleSoft in New York State and found only one connection.

On the other hand, if you want to reach out to people you went to school with to reconnect and network, then Classmates is the way to go.

A WAR STORY

Dave Opton

One Classmates.com member, a Notre Dame alum, read in *BusinessWeek* that more CFOs attended his alma mater than any other university, so he obtained the list and wrote to them all. His "good old college try" netted him 3 interviews and one offer.

Another member leveraged his college connection when he learned his school was going to be in the NCAA tournament in Ann Arbor, Michigan. As a demonstration of school spirit, he decided to attend the event, but not before attending a professional association meeting. At the meeting, he learned of an Ann Arbor position that perfectly fit his credentials, so he scheduled an interview while he was in town for the tournament. He became happily employed in a new location as a result.

Dave Opton, president, ExecuNet (www.execunet.com). Reach Dave at www.linkedin.com/in/dopton/.

> **Other Alumni Networks**

If you're looking to make inroads with Fortune 1000 companies, then use a keyword search in Google to see if they have a corporate alumni web site. Many do and it's the easiest way to find people. The command for Google is "[name of the company]" and alumni (see Figure 8.3).

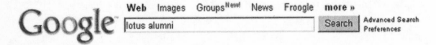

Figure 8.3   Alumni approach.

If former employees have an alumni site, this will find it. We were looking for Lotus Notes people recently and found this site through that query: www.axle.org.

GUERRILLA INTELLIGENCE

Women and Networking

Penelope Trunk

One of the reasons the glass ceiling persists is because networking is key to getting ahead and women are not as effective as men at building a network. For one thing, men, more than women, are likely to be invited out to dinner (since men are doing the inviting). Also, men, more than women, are likely to have the time to network outside the office (since women are the primary caretakers of children even when both spouses work).

If you are a woman who thinks you do not have a problem networking, you are wrong: when men entertain clients at basketball games and strip clubs, you are not invited. Don't tell me you don't work with men like that. How would you know? They'd never tell you. Additionally, men talk differently to men than to women. The subtext of an all-male conversation is let's-be-friends. The subtext of a male-female conversation is let's-have-sex.

So women need to approach networking differently than men. Women are at a disadvantage and need to figure out ways to get ahead in the game. Here are some times when men don't typically network, but women can:

➤ *During work hours:* While men tend to network before and after work, women usually feel too strapped for time for that. So women should concentrate on creating a network during office hours. This means setting aside time to speak informally with people inside your office and taking long lunches with people from other companies. This sort of schedule requires careful planning to start and maintain relationships—something women are usually better at than men.

➤ *During family time:* Most moms work. So get to know the parents at soccer games or at gymnastics practice. You never know who might be there, especially on the weekend. In many cases, you will spend as much time with these parents as you do with some of your coworkers. So make the time count for your career.

➤ *During book clubs:* The recent flurry of book club groups has not caught on among men, but women love them—even high-powered women you'd expect to be too busy to read *Middlemarch*. So while you're at the book club, don't be timid about letting people know what you do, and how you can help them. In that context, they are likely to reciprocate.

➤ *At the gym:* It doesn't matter how busy you are, how many kids you have, you have to get some form of exercise. Sadly, most moms do not take this advice to heart, so the women at the gym are usually the single, no-kids, high-power types—great for networking. If you start going on a

(continued)

regular schedule, you'll meet the other people who are on your schedule—men and women.

Each of these situations will be awkward for most women because generally, women don't like mixing business with pleasure. But here's my advice to you: get over it. Men do it all the time. In fact, for many men, there is rarely pleasure to be had unless it's mixed with business. So if you want to compete in a man's world, which corporate America definitely is, then you need to take the small opportunities you have and work them as hard as you can.

Penelope Trunk is the New York-based author of *Brazen Careerist* (New York: Business Plus, 2007). She has started Internet divisions at Fortune 500 companies, founded 2 technology-focused companies, endured an IPO, a buyout, and a bankruptcy. Contact her through www.linkedin.com/in/penelopetrunk/.

■ THE KITCHEN SINK APPROACH

While I would advise you not to specifically count on your friends and relatives, you would be remiss as a guerrilla if you did not use every possible tool. So, involve all your friends and colleagues in your job search.

Many companies post jobs internally before going to newspapers or third-party recruiters, or have referral programs that pay employees a bonus for referring people. Ensure that your network of friends has your resume in electronic format and permission to forward your resume to hiring managers on your behalf. When referred by a colleague within your network, always ask the referrer how you should follow up. Some people will want you to call, others won't. You need to abide by their wishes or they will not refer you again.

GUERRILLA TIPS

➤ Start with the people you know best. This encourages you to make the calls, and it's a great way to ease into networking because they'll be nicer than strangers.

➤ Don't jump right into your agenda; start off by asking them, "Is this is a good time to talk and what's new?" They'll get around to asking about you soon enough.

Your goal is to get referrals. So how do you ask in a manner that won't put people off? Generally, it is better to be subtle, so instead of "Can you give me the names of all your friends?" try "Who else should I be talking to?" or "I could really use your advice on something." People like to be asked for advice because you're acknowledging them as an expert.

If you're wondering what to ask, try these openers:

➤ Are there any groups or organizations I should join?
➤ Are there any books or publications I should read?
➤ Is there anyone else I should be talking to?

And my 2 personal favorites:

1. What would you do if you were me?
2. Whom would you be talking to?

Dig for information about industry trends or trends in your functional area or specialty. Listen for plans for new products or services. Seek out emerging markets, hidden jobs, and companies that are hiring. Focus on anything change-related. Change equates to opportunity.

Whenever you network, it is your responsibility to set the stage and ask how much time they have. State your purpose clearly and directly. Share your excitement and enthusiasm. Ask for advice and ideas. In general, listen more than you talk. This meeting is a courtesy call that must reflect well on the referee or they won't continue to help.

A WAR STORY

Ross Macpherson

One of our clients worked for a large financial institution and desperately wanted to move up in the company, but kept hitting barriers in HR (not enough experience, not the right education, etc.). When we were working on her resume and job search campaign, she mentioned that the person she really needed to get in front of was a divisional president. Since she couldn't work "within the system" at her firm to show him how great she was, we devised a long-range plan to work around it.

The president in question sat on the board of a local nonprofit, a cause that both he and my client were passionate about. This was her way in. She volunteered her services with the organization and quickly developed a name for herself as a dynamic and innovative thinker who could really make things happen. Within a short time, she found an opportunity to meet her president at a fund-raising gala and introduced herself as the person who worked on the "X" campaign. She also mentioned that she happened to work for the same company (what a coincidence).

After making the initial contact, over the next year she did more great things for the nonprofit, had more opportunities to shine, and quickly found herself on his radar. At one of their next meetings, she mentioned where she'd really like to see herself in their company, threw in a few of her ideas, and asked his advice. Knowing now how good she was, he recommended a few people and even offered to contact them on her behalf. With a strong testimonial from the company's president, it wasn't long before she landed a high-profile strategic role more suited to her abilities (she also stayed on with the nonprofit where she continued to do great work and has been asked to fill a major leadership position on a full-time basis). It was a unique case where shining outside the company helped her move up inside it.

Ross Macpherson, president, Career Quest (www.yourcareerquest.com).

Chapter 9

Fearless Warm Calling

A Fresh Alternative

It's not whether you get knocked down; it's whether you get up.

— VINCE LOMBARDI

Although you may be a top-notch engineer, mortgage broker, or what-ever, when it comes to getting interviews, I have observed that many sharp people—to use a metaphor—couldn't close a paper bag much less an employer. Hang tight, I'm going to show you how to "warm call" an employer and land an interview.

■ FIRST CONTACT

The majority of job-hunting books I've read and courses I've reviewed stress cold calling (or dialing-for-dollars, as it's often called) as one of the best ways to land an interview. "It's a numbers game" they say, "just have faith, make the calls, and you'll be successful—eventually." Now there is a certain amount of truth in it. Cold calling is a numbers game but it is also demoralizing, frustrating, and the fastest most unsatisfying way to burn through your list of prospects.

Think about this dialing-for-dollars approach for a minute. You've executed your job hunting from a plan. You analyzed your skills, wrote an enticing resume, and built an online presence. You've spent count-less hours, even weeks, gathering information and logically assessing your value added against your list of prospective employers. Now the

203

time has come for you to make that all-important initial contact with an employer—this is where nonguerrillas blow it.

Every single day for the past 20 years, I've heard some iteration of the following:

> *Hi, Mr. Employer. My name is Pam and I am a marketing expert with well over 20 years of experience. I have been following your company for some time and am quite impressed with some of the recent successes. I would like to see if there would be an opportunity to meet with you and discuss how my qualifications and experience could serve your company.*

Sounds nice enough, doesn't it? But it doesn't work. This is a new millennium, and that is an old and tired approach. Seriously, Mr. Employer is going to politely get rid of you. He will ask you to send a resume (the number one way to get rid of a job hunter) or refer you to someone in human resources, who'll tell you they're not hiring, "but we'll keep your resume on file." So if this tried-and-true method has run its course, is there a better way? The answer—fortunately—is yes!

■ YOUR ALTERNATIVE

I would love to take credit for what I'm about to teach you, but that wouldn't be fair. First off, the base methodology and principles are not mine. Second, the ideas in Thomas Freese's book *Secrets of Question Based Selling: How the Most Powerful Tool in Business Can Double Your Sales Results* (Naperville, IL: Sourcebooks, 2000) (www.qbsresearch. com) were brought to my attention by Daniel Houle (www. danielhoule.com).

As a successful headhunter and guerrilla marketer myself, I was intuitively doing what Freese teaches, so when Daniel introduced me to the book, I wasn't shy about integrating the question based selling (QBS) principles into my firm. Tom's fresh approach helped me keep Perry-Martel International flying high at a time when most of our competitors crashed and burned.

Freese's premise is that people sell to people. Although this might not be a revelation, it's critical that you understand the instinctive psychological process that interferes with the sale by pitting you and the employer against each other—why the employer is looking for a reason to say no.

Interviews are adversarial because our natural defense mechanisms come into play every time someone tries to sell us something.

Freese refers to this defense mechanism as mismatching; and all humans do it.

Mismatching is a form of disagreement. It is an instinctive and emotional behavior that causes people to respond or push back in a contrarian manner, usually by taking the opposite viewpoint on what's being said.

It's important to realize that mismatching isn't something we do consciously. We do it mostly because we want to add value to a conversation. The easiest demonstration of this is perhaps the following exchange between 2 people about the weather:

Person A: Well, it's supposed to be really nice this weekend.

Person B: I heard that we may get showers Sunday afternoon.

Person B's intent was really to share an additional tidbit of information, but at the same time, dispute the assertion that was made by Person A.

Mismatching is common in the first phase of a sales process because—let's be honest—we all get defensive when a salesperson calls. Think of the way you answered the phone the last time a telemarketer called you at dinnertime; that's how an employer usually feels when someone is trying to score an interview. As can be expected, mismatching often leads to outright rejection. Most salespeople who fail do so because they never learn how to avoid mismatching.

Freese's first rule is to limit your exposure to mismatching by memorizing the following sentence, which summarizes the QBS approach: "You don't sell by telling but by asking."

So what does this have to do with finding a job? Everything! Landing your dream job is all about closing the ultimate sale, where what you are selling is yourself. Applying QBS techniques minimizes your exposure to mismatching and increases your ability to close the sale. This doesn't mean that you will no longer need persistence—quite the opposite. In this day and age of e-mail, voice mail, beepers, cell phones, Blackberries, and caller ID, prospective employers can effectively block your call.

QBS makes use of 4 strategies to reduce the risk of mismatching by showing you how to:

1. Ask more questions and make fewer statements.
2. Establish your credibility with the prospective employer from the start.

3. Pique the prospective employer's curiosity to neutralize mismatching.

4. Build momentum to quell the mismatching instinct.

➤ **Strategy 1: Ask More Questions and Make Fewer Statements**

It is nearly impossible to mismatch a question. Aside from helping you avoid mismatching, asking more questions uncovers the very opportunities you need to showcase your experience and accomplishments. Asking the right questions will not only help you validate an employer's current opportunities but could change the employer's perception about latent opportunities.

A prospective employer might be considering hiring someone with your skill set sometime in the future—what we would call a "hidden job"—but after listening to your thoughtful questions, the future need has gained an immediate urgency.

Question based selling applies to finding the ultimate job. It is about getting prospective employers to want to hire you, to eagerly answer your insightful questions and be more than willing to listen to you.

➤ **Strategy 2: Establish Your Credibility with the Prospective Employer from the Start**

The challenge job seekers face is that they need to communicate a sense of the value added they can bring to a prospective employer. This can be particularly challenging when they have no common relationship to leverage, that is, someone who can be used as a personal reference.

Asking questions will reduce the prospective employer's need to mismatch you. But asking the right questions will go a long way in establishing credibility.

Salespeople are trained to ask open-ended questions and to give the impression that they're interested in what the customer has to say. What they're really doing is fishing for an opportunity to explain that they can provide the solution, or answer, to a problem that the prospect has described.

You establish credibility by avoiding open-ended questions like: "What does your company plan to do in the next five years?" and replacing them with short diagnostic questions. Diagnostic questions are close-ended and designed to elicit specific answers. In the following dialogue, a high-tech job hunter makes use of diagnostic questions:

Job hunter: May I ask you a question?

Prospective employer: Sure. What's up?

Job hunter: How many net-native applications in the CRM field do you now consider as direct competitors to your standard desktop product offering?

Prospective employer: Uum.... At this time, there are probably three net-native applications that offer functionality similar to desktop software.... And that's aside from all of the other net-native applications that keep popping up every couple of weeks.... Some of them being open source too.

Job hunter: How many months would it take to move your current application to more of a net-native model?

Prospective employer: Well, we did evaluate the ASP model several years ago and at the time, we felt it would probably take about 12 to 18 months to reengineer our software.

Job hunter: At what intervals are new upgrades being offered by your net-native competitors?

Prospective employer: On average, perhaps every 4 months.

Job hunter: Have you looked at the .NET framework or other Web services platform to port the functionality of your software so it can be delivered via the Web?

Prospective employer: Yes. We formed a task group a couple of months ago, and they should be presenting their recommendation shortly.

And so it goes. A similar dialogue could happen in any industry. By using these diagnostic questions, the job hunter is inferring that she has a good grasp of the Web services model and the real threat that it poses to a traditional desktop software vendor. In this example, the questioning technique served to establish the immediate credibility of the job hunter with the prospective employer. Question based selling has the potential to transform an ordinary interrogative interview into a business discussion, allowing the job hunter to expand the scope of the questions and initiate a relationship with the employer.

Applying this technique to your job hunt will help to uncover the employer's needs that your skills, experience, and talents address in a natural uncontrived manner.

Other Examples of Lead-In/Follow-Up Questions
Marketing Communication

Job hunter: May I ask you a question?

Prospective employer: Yes, if you make it quick.

Job hunter: How many trade shows are you planning on attending in the next 12 months?

Prospective employer: Currently, we are planning to attend 6 events, with perhaps another 2 to 3 events being considered.

Job hunter: Do you have defined specific goals for these events in terms of how many new leads are to be collected, prospective customers to be met, and/or major announcements to be made? How do you quantify your ROI for participating at these events?

Prospective employer: Uum ... well, we usually look at the number of new customers that we sign up in the 8 to 12 months following the event.

Job hunter: Do you build a communication plan for each event, which would outline deliverables and timelines tied to communication with existing/prospective customers, as well as media representatives and key opinion leaders? [You may be surprised to learn most companies don't have such a plan in place.]

Web Site Design

Job hunter: May I ask you a question?

Prospective employer: Most certainly. What's on your mind?

Job hunter: I noted on your web site that quite a few of your customers are in the public sector.

Prospective employer: That is correct.

Job hunter: Have these customers inquired about meeting compliance with the new accessibility standards as outlined in standards like W3C A, W3C AA, and U.S. Section 508?

Prospective employer: As a matter of fact, more and more organizations are inquiring about this.

Job hunter: What are you advising your customer to do in terms of migrating to such compliant web sites?

The bottom line is this: If you have any in-depth knowledge of a subject that would enable you to contribute to an organization's success, you should be able to phrase 10 to 15 questions that would undoubtedly position you as an expert. Of course, make sure that you can answer these questions; otherwise it could get quite awkward if the prospective employer turns the table and questions you.

Better still, be ready to give concrete examples of how you could apply your knowledge in response to these diagnostic questions. Be smart about it. Make sure that you have a signed contract before answering too many questions. You have knowledge that prospective employers want to make use of, but that knowledge should not be offered for free.

GUERRILLA INTELLIGENCE

Are You Outstanding?

Matt Massey

To be outstanding is tough and it's not for the faint of heart. We connect every day with people who are uninspired and unmotivated. Individuals who are either too lazy or too whatever to challenge themselves to be better by setting standards for themselves that help them rise above the crowd. My recommendation is *THROW OUT THE STATUS QUO.*

Now, think of your last 3 job interviews—what did you do to put yourself above your competitors? What did you do to make the customer, prospect, or interviewer want to work with you? How did you engage them? Did you make a positive lasting impression? If you relied on the status quo, odds are the answer is no.

Now think about your next interview. What are you going to do to make that person want to hire you? How are you going to stand out from the 20 to 50 calls and countless e-mails he or she receives every day from people just like you?

Here are 3 ideas to help you stand out and outsell your competition.

Get Research-Ready
Before you make contact, research the prospective employers. Dig deep. Look for recent announcements or changes that may open doors. When you're informed about their business, you can speak to how your product, service, or your experience is relevant within their world.

(continued)

Become an Instigator

Being an instigator is tough to strive for. You have to be personally and professionally committed to breaking away from the traditional and throwing out your own status quo first. You need to demonstrate your value and professionalism on day one and build a relationship that will be the impetus for getting them to throw out their status quo and make decisions that will positively progress the sale of *you* within their company.

Get in the 2 Percent Club

I have a customer, Neil, who when we first sat down to discuss how he wanted to generate new business and how he wanted to differentiate his company, told me he wanted all of his customers and prospects to know that he and his partner were in the 2 percent club. Puzzled and thinking he had been recognized with some award in their industry, I asked Neil what he meant. Neil explained that if you put 100 salespeople in a room and told them the exact steps they needed to bring in a million dollars in business each year, only 85 of them would leave the room intent on following those steps. Within 2 weeks, only 40 of those 100 salespeople will still be following those steps. Within 2 months, maybe 15 or 20 of that original group would still be diligently following the path to revenue. Then finally, within a year, only 2 will remain. *Two salespeople out of the 100 will have followed through.* Get yourself into the 2 percent club by becoming more disciplined and diligent in your everyday activities and you are guaranteed to succeed no matter the position.

If you begin executing on these 3 tips today, I guarantee, within a month you will be on a path to becoming one of the top 2 percent. You'll get there because you are challenging yourself to be better prepared to create new customer relationships and to be *outstanding* in a very competitive landscape. Strive *to stand out or to be outstanding.*

Matt Massey is president of drive2 Inc., a demand creation and lead generation company. He can be reached at www.linkedin.com/in/drive2/.

➤ **Strategy 3: Use Curiosity to Neutralize the Mismatching Reflex**

Intrigue and mismatching do not coexist. Prospective employers cannot be intrigued and at the same time want to mismatch you. Your aim is to have employers become so curious about you that they will actually lean into the conversation. This helps facilitate an in-depth discussion, where you will be able to present your value added in the best light.

Leveraging Voice Mail

As you begin to set up interviews, you will run headfirst into the employer's voice-mail system. Immediately seize this opportunity and leave an intriguing message.

A typical all-too-common voice mail sounds like this:

Hi, Mr. Perry. My name is Frank and I am a marketing expert with well over 20 years of experience. I have been following your company for some time and am quite impressed with some of the recent successes. I would like to see if there would be an opportunity to meet with you to discuss how my qualifications and experience could serve your company.

Instead, try something like:

Good afternoon, David. I'm calling you because I have a question that only you can answer. Could you please call me back at [phone no.] before 4 PM?

Or the something-made-me-think-of-you technique: where you find additional information about the employer that could be used to prompt a callback:

Good afternoon, David. I'm holding a copy of an article published in the Wall Street Journal *that mentions you in a review of the industry, and I have a question. If you would, please call me back tomorrow at [phone no.] before 10 AM?*

Or:

Good afternoon, David. I just got off the phone with your partner Anita and I have a question. If you would, please call me back this morning [phone no.] before 11 AM?

The last tactic makes use of what's called an associate reference. You infer a discussion with a colleague of the employer. The employer is definitely curious as to what his partner, Anita, might be up to. She's very competitive, you know.

Your goal in eliciting curiosity is to engage the prospective employer. Freese's book offers examples for using these strategies in a sales situation. With a little work on your end, you'll easily be able to adopt it for your job hunt.

➤ **Strategy 4: Momentum Helps Reduce the Mismatching Instinct**

We've already recognized that hiring managers are at risk when they hire someone. A poor hire might cost the employer money or the hiring managers their job. By using Freese's Herd Theory, you leverage both the employer's need to limit risk and to appear savvy. You highlight and emphasize what everyone else is doing. In the following message, the job hunter discretely educates an employer about the direction taken by other companies (competitors), motivating the employer to follow the herd or risk being left out:

> *Hello, Mr. Perry, my name is Daniel Houle. You may recall that a few weeks back I sent you a series of white papers I authored on the impact of the software-as-a-service-delivery model on traditional software vendors. As I indicated in the accompanying letter, I plan to release some complementary information to these white papers in the next 7 to 10 days. Frankly, several companies have already asked for the follow-up documentation as well as an interview: ABC Company and DEF Inc., to name just a couple. I am following up because I have not received word from your company, and I wanted to make sure that you didn't get left out.*

The last sentence of this voice mail will elicit the following reaction from the employer:

> *Left out of what ...? I better call him back if ABC Company is interviewing him already.*

This is an especially effective strategy for setting meetings with senior executives. However, it will require you to actually have written the white papers and done the research work. A guerrilla would simply recycle previous work whenever possible.

The strategy comes with caveats; you'll need to have established some credibility with the prospective employer if this voice mail is to have the desired impact. Creating a bidding war without having other bidders lined up is gutsy at best and could be disastrous if you're discovered. It is best to use this tactic as part of a well-planned campaign where you have at least one initial interview scheduled.

Run through a few practice drills on undesirable companies in preparation for the big game.

GUERRILLA INTELLIGENCE

Stay Away from the Human Resources Department
Daniel Houle

Your dream job is probably the most gratifying "sale" you will ever close in your life. As in any sale, selling yourself will have nothing to do with telling them why they should hire you; remember, selling is not telling. Once you're in the interview, ask more questions and make fewer statements.

To avoid mismatching, engage the employer with:

➤ Intriguing questions (voice mails) to elicit curiosity

➤ Concise diagnostic questions to establish your credibility

➤ Slightly negative questions to obtain factual and accurate information

➤ The Herd Theory to convince prospective employers that they could ultimately be left out

Stay away from the human resources department because they are paid to mismatch. Human resource people have a role similar to that of your body's natural immune system—essentially keeping out germs (bad employees) that could make the company sick. By nature, they are risk-averse, err on the side of caution, and mismatch out of habit. You have little to gain with human resource people because unless you are a human resource professional, they will not make the final hiring decisions.

Thomas Freese's book is a must-read for any sales and marketing professional who is serious about landing his or her dream job, and it won't hurt for non-salespeople to read it as well.

Daniel Houle is a successful product management and marketing executive. He may be reached at (www.danielhoule.com).

--- **A WAR STORY** ---

Deanna J. Williams Sr.

My phone rang and it was a salesperson who was pursuing me for an outside sales position I had advertised in the *San Jose Mercury*. He said he wanted to see me right away. He had something to show me and he knew that once I saw it, I would be so impressed that I'd hire him on the spot. Now I was sitting there thinking this guy is pretty full of himself, but I was also impressed with his self-confidence and persistence. I explained that I had to be in a meeting in 20 minutes. He insisted he could be at my office in less than 1 minute. I protested, saying I didn't see how that was possible and that I really thought we should find a time to talk after my meeting. He kept insisting that if I would just give him a chance he promised that he could meet with me in less than 1 minute, and if I would just look out the window, I would see why. As I strained to look out the window, I saw a fellow sitting in a red Mustang, talking on his cell phone and waving at me. I had to laugh at his dogged pursuit and creativity. Yes, I did let him come in before the meeting and, yes, I did hire him. He was one of the best salespeople we ever had and one of the most creative in finding ways to open doors to potential customers.

Deanna J. Williams, contract recruiter, dwilliam3185@earthlink.net.

Chapter 10

Creative Ways to Find a Job

Breakthrough Strategies

You've got to say, I think if I keep working at this and want it badly enough I can have it.

—Lee Iacocca

Perhaps networking and warm calling aren't for you. You should add them to your mix anyway. Here are some alternative methods we've used in our Boot Camps.

■ BECOME THE EXPERT

You can become recognized and branded as an industry expert by writing and producing a newsletter. All you really need to do is summarize best practices—add your experience or comments—print and mail it. When you send a newsletter with topical information that's actually useful, employers may recognize your name when you telephone, making them more likely to take your call. When they in turn are looking to hire someone with your expertise, you're likely to be one of their first calls. Here are some useful guidelines:

➤ Newsletters should be 1 to 4 pages but no longer.
➤ Summarize lengthy pieces and refer the reader to your web site for the full text version.

➤ You can dress up the newsletter without breaking the bank by using preprinted paper from companies like Paper Direct (paperdirect.com).

■ WRITE A WHITE PAPER—FOCUS ON A HOT TOPIC

This is just like producing a newsletter but you only need to do it once and you can reuse it until the topic falls out of vogue. Summarize the industry pundits and then offer your own take on it. Read up on a hot topic like VoIP [voice over Internet protocol] and write a 10- to 15-page summary linking it to your industry. A hot topic like VoIP will have effects on every industry in America, but you need to concentrate on what's important to your sector. Call some of the more quotable people you discovered during your research and interview them for your own piece. Ask them for feedback before you publish. Print and distribute it, for example:

➤ Mail it to employers you want to work for.

➤ Make it available electronically for e-zines.

➤ Send it to business publications as a possible article.

➤ Send it to trade publications relevant to the industries you have targeted for your job search.

➤ Allow other publishers and editors to use your White Paper as long as they include your byline, e-mail address, and web site URL.

■ USE "THANK-YOU" NOTE ENVELOPES

Everyone's face lights up when they see one of those little envelopes that are peculiar to "thank-you" note cards—those tiny little 4 × 4 white envelopes with barely enough room to write a name and address on the front and a return address on the back. Fold your resume and cover letter together carefully until they fit inside and then mail it:

➤ Don't use labels, address each one by hand.

➤ Use this technique around any holiday—Christmas, New Year's, Fourth of July, and so on.

➤ Use a small, tasteful stamp.

➤ If you feel you can afford it, use a stamp with your picture on it. In Canada you can put any picture you wish on a stamp. Details on their Picture Postage program can be found at www.canadapost.ca.

➤ To really get noticed, use a stamp with their logo on it and send them the rest of the stamps.

■ SEND HALF OF YOUR RESUME

First, find a company you want to work for. Write a compelling cover letter describing why you are a good fit, pointing the receiver to the enclosed curriculum vitae (CV) for further information. Don't seal the envelope and don't enclose a CV. They'll think the CV fell out in the mail. Wait for the phone to ring; speak to the hiring manager personally, engage in a conversation, and sell yourself shamelessly. (This tip comes compliments of Matt Foster, managing director, CVO Group at www.professionalpeople.com.) In addition:

➤ Use high-quality stationery.

➤ Make sure the letter fits snugly in the envelope so it doesn't fall out.

➤ Ensure your phone number is on the cover letter.

■ SEND A LETTER STATING YOU ARE OVERQUALIFIED

Send your resume and a cover letter which states "It'll appear obvious from my resume that I'm overqualified for the job you advertised, so let me tell you why you should interview me and consider super-sizing your opportunity." Write a bulleted list of 3 to 5 benefits you think they might be interested in. Close the letter saying something to the effect that "I am old enough to have already learned from my mistakes—so my experience is more cost effective than a more junior person. In a few months, or years, you'll need to send those folks to training to upgrade their knowledge, whereas I come fully equipped to do the next job, too." Then:

➤ Point out any certificates or advanced training that you already have that someone in that job might be expected to acquire.

➤ Show you are already qualified to do the next position too.

➤ Point out any retraining allowances or incentives employers might be eligible for if they hire a more seasoned person.

―――――――――――― **A WAR STORY** ――――――――――――

Allan Zander

I was looking to get involved with a very large hospital project with the major hospitals in a large city. I knew that my working on the project would require the buy-in from the hospital chairmen. I knew they knew of me but we had never met and I needed to shine above the pack. At the time, there was a serious concern in the hospitals that the executive management didn't care about the patients but cared more about the financial aspects of the hospitals, and I also knew that they tended to decorate their offices with collectible items.

I sent each chairman a big box with a note that said "My name is Allan Zander and I have been working within the healthcare market for over 6 years now in a variety of consultant capacities. I recently noticed that you enjoyed collecting rare items and I knew that you would appreciate this collectible Teddy Bear from Harrod's of London." When they opened the box, there was no bear—only another note that read "but not nearly as much as the sick children in your children's critical care unit. I have donated the bear to them in your name. If you would like to learn more about how I can help you bring new technology into your hospital while allowing you to show that you have great caring for your patients, please give me a call." They all called me and a few weeks later I was the lead healthcare consultant on a major multimillion dollar initiative.

Compliments of Allan Zander. He may be contacted at ajzander@hotmail.com.

GUERRILLA INTELLIGENCE

Be Your Own Recruiter with E-Mail Marketing

Joseph Nour

Most people think of e-mail marketing as a way for businesses to promote products or services by sending thousands of e-mails. Guerrillas understand they can use it stay in touch with prospective employers on a one-to-one basis, too. Let me give you an example.

Let's say you're a marketing professional seeking a communications director position with a growing company. In addition to your resume, you have an electronic portfolio showcasing some of the best work such as brochures, advertisements, sell sheets, and published articles. In most cases, the only chance you'll get to share your portfolio is when you get to the interview stage, but you know that if potential employers could actually see some of your work up front, your chances of quickly finding the right job would dramatically improve. E-mail marketing can provide the vehicle for you to do just that.

With e-mail marketing, you can provide your contacts with regular samples of your work through a monthly e-newsletter with Web links to published articles or to your blog. It's a great nonintrusive way to enhance your mindshare. The first step is to build your *opt-in e-mail list*. Include your professional contacts as well as recruiters and those recruitment services that your company may be using.

A best practices e-mail marketing service should offer a host of features including:

➤ On demand online access

➤ Tools for helping you grow your opt-in e-mail list

➤ Easy-to-use tools for quick e-mail campaign creation

➤ HTML templates for newsletters, e-cards, promotions, and so on

➤ Campaign tracking and reporting features

➤ Automatic CAN-SPAM compliance

➤ Image hosting for uploading captivating images to enhance your campaigns

(continued)

Take advantage of the metrics and tracking reports to see who opened your e-mail and the specific content they clicked. Use this information to follow up personally with those who showed a clear interest in what you have to offer.

Here are a few more useful tips to specifically aid your job search:

➤ Keep your e-mail as short as possible.

➤ Tease them with the e-mail message and get them to click to your resume, online portfolio, or blog—you want to hook them, NOT pitch them.

➤ Keep it personal—use the mail merge functionality so all of your contacts receive a personally addressed e-mail. If your e-mail looks like a bulk or mass mailing, your recipient is less likely to read it or respond.

➤ Use HTML so you can get the advantage of tracking, but keep it simple!

➤ Spend most of the time on the top 3 inches of the e-mail; it's what they see if they are using "preview" in Outlook.

➤ Ask them to forward the e-mail to other colleagues who may be looking for your skills.

➤ Spend time on your subject line—legally it can't be misleading and it must reflect the contents of the e-mail, but you want to make it punchy.

➤ Does it look like spam? Send a copy of the e-mail to yourself and see if you'd open or delete it unread.

➤ Always use both first and last names in the "from" line—most people assume mail from Lily or Irene or any other first name only person is spam.

Attachments = viruses in my mind. I have never opened a resume from someone I didn't know that came as an attachment—EVER. If the resume wasn't in the body of the e-mail, it was an immediate delete.

Joseph Nour is CEO of Protus IT Solutions, owners of www.campaigner.com, an e-mail marketing service for small-to-medium sized businesses. Access a free trial as well as tips, webinars and other resources at www.campaigner.com.

■ E-MAIL CHAIN LETTER

Take a list of 20 companies you want to work for and send an e-mail to everyone you know asking them to read the list to see if they know anyone who works at any of the companies. Ask them to contact you if they do so that you can ask for a referral. Finally, ask them to forward your e-mail message to 10 more people. (We've learned that this does not work for lobbyists.) Note:

> ➤ If you e-mail your list to 10 people and they e-mail it to 10 people and . . . within 4 cycles, you have covered 10,000 people.

> ➤ Don't ask people to e-mail to more than 10 people because they just won't do it.

> ➤ Put your e-mail address in the message so people can e-mail you directly.

> ➤ Only include your phone number if you don't mind having people call you.

> ➤ Don't put anything in the letter you wouldn't want a stranger to read.

> ➤ Put your name and e-mail address at the top of the message in a "From": salutation, so the reader can find your coordinates quickly.

> ➤ Do not do this if you're currently employed!

■ PRESS KIT

People make all kinds of claims about their skills and abilities when in fact they're not true, so it's little wonder that employers are naturally skeptical. So if you have won awards, have been quoted in the news, or have any other type of proof that your accomplishments really do exist, build a portfolio and send it with your cover letter and resume. I've done this myself many times, first as a job hunter and then later as a headhunter in search of projects. A picture is worth a thousand words and an article, reference letter, or thank-you note from a client, is worth a thousand more. For example:

> ➤ If you're a student looking for your first real job, send a transcript of your marks. It probably doesn't matter but it might, especially if you kept a high GPA and a part-time job.

> ➤ Copies of articles and awards should be included.

> ➤ Don't send originals because you may never get them back.

➤ In articles, highlight the part about you so they don't need to search.

➤ Bring these items with you to an interview as well because the individual items in the Press Kit make good talking points.

■ SEND ARTICLES AS A FOLLOW UP AFTER AN INTERVIEW

Sending an article to a hiring manager with a simple note like: "I thought you might be interested in this" is a great door opener. The trick is to find something that is truly helpful to them in their job. You can uncover potential needs by doing a search through Google for position papers they may have presented or to see what their competitors are announcing by way of new products—and let them know. I know several people who have landed great jobs by doing this. Here's what to do to find articles using search engines:

➤ Use the alert system at Google to keep you up-to-date on subject areas of interest to your targeted employers: www.google.ca/alerts/.

➤ Magazines usually have electronic editions.

➤ Photocopies work best because very few people bother to do this anymore. Also, the photocopy will stay longer on their desk. It may even be passed on to other staff members who could be hiring.

➤ Keep your contacts through this medium to a maximum of once every 3 weeks.

➤ Don't bombard people.

➤ Make sure you send a personal note, even if you send an e-mail clipping.

■ DISTRIBUTE A BOOKLET

Write a booklet with information relevant to your industry and give it away. Everyone loves a freebie, so give away something that demonstrates your expertise. I designed, wrote, and distributed a free booklet on how to do a reference check correctly, entitled "Don't Hire a Liar" (see www.perrymartel.com). It subtly points out the benefits of using a professional like me when hiring. The booklet hot-links to a supplemental software program for reference checking that my firm sells. Here are some ideas:

➤ Link to your web site, e-resume, or blog.

➤ Give the booklet away electronically.

➤ If you send a printed version, indicate where the recipient can get extra copies for colleagues.

➤ Advertise it on your web site and those newsgroups frequented by hiring managers in your target market.

A WAR STORY

Jill Tanenbaum

My most recent hire sent me a beautiful hand-designed booklet that contained the best samples of her design work. She didn't just e-mail me a link or send a resume. The fact that she went over the top to design the booklet was impressive. In fact, her experience on its own wouldn't have gotten her the interview, much less the job. But the booklet did it!

Jill Tanenbaum, president, Jill Tanenbaum Graphic Design & Advertising (www.jtdesign.com).

■ CALL HUMAN RESOURCES

I know this sounds like heresy, but there's method in my madness. Call the human resources department. Ask what outside agency or third-party recruiting firm they use. Why? Two strategic reasons. First, any human resources person will immediately ask why you want to know. To which you answer, "I've been to your web site and I understand that you're not looking for someone with my skill set right now but the agency you use may be dealing with other firms—so I guess I'm looking for a recommendation from you." If they don't press you for an interview, insist on knowing whom they use and why.

People in human resources love saving money on fees, so they may try to hire you directly. They tend to group together by industry and make referrals.

Getting a referral from one of their customers will ensure an agency gives you special attention. In addition:

➤ Always ask for the name of a specific person and their direct dial number.

➤ Get permission to use the human resources manager's name as a reference.

➤ Ask if they personally know of any other companies that could make appropriate use of your skills.

➤ Send them a thank-you note with a copy of your resume to keep on file.

A WAR STORY

Lauryn Franzoni

A methodical strategy paid off for this ExecuNet member who was very active in her local human resources groups. She contacted the national headquarters for the names of local chapter presidents, and mounted a campaign of contacting each one every 2 months. Her persistence paid off when she received an offer.

Lauryn Franzoni, managing director of ExecuNet (www.execunet.com).

■ WRITE A CASE STUDY

Write a case study that showcases your skills. This could be as simple as a coveted client you sold or as complex as a new product you helped introduce to the market. Send the study to firms that have needs similar to those emphasized in the study. Not only do you get to showcase your writing as well as your research and analysis skills, it demonstrates your business acumen. Did you establish an innovative compensation program for resellers that increased sales and decreased spoilage or returns? This is a big deal in retail, where 90 percent of profits are lost due to returns. Try this:

➤   Choose an example that builds your credibility with your targeted employers.

➤   Results that would be of interest to a potential employer include increased efficiencies, new marketing techniques, and new or different distribution channels.

➤   Areas that would be promising include:

    ➤   *Sales/marketing:* Distribution channels

    ➤   *Manufacturing:* Just-in-time (JIT) inventories

    ➤   *Operations:* Enterprise resource planning (ERP) systems

―――――――――――――― **A WAR STORY** ――――――――――――――

Bill Humbert

A college recruit graduated from an architecture program and wanted to work for Marriott designing hotels and hotel rooms. Prior to graduation, she contacted the architecture group at Marriott. They interviewed and liked her but did not have any openings. She asked if it was okay to keep in touch. Every couple of weeks, she would send a design for a room, a balcony, a lobby, a hall area, a convention area. Finally, after 6 months of constant contact (and probably to get her to stop sending designs, they did not need), Marriott hired her.

Bill Humbert, The Humbert Group (www.recruiterguy.com).

■ PREPARE A COMPETITIVE ANALYSIS

Do a competitive analysis on one of your targeted employer's products and send it to the president or vice president of the targeted firm. People assume that all companies keep up to date on their competitors, but this is rarely the case. Most companies don't have the budget or the ability internally to remain aware of best practices. Your piece will likely be most welcome. Follow these suggestions:

➤ Focus on companies that are direct competitors of those you want to work for, not your own company.

➤ Potential employers need to get something out of reading the piece.

➤ Use graphs and charts wherever possible because people like visuals.

➤ Make it only as long as it needs to be.

➤ Offer to share your primary research if the company is interested.

A WAR STORY

Ross Macpherson

I worked with one client who specialized in retail merchandising (point of purchase [POP], planagrams, etc.). After developing her resume, we discussed putting together a targeted job search campaign to go after some of the bigger players in retail. While working out her "unique selling proposition," she made the claim that she could walk into any retail environment and recommend how they could make more money through better merchandising. I asked, "Can you really back that up?" and suddenly her plan was born.

My client targeted 5 major retail outlets, went to a number of their locations, and made detailed notes on what she saw and how she would improve it. The first company she contacted was a major outlet with offices located in the building over the store. She walked into the offices, asked to speak to the person in charge of marketing, and was told he was in a meeting until 11:00 A.M. She scribbled a quick note on a piece of paper that read, "I've just spent 30 minutes in your store. I found 3 merchandising inconsistencies and identified 7 ways that should increase your sales by about 12 to 15 percent. My name is _____ and I will be waiting in the coffee shop downstairs."

She told the receptionist, "Please hand this to him at the end of his meeting. It's very important," and she walked out.

Shortly after 11:00, the vice president of marketing came downstairs, met her in the coffee shop, and she spent the next hour walking through every corner of the store with him discussing her findings. Although no such position existed, the vice president hired her as their new director of merchandising.

Compliments of Ross Macpherson, president, Career Quest (www.yourcareer quest.com).

■ CLASSIFIED ADS

Buy a classified ad in the newspaper. Have a title that describes your ideal position (Cost Accountant, Project Manager, Marketing Manager). Bold the title and describe your features in 25 words or less. The more space you use, the more it costs. Here's what to do:

➤ Use acronyms. For example, a cost accountant could advertise: CA 10 yrs exp in manufacturing. Excel, AccPac, Ref. More info 555-1212 (also works on Facebook and Craigslist).

➤ Bold your headline so it jumps off the page.

➤ Plan on running it for 2 to 4 weeks.

➤ If you can't afford every day, ask which are their busiest days.

➤ Propose a swap, a deal where you trade your expertise instead of paying cash.

➤ Ask if you can run a box ad and pay only for actual leads.

■ WRITE A BROCHURE

Do a brochure instead of a resume. This is a great way to find temporary or contract work leading to a full-time position. Send the brochure to your target group. Speak to their needs on the front cover. Profile your projects and accomplishments on the inside flaps (use one of the inside flaps for quotes from your references). Reserve the back panel for your mini bio. Include a photo if you're good looking (see GM4JH.com/007.html for examples). In addition, do the following:

➤ Hand-address the envelope you mail it in.

➤ Buy glossy brochure paper for your laser printer. I order mine from Paper Direct (www.paperdirect.com).

➤ Lead with your best foot.

➤ Keep the copy short.

➤ Make sure your address and contact information are easy to find.

■ CONSULTANT LETTER

Employers often prefer to "try before we buy" prior to making a permanent offer, or to bridge the gap while they are looking for a permanent employee, or a way to hide the extra headcount in their "variable" costs. Many people get their start this way. Robert W. Bly has a letter in his book, *The Encyclopedia of Business Letters, Fax Memos, and E-Mail* (Franklin Lakes, NJ: Career Press, 1999), that he suggests using to land consulting or freelance jobs. It starts this way:

> *Is freelance a dirty word to you? It really shouldn't be. In public relations, with its crisis-lull-crisis rhythm, good freelancers can save you money and . . .*

What a great opener for starting a discussion. Use the possible contact as an entrée to a permanent job. Great places to start looking for consulting gigs are www.guru.com, www.net-temps.com, or www.elance.com. Or, simply target companies you're interested in and:

➤ Focus on the employer's needs, not yours.

➤ Dismiss their concerns about hiring a consultant by quickly stating the benefits in the first paragraph.

➤ Provide letters of reference from former employers.

➤ Give the employer your absolute best effort because you may be auditioning for a permanent job.

➤ If you're not hired full-time, ask for referrals to other departments, divisions, or companies that they think might benefit from your services.

■ TEMP TO PERM

The temporary help industry employs nearly 2 million Americans on any given day. "Temping" is a multibillion-dollar industry. This is a great way to break into a company through the backdoor. Remember, employers hire from within first, so it's to your advantage to already be there. Although there may not necessarily be a lot of firms hiring people on a full-time basis, there are probably a lot of firms that can afford to hire someone for 1 day a week. Try this:

➤ Market yourself as a "Top gun for hire." A good rule of thumb on what to charge is 1.6 times your previous daily rate.

➤ Try to get hired for full days not half days.

➤ Ask the employer to provide parking.

➤ Invoice people every week.

■ AUDITION

It worked well for the people on *Survivor* and *The Apprentice,* so why not you? Produce a video, burn it on a CD or DVD, and distribute it to potential employers. Keep it tasteful and highlight the results you achieved on 1 or 2 projects. Ask for an in-person interview. If you have video editing software, you can burn your own copies for less than $2, complete with the box. In addition, do the following:

➤ Use a DVD box because you can tuck a resume inside the front cover.

➤ At the beginning of each video, tell the employer why you're interested in working for the company.

➤ Talk about the research you did to conclude the company is a good fit for your skills.

➤ Highlight accomplishments that would be of interest to this employer.

➤ Ask for an in-person interview.

A WAR STORY

Jim Moens

I had recruited a young guy (very early 20s) for a visual basic developer position at one of my clients. He had a 2-year computer science degree and had been working for a year and a half to 2 years as a sort of one-man IT department for a very small, rural manufacturer. He did it all: programming, networking, support, you name it. The day before the interview, he and I met for lunch. He brought along his laptop and proceeded to show me how he had developed an application for my client, based on information he had gleaned from me, their web site, and other sources. He had been working on it every evening for the past week, and it was most impressive. Good functionality, slick interface, intelligent use of technology... simply awesome. The day of the interview came and went. He did well, just as I had expected, but we were a bit nervous. Another, more experienced programmer had applied on his own and interviewed as well. I spoke with the client just after he had made the decision to hire my candidate. He stated the deciding factor was (no surprise) the "home brew" application my candidate had developed. It proved, in one fell swoop, that he could, without a doubt, do the job, and perhaps most important—that he wanted it more.

Compliments of Jim Moens, owner, SearchWorks at www.searchworkscareers .com.

■ DON'T TRY THIS AT HOME

There's an obvious benefit to out-of-the-box activities that bring you to the attention of employers. There is also a real danger of crossing the line and doing something in poor taste or that puts you or the employer at risk. Here is an example pulled from the pages of the *Montreal Gazette*:

The job hunter hoped his resume would land him an interview. What he got was the attention of the bomb squad. The man was arrested after he included his CV in a ticking package left in a Montreal marketing firm's washroom last month. It was his way of drawing attention to the application, as he was among 400 contenders vying for six paid internships. The 24-year-old didn't get the job but he did get charged with public mischief. He had handed the receptionist an Arabic newspaper with a note alerting her to the ticking parcel in the men's washroom, police said. At a time of heightened concerns over terrorism, the package raised the specter of a bombing. Montreal police evacuated the company's building. Later, police discovered the package was harmless. It contained a metronome—a device used by musicians to help maintain rhythm and tempo—along with the candidate's CV.

GUERRILLA TACTICS

➤ Be bold!

➤ Be passionate!

➤ Be creative!

➤ Be tasteful!

➤ Be safety conscious.

➤ Be image conscious.

➤ Enlist a personal army of helpers.

➤ Offer a reward to anyone who helps you secure an interview or job.

➤ Don't do exactly what others have done recently.

Part

IV

Your Guerrilla Job-Hunting Campaign

Chapter 11

3 Sample Campaigns

The Force Multiplier Effect in Action

Take time to deliberate, but when the time for action has arrived, stop thinking and go.

—NAPOLEON BONAPARTE

As explained in this book, there are numerous weapons and tactics that you can use in job hunting. By opting to use multiple weapons and tactics in a unified plan of action, you will significantly enhance your prospects and probability of success. That is the power of the Force Multiplier Effect (FME).

The weapons and tactics you choose will be unique to your situation. The following 3 real-life examples may not be the best ones for you, so don't feel compelled to copy them. Instead, be inspired by these job hunters who had the courage to drop their old tired ways and try something new. They are my friends—and I know their stories—because like many of my other friends, I advised them.

■ EXAMPLE 1: TOM WEISHAAR

➤ *FME mix:* E-mail, web site, chronological resume, Extreme Resume, Internet ads, networking, cold calling

➤ *Target job:* Executive, business development, or marketing

In his campaign, Tom combined multiple marketing weapons and multiple avenues of attack to enlist the aid of people in his network.

235

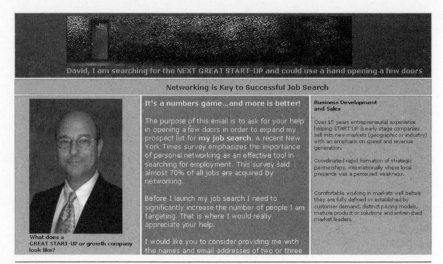

Figure 11.1   Tom Weishaar.

Tom combined e-mail marketing with his personal web site and a follow-up call. Later Tom's campaign morphed to include an Extreme Resume and web advertising.

My first interaction with Tom was over coffee. One morning, while I was working on my first coffee, an e-mail popped up on my screen (Figure 11.1).

You have to love it. His tone was total chutzpa. Talk about attention getting. Wow! I immediately telephoned Tom. I was curious to know how he found me. This was, I learned, a cold call. I also learned that Tom was using a new software service from Protus IT Solutions (www.campaigner.com).

Tom had seen my advertisement on VentureWire and decided to contact me using the GotMarketing technology. We spoke on the phone for perhaps 15 minutes, and I was so impressed with him (exactly what he was counting on) that I discussed a few of my upcoming requirements. While Tom wasn't a fit for any of my current search assignments, he managed to convince me that he was money in the bank for an aggressive recruiter like me. (Yes, I bought that.)

I asked his permission to do a 1-page Extreme makeover version of his resume so that I could market him properly (check www.weishaars.com). Tom also agreed to change the picture on his web site to one in which he was wearing a suit and tie. Image is important.

Tom made all the changes I requested. Before I could begin a marketing campaign, several clients called and booked all our time with searches. When I had time to speak with Tom, it was all over. I didn't have a chance!

Unbeknownst to me—and I should have known, shame on me—Tom is a true guerrilla marketer. He took my Extreme Resume idea and adapted it to his situation. Armed with the new resume, he launched an assault. He targeted CEOs across the United States with an innovative ad campaign, followed by a 1-2 punch with his resume and web site.

Using online magazines like VentureWire, Silicon Alley, Tech-Wire, and PotomacWire to generate inquiries, Tom placed the "Resume" ad reproduced here:

RESUME: NEED TO CLOSE NEW BUSINESS NOW?

VP Business Development—SALES CLOSER!

Tom Weishaar

Tom Weishaar is a Sales Closer and Start-Up Business Development executive who excels at rapid closure of high level, complex deals and new market penetration. Extensive Bus Dev, Direct and OEM Sales experience. Start-Up experience includes Internet, ECommerce, Security, Enterprise Software, and Handheld Mobile Computing with strong international exposure. Rapid engagement strategy, time compression, and closing in new markets without the advantage of brand or franchise are unique strengths. Review comprehensive history with full references at www.weishaars.com.

The ads were a lot less costly than being unemployed. Every ad was hyperlinked to his web site, allowing readers to instantly link to his web site and read his resume. He teased readers just enough to get them to his site and then pummeled them (subtly) with his accomplishments—a great strategy.

When interviewed for this book, Tom had this to say about his campaign:

The results were numerous and across the board. First, it instantly drove eyeballs. Second, it kept me busy and engaged in networking with other executives who thought the idea was cool and wrote me with their thoughts. Some of them, more than a few in fact, followed my lead. Hundreds of phone calls and e-mails, many phone interviews, and several face-to-face interviews were directly attributable to the web site. The web site attracted at least three job offers that I would never have seen otherwise. Most importantly, the web site worked in concert with my CV. Together, they were a significant marketing force. The CV was strongly worded, and the web site allowed for the depth and granularity one can only take in that form. While talking to the recipient of my cold call, I would ask, "By the way, are you in front of a browser?"

... If you can walk a prospective employer through your web site, you're halfway there!

Yes, it worked. So well in fact that Tom has continued to use this mix as his approach. He's even updated his web site to give it a fresh look. This time instead of spending weeks building it from scratch, he bought a template from Templatemonster.com and modified it. Tom's new web site is a good example of how to build a web site specifically for job-hunting purposes.

➤ The Key to His Success

Tom used a variety of weapons to get a prospective employer's attention. In the final analysis, the key to getting the interview and closing on an offer was calling early in the morning to follow up and step the employer through his web site.

■ EXAMPLE 2: ALLAN PLACE

➤ *FME mix:* Extreme Resume, personal letter, follow-up call
➤ Target job: Sales

The economic downturn in the tech sector in 2001 affected most companies. In 2000, if you interviewed in jeans, a blue Mohawk, and a T-shirt while extolling the virtues of anarchy, you very likely would have received a job offer. Not so just 2 years later. It was soon an employers' market, with viable companies cherry picking from the large and growing base of newly laid off, talented people.

Allan launched his campaign with an aggressive mix of the traditional methods that had always worked for him in the past—cold calling and traditional networking.

Allan started with some basic assumptions:

➤ Difficult job markets still produce perfect "fits."

➤ Finding a job is a job. Spending only 4 hours a day would not produce results.

➤ He could rely only on himself to find work.

➤ He would not rely on headhunters, job boards, web sites, newspapers, or friends.

— Most job seekers see headhunters, job boards, web sites, newspapers, or friends as primary lead sources. Here's why: they are easy to access; they are the path of least resistance. "Too many dogs sniffing at the same gopher hole."

— The best positions never get advertised.

➤ His best chance was to target specific companies, determine the right contact, get that person's attention, and develop a position. He chose this route because:

— Fewer people would be willing to spend the time required.

— The best positions are either created or not advertised.

— Where no position existed and one could not be created, he would at least have created some level of rapport with the decision makers that he could draw on if a position developed.

— It is easier to position yourself for a job when the job doesn't exist.

Allan's Force Multiplier Effect in more detail:

➤ Develop database of potential employers in selected industries.

➤ Conduct research.

➤ Discard companies that did not represent a good fit.

➤ Contact selected companies.

➤ Arrange interviews.

➤ Register on job bulletin boards.

➤ Contact headhunters.

➤ Respond to posted advertisements.

➤ Develop Database of Potential Employers in Selected Industries

This database of 134 companies came from the *Ottawa Business Journal* in the following sectors:

➤ Aerospace, defense, and security technology
➤ Electro-optical/photonics
➤ Internet technology and e-commerce
➤ Semiconductor
➤ Software
➤ Telecommunications, satellite, and mobile communications

➤ Conduct Research

This took between a half-hour and 1 hour for each company:

➤ Industry
➤ Product
➤ Company
➤ Position
➤ Growth path

➤ Discard Companies That Did Not Represent a Good Fit

➤ Fifty companies were discarded for the following reasons:
  – They were struggling in the marketplace.
  – Allan's background was not appropriate for the product/business model.
  – Other indefinable reasons disqualified them.

➤ Contact Selected Companies

➤ Each selected company was contacted for the names of the vice president of sales and human resources.

➤ Broadcast letters were sent to each of these vice presidents.

➤ Follow-up calls were made to determine and explore current or anticipated employee requirements. In almost all cases, they were not filling immediate opportunities. Allan would engage with the vice president to determine and explore company growth and future directions.

➤ Current points of pain:

— Poorly performing sales representatives

— Limited success in challenging geographic or vertical markets

— Insufficient sales bandwidth

— Evolving business model (e.g., geographic to vertical)

— Resumes forwarded if appropriate

➤ **Arrange Interviews**

➤ If he sent a resume, he did additional research as preparation for the follow-up call. It also allowed him to further qualify the company for fit. In a few instances, he discarded the company from the prospect list.

➤ If he was still interested in working for the company, he would follow up and try to set up an interview. People do not hire resumes; they hire people. The only purpose of his resume was to elicit interest and prompt a meeting in front of decision makers.

➤ It was assumed that no immediate openings were available. However, companies are always looking for good talent. "Even though you may not be hungry, there is nothing wrong with looking at the menu." Simply put, even if he knew there was no immediate career opportunity, he would try to arrange an interview. Spending 30 minutes with a prospective employer benefited both parties:

— Sales opportunities could appear quickly.

— The vice president of sales/human resources might be able to refer him to someone in their network who was looking.

— It provided interviewing practice.

— It was an opportunity to establish a rapport that might be valuable over time.

➤ Interview preparation averaged about 5 hours per company.

— Product

— Industry

— Competitors

— Position

➤ **Register on Job Boards and Respond to Posted Advertisements**

➤ Monster

➤ Careerbuilder

➤ Various others

He searched the web sites and responded to a limited number of opportunities. Typically, they were being handled through head-hunters.

➤ **Contact Headhunters**

➤ Allan only contacted a few headhunters. If a headhunter believed Allan was trying to work with too many competitors, there would be less interest in trying to place him.

➤ **Results**

Initially, his results were dismal. Job boards, recruiters, and traditional networking were a complete bust. There were plenty of lunches and kind advice but no offers. After many months, he decided to try a targeted approach to marketing himself. He designed a 1-page Extreme Resume based on the qualities employers look for, as outlined in Table 2.1. He sent his resume with a customized letter to just 2 employers that he had closely researched. Both employers made offers.

When I asked him why this approach worked for him, his answer, which may surprise you, was:

> *I forwarded the letter I wrote using the techniques laid out in your book. I called when I indicated I would. They [the employer] requested my full resume. I forwarded a full functional version that summarized my background under select headings, as suggested in your book. At our first meeting, the employer indicated several things during our discussion:*
>
> ➤ *He received literally dozens of resumes and phone calls weekly. He responded to none—ever!*
>
> ➤ *He had all his calls screened to reduce the number of job seekers who got through.*
>
> ➤ *He told me that the main reason he took my call when I followed up was that my approach was unique. I did not throw a resume at him hoping he liked what he saw. Neither did I call repeatedly.*

Allan created his own job where none had previously existed by triggering the value requirement in each company. He did that by focusing on the prospective employer, not himself. He made heavy use of the employer's needs as described in Table 2.1.

➤ Summary of Activities

Companies contacted	150
E-mails sent	450?
Calls placed	1,000?
Resumes forwarded	85
Interviews: first round	35
Interviews: second round	22
Job offers	4

➤ The Key to His Success

Initially, Allan used a variety of weapons to no effect. Shifting his approach, rather than doing more of the same, changed Allan's results. The key to securing interviews with both of his targeted employers was following up his Extreme Resume, which had been designed specifically to target each employer's needs.

GUERRILLA INTELLIGENCE

Surviving beyond Hopelessness

Deanna J. Williams

I knew a young woman whose husband had left her 1 month before she had her lungs burned with hydrofluoric acid at work. She had been laid up for a year and had 2 children to support by herself. She could no longer work around acids per her doctor's orders, so she had to start all over. She had no formal education other than a high school diploma but she did have a strong will to survive. She tried desperately to find work, but when asked if she had ever had an industrial injury she admitted that she did, although it was through no fault of her own but rather that of a faulty vent that was not properly working. The interviews seemed to stop immediately after she disclosed her injury and she never heard from the companies again.

(continued)

After many months of this, she decided she needed to try something new. The young woman decided that with her experience in the semiconductor industry, she could use this experience to become a recruiter and hire people to do the work that she could no longer perform. She went to a temporary agency that was looking for a nonexempt recruiter with a couple of years of experience. Although she did not have the required experience, she did her research on the agency and looked at their want ads and acquired a couple of resumes from people she knew whose backgrounds fit the job descriptions. When she arrived at the agency she told the manager that she knew what kind of people they were seeking to hire and produced the resumes she had collected.

The manager listened intently but wasn't totally convinced yet, so the young woman told him she would work for free for 1 month and if she couldn't meet his hiring expectations during that period, she would leave and he would not have to pay her for her services. However, if she did produce what he wanted he would have to pay her for the time she had worked with a bonus at the end of the month for achieving her goals and a full-time position with the company. The manager thought about it and took her up on her challenge. She not only succeeded in producing what the manager had given her but she also went beyond what he expected. After 5 years with the company, she went on to receive several promotions and was eventually offered a position as a manager. That woman has been in the recruiting industry for 35 years and earns a 6-figure income annually.

Deanna J. Williams, www.linkedin.com/in/deannajwilliams/.

■ EXAMPLE 3: CHELSEA TEGAN

➤ *FME mix:* Networking, competitive analysis, functional resume, personal letter, market research with a white paper

➤ *Target job:* Technical lead

In Chelsea's own words:

I also started to research, not just companies to work for, but their businesses. When I chose a company that I thought I should pursue, I asked for an introduction. Before that meeting, I completed

two or three days of research on their business, competitors, and general issues. The day before the meeting, I summarized this in an e-mail to my contact (generally the CEO) with the comment that this is what I understood about their business and that there were questions about their business I would like to explore. The conversations I had were good ones, where we were discussing topics of mutual interest (the contact's business is always of interest to that contact). In every case, I left the meeting with someone who had a future interest in my whereabouts.

Other notes:

I quickly found a company I wanted to work for. I realized it by the way the CEO responded to my questions. Essentially after about 15 minutes of discussion, he looked at me and opened up, "This is what we are really lacking, and if you can do this, we are interested." He talked for 45 minutes. Now, this company was bound by commitment to the board not to hire anyone in this position until next budget round, about a year away. I had researched the company and heard only good things about the business and the management. So I was intent on joining.

➤ *I asked the CEO if I could have several business contacts phone in to him as references, which he agreed to.*

➤ *I continued to research the business and tried to find ways to provide service even though none had been required.*

➤ *I made sure to be friendly, never expecting them to "get back to me right away." Having been in a leadership position myself helped. I knew that 2 weeks for an answer is okay sometimes.*

I realized that making things easy for people was important, but positioning was important, too. A junior person usually communicates by e-mail, a senior person is generally confident enough to pick up the phone and call. However, e-mail is easier to answer. And I knew it was my job to sell into this account. So over the summer, I ensured that I phoned both senior contacts roughly once a month with something that I felt might be of value to them. If I reached voice mail, I mentioned at the end of the message that I'd send the information in an e-mail for their convenience. And then I immediately followed up with an e-mail with the subject line "follow-up to phone call." (This worked not only with the target company but with several "plan B" companies. It was a combination of establishing a relationship, while offering the contact convenience of response. It was a simple approach that focused on making it easier for them, not for me.)

After a particularly long conversation with two senior individuals, I took it upon myself to summarize what we had discussed and also to add input from my own experience about the challenges they might face in accomplishing their aims. In this case, the company was successful with customers in an old structured industry, but this industry was not growing and they needed to open up new markets. Because I believe strongly in giving value before asking for value, I went over several cases where I had seen this before and simply offered some ideas about how others had handled it.

The process started at the end of May and I came on board at the start of November. That's about the standard six-month sales cycle for high-value products.

Finally, I accepted the advice and assistance of an executive recruiter friend of mine, who offered an idea. He made an executive search database open to me where I could look for contacts in the industry this company was in. I found several good contacts. As a small "market research firm" (not a lie at all!), I asked them an interesting question about the use of this company's technology and got some responses. I provided this to the firm as an additional and useful contact.

I found out the difference that attitude makes. It is not about being arrogant; it is about being able to see the other person better because you are confident enough to forget yourself.

➤ The Key to Chelsea's Success

The key to securing the interview was networking into each company and then following through with a competitive analysis. As a guerrilla, Chelsea focused on the needs that employers weren't aware they had.

■ SUMMARY

When I decided I wanted to be a headhunter, I didn't understand that not having direct sales experience was a detriment. At 25 years old and a whole 3 years' work experience, I thought I was "hot stuff." Interview after interview, the search firms in town couldn't see what I saw in myself and why I wouldn't take no for an answer. In my mind, I was simply failing to articulate my value correctly. In the end, the owner of the first firm actually turned me down 12 times over 3 months. I just kept thinking of reasons to get back together and reiterate why he should hire me. Thirteen was my lucky number.

Chelsea, Allan, and Tom profited from leveraging a suite of tactics and weapons to precisely target employers and climb above the "background noise" of a supposedly lifeless market.

Which tactics will you use? Experiment—be bold—let your real personality and passion shine through, and remember "no" just means, "Not today."

GUERRILLA INTELLIGENCE

In Case of Emergency, Break Glass

Harry Joiner

I was unemployed and broke during the last recession. I had been laid off from my job at a software company, and with a wife, 4 kids, and a pricey mortgage—things were pretty stressful. Panic attacks were a daily occurrence. Whatever you're going through right now, I can relate.

Looking for a job when you're unemployed is tough. I'm not sure where I heard this statistic, but you should be prepared to spend 1 month looking for a job for every $20,000 of base salary. So, a $100K job could take 6 months to land.

During that 6 months, hiring managers always seem to migrate from one set of concerns about the candidate to another. The migration looks something like this:

Month 1 to 3: The hiring manager wonders to himself "If you're so good at what you do, why did your company fire you?"

Month 3 to 5: "If you're so good at what you do, why are you still looking for a job?"

Month 6 and longer: "What's wrong with you?"

During my own job search, I reached month 4 and realized that I was going to hit month 7 or 8 without any problem. So I printed up some business cards, slapped up a web site, and

(continued)

started telling everyone that I was a "business development consultant."

One small problem: hiring managers began to see me as an unleadable entrepreneur who would be too much of a maverick to bring on to their sales teams. All hiring managers want someone who will plug-and-play right into their organization—someone who can lead and be led. One hiring manager told me that he would *interview* me only after I had taken down my web site. Right.

As I was driving home that day I thought to myself: "What *exactly* would I do if I had to find a decent job in this economy in six weeks or less?"

I have never addressed this question in my blog, nor have I ever seen anyone else tackle it. It's one thing to read a job search book that's filled with theories about finding a job when you're unemployed and desperate. It's another to actually do it.

What you are about to read assumes that you will continue to run a conventional job search, complete with cold calls to recruiters, job board resume submissions, and chicken finger networking events. And the reality is that if you make +$100K per year, the following method might not work. You'll need to take a more traditional approach. But if you can settle for a lower paying job, then here's what I like to call the *"Any port in a storm"* blitzkrieg job search method:

Step 1
Collect yourself. Not too long ago, my 12-year old son, an aspiring Eagle Scout, brought home a copy of the *U.S. Army Survival Manual*. I swear, this book reads like a job search guide—at least as far as the mental conditioning aspects are concerned. The Guide mentions 10 personal qualities required to survive in a life-threatening environment. They include:

1. Being able to make up your mind.
2. Being able to improvise.
3. Being able to live with yourself.
4. Being able to adapt to the situation—to make a good thing out of a bad thing.
5. Remaining cool, calm, and collected.
6. Hoping for the best, but preparing for the worst.

7. Having patience.

8. Being able to "figure out" other people—to understand and predict what other people will do.

9. Understanding where your special fears and worries come from, and

10. Knowing what to do to control them.

Don't those tips apply to a desperate job seeker?

I have seen my own career crash and burn this century, and I know from experience that not only will you survive it—but, if you are cool headed, you can also emerge from it with a higher-paying, more fulfilling job than you had before. Just relax. Your anxiety is like your skin color: there is nothing you can do to change it.

You can manage your anxiety with prescription medications, but basically you are going to have to deal with it yourself. Freaking out won't help you survive. In fact, it will only make things worse—and then you'll *still* have a problem. Anxiety adds no value. I know what I'm talking about. Simply inhale. Hold it. And exhale. Now lock and load.

Step 2

Make *sure* your former employer will give you great references. Preferably, they should do this in writing on an undated letter on their letterhead. This letter will be added to the envelope you prepare for Step 6, so don't let your former employer slide on this. Good references are a MUST.

Step 3

Call a bunch of nonprofits and ask them if you could work for them in a white collar capacity for *free* 1 or 2 days a week while you look for a new full-time job. After you see Step 6, you'll know what you are going to be doing with the other 3 days a week.

Call 50 nonprofits if you have to. You'd be amazed at how tough it is to get a job working for free, but you must persevere. Job One is being able to look a human resource (HR) manager square in the eye when he or she asks you, "So, what have you been doing in your free time?" because nobody wants to hire a victim.

(continued)

Tell the HR manager that you are working at such-and-such a charity, "because you have always believed in the cause, and now—thank heaven—you have a couple of days a week to give back to society." Now you have gone from being a victim to being a positive, outcome-oriented survivor who can make lemonade out of lemons. PLUS—and this is a big plus—you can put the nonprofit on your resume and use them as a reference. It's a beautiful thing.

To find nonprofit organizations, check out www.Guidestar. com, a database of more than 1.7 million nonprofits.

Step 4

Order some nice stationery from an excellent stationer. Make sure it's nice because you want it to reflect well on you. There is no point in being unprofessional. Time is of the essence, so first impressions will count for a lot. I use a thermographed "house linen" weight paper from ReavesEngraving.com, but you can use any stationer that has a similar quality product. Get the matching envelopes and business cards. $500 should cover it. It's a small investment to make in your career.

Step 5

Rewrite your resume and prepare a nice sales letter. There's a cottage industry around resume writing, so I won't get into it here except to say that you need to have a hard-hitting "metrics rich" bullet-pointed resume. The law of specificity applies. Odd numbers work best. Your resume must highlight verifiable, concrete accomplishments such as:

➤ Increased sales in XYZ category by $47,215 in Q2 2006.

➤ Decreased distribution costs by $17.61/pound by renegotiating truck leases.

➤ Reorganized shipping and receiving workflows for a savings of $12.41/case.

You get the idea. This goes back to the comment about being able to plug-and-play in any company.

About the cover letter: the best cover letters are actually written in the "Problem/Agitate/Solve" format. Google that to see what I'm talking about. The master of sales letter writing is Gary Halbert. Google him, too. Without being long-winded here, you want to write a letter to the head of the company function in which you'd like to work, like *Dear Sales Manager, Dear CFO,* or whomever.

Then start off with an honest opening sentence like "I stopped by briefly today to apply for a job. I have no idea if you are hiring, but even if you aren't—I think I could be of value to you."

Then simply provide a bullet-pointed laundry list of ways that you could help on a full-time, part-time, project, or interim basis. Give some affordable no-strings attached staffing options. Again, position your needs honestly in a way that he or she can identify with—and profit from.

Why such over-the-top honesty? Because hiring managers are busy and they are not expecting such an honest approach. It will catch them off guard because it's true. It's completely without pretense. Hiring managers love that.

Step 6

Cold walk buildings. You are looking for full-time, part-time, temp, interim, project, and seasonal work to get you through your job search. You can work from their office or from home. You have a computer with Internet access.

A local Atlanta phone company, Cbeyond Communications, has come out of nowhere in the past few years to carve a nice niche in the hotly competitive small business market. Its sales reps are known for going into high-rise buildings and popping in on office managers to solicit new business. Of course, unannounced solicitations are strictly forbidden in most high-rises, but that hasn't stopped Cbeyond's sales reps, who rarely get busted by security.

How Do They Do It?

By starting at the tenth floor, then going to the first floor, then working the ninth floor, then the second, then the eighth, then the third, and so on—finally stopping in the middle.

Why the Strange Pattern?

Because when tenants call security saying that there's a solicitor on the tenth floor, security goes to the ninth floor to wait for them. But by the time Cbeyond gets to the ninth floor (after

(continued)

having spent 30 minutes on the first), security has left the scene. And on it goes, a goose chase that ends with Cbeyond having canvassed the entire building.

If I were in insurance, legal services, or accounting, I'd swipe this tactic.

THE ONLY GOAL IN DOING THIS IS TO MEET ENOUGH PEOPLE TO GET CALLED IN FOR A REAL INTERVIEW.

Nobody is going to get hired on the spot with this plan. However, if you *do* meet the sales manager on the first visit, simply say:

> Look, I know you are busy, but I'm looking for a new job in this geographic area. The envelope contains a cover letter and my resume. I have no idea if you are hiring or not. My only objective in stopping by was to position myself as a possible resource for your company. Obviously, I have enough guts and tenacity to knock on doors—but I'm decent enough not to be pushy. Kindly review my resume and let me know if you'd like to meet for a regular interview. That will give both of us some time to do our homework on each other. Otherwise, perhaps you can pass my resume along to a local friend who is hiring. Okay??

Now clearly, it takes nerves of steel to pull this off—but people did this type of thing during the depression. And business-to-business salespeople do this every day.

Remember that desperate times call for desperate measures, and if you just lost your job and you are not niched to a particular industry and you are almost out of cash and have kids to feed, then what I have written is a fairly good game plan for getting out an collecting noes—the most time honored way to get to yeses there is.

Harry Joiner is a well-known marketing recruiter based in Atlanta, Georgia. His blog, MarketingHeadhunter.com, is one of the world's most widely read blogs on careers in marketing, and his forthcoming book *The Over 50 Job Search* is expected to be published in 2010. You can see the book's weblog at www.Over50JobSearch.com

Chapter 12

Hand-to-Hand Combat

Winning the Face–to–Face Interview

The first one gets the oyster, the second gets the shell.

— ANDREW CARNEGIE

As competition for customers, market share, and profitability intensifies, understanding what makes an organization effective and which levers to pull to improve financial performance are critical. High-performing companies consistently hire doers—go-getters—at all levels in the company. Innovation, creativity, perseverance, and leadership are the key levers for success.

As a guerrilla job hunter, your strategy has been to appeal to an employer's core need to make money, save money, and increase efficiencies. Combining those needs with elements from the New Value Table (see Figure 2.1) produced a winning resume that secured interviews. Now you must deliver on your marketing.

■ BUILD YOUR STRATEGY AROUND THE EMPLOYER'S EXPECTATIONS

You will meet 4 general groups of decision makers during interviews. Each group requires a different strategy. Each has a different agenda that you must focus on.

253

The groups are:

1. Senior executives
2. Hiring managers
3. Human resource managers
4. Corporate recruiters

➤ Senior Executives

➤ Even if you are not seeking a senior executive role, executives look for similar things from all candidates, so understanding their perspective will help you position your accomplishments accordingly. By the way, that is the first thing they look for—accomplishments.

➤ Executives want to see a lot of recent accomplishments and understand the specifics. They need to know how your accomplishments can translate into success for them if they hire you—even before they interview you.

Executives also look for:

➤ *Outstanding leadership qualities:* A demonstrated ability to create and communicate a vision and then build a team to carry it out

➤ *Honesty and integrity:* A well-principled person whom people trust and who can build shared values throughout the organization

➤ *Intellectual capacity:* The ability to make quick, solid decisions in tough competitive environments

➤ *Intensity:* The capacity to create a deep level of trust among their staff and create an energy-charged, enthusiastic environment

➤ *Passion:* An unrelenting drive to leave a positive mark on the organization that is not driven by money or power

➤ *Work ethic:* A warriorlike resiliency that allows you to persevere, no matter how difficult the task

➤ Hiring Managers

Hiring managers are the people you will work for directly. They are mostly interested in accomplishments specific to their area of the business. Moreover, they want to know how your accomplishments can translate into success for them personally.

Here's what else hiring managers may look for:

Technical Competencies

➤ *Proactive:* Do you embody a forward-thinking, proactive mindset beyond the person's immediate function?

➤ *Focus on results:* Can you recruit a quality subordinate team and get them working together, to generate high levels of performance?

➤ *Smart:* Do you have a strong intellect, coupled with pragmatism and pure common sense?

Business Intelligence

➤ *Budget conscious:* Do you understand the critical importance of cash? Do you watch expenditures as an entrepreneur would, or simply spend knowing your paycheck and benefits will come, no matter what?

➤ *Judgment:* Do you have the ability to deal with novel and complex situations where there is no history or road map?

➤ *Customer focused:* Do you understand how the industry and marketplace work?

Emotional Intelligence

➤ *Persistence:* Can you drive programs to successful fruition? Are you highly self-motivated?

➤ *Empathy:* Do you have the ability to connect with employees and customers?

➤ *Stamina:* Do you demonstrate a built-in unrelenting drive to succeed?

➤ **Human Resources Department**

Human resources (HR) has concerns that go beyond those of hiring managers and executives. HR is also interested in your overall fit with the company's core values and culture—your relationship intelligence. The people in HR look for the following attributes:

➤ *A fit with the next job:* How easily can you move up as the company grows? HR will consider your qualifications for the next job because an upwardly mobile person eases their burden for succession planning and improves their department's return on investment (ROI).

➤ *Ability to fill a gap in the management mix:* Good coaches know their relative offensive and defensive strengths and make trades accordingly. Likewise, smart HR managers understand their organization's strengths and weaknesses and will seek to complement, not replicate them.

➤ **Corporate Recruiters**

These are a company's internal recruiters, junior members of the HR team. More often than not, if you respond to a newspaper ad or job posting, a junior staffer will be the first person to assess your qualifications. The irony of tasking a company's least qualified employee with the responsibility of acquiring its human capital assets probably hasn't escaped you—but that's reality.

Recruiters are often left to figure things out on their own. At a minimum, they have to compare candidates against a list of stipulated skills or abilities. If you have the exact skills you make the cut—if not, you're out. They have a lot to lose professionally by recommending someone who is not qualified. Some people have said that these people might not know good credentials if they slapped them in the face. They can't read between the lines. Tailor your response to exactly what was advertised. Here's how to give corporate recruiters what they are looking for:

➤ *Work experience:* Tell them how your experience fits their opportunity. You have to connect the dots for them subtly.

➤ *Goals:* Your short- and long-term goals must be reasonably in line with the opportunities for advancement.

➤ *Personality:* Chemistry and cultural fit between you and your coworkers is critical. Find out what "type" they hire ahead of time. Call someone who works there.

➤ *Communication skills:* Written and verbal communication skills are becoming increasingly critical as the global marketplace evolves. Demonstrate your ability to listen effectively, verbalize thoughts clearly, and express yourself confidently.

➤ *Image:* Junior people are easily impressed by an appropriate ensemble, so dress for the part you want, not the one you currently have. They'll mentally compare you to their image of the group you'll be working with. When in doubt, overdress 2 levels above business casual.

➤ *Knowledge of the company:* Recruiters expect you to be as enthusiastic about the company as they probably still are. Make sure you read everything on the company's web site. Don't waste their time by asking questions you should already know the answers to.

■ THE INTERVIEW MINEFIELD

The most common way people gain entry to a company is through an ad or referral, starting the process at the bottom of the chain of command. As mentioned, the corporate recruiter is the person who is least likely to understand your potential and has the most to lose by recommending you so their natural tendency will be to do nothing.

Traditional job-hunting methods will expose you to a minefield fraught with booby traps. As you advance each successive level up the chain of command toward the final decision maker, you risk being eliminated. After the company finally does make you an offer, it will be subject to an excruciatingly detailed reference check and yet another opportunity for you to be eliminated.

For most job hunters, diagrammatically, interviewing looks like this:

Recruiter → Human Resources → Hiring Manager
→ Executive → Job Offer

The lower down the chain you begin, the more people there are who will need to approve of your hiring, and therefore the more hurdles you'll have to clear. Luckily, the opposite is also true.

➤ Navigating the Minefield

As a guerrilla, you've been trained to attack weak points. The higher up in the organization you begin, the fewer people you need to satisfy, and the closer you'll be to an offer.

Executives have a macroview of the industry, their business, and skill sets. They're more interested in what you're capable of doing for them in the future than in dissecting your life story. Executives have more experience hiring and tend to make quick gut-level decisions with little validation. So, you should always aim to begin your job hunting in the executive suite.

Guerrilla interviewing looks like this:

Executive → Job Offer

Or in the worst case scenario, this:

Executive → Hiring Manager → Job Offer

When you start at the top, you can get an offer without meeting anyone else. Executives have authority to make an instant hiring decision and have a mandate to continuously "talent hunt" for the whole company. They're the only people who have that macroview of the company's needs. When an executive passes your resume down to a hiring manager with a note saying, "get a hold of this candidate" or "looks good," it's much easier to get an offer. If you think that's simplistic—boy, are you ever wrong! Headhunters work with senior executives for a reason—they can make decisions quickly and efficiently.

➤ Focus on the Employer's Goals

What you're ultimately "selling" during an interview are those elements of your background, skills, and personality that can make a significant contribution to the company. Your potential contribution will be weighed against the cost of a bad hire. If they make the wrong choice, at minimum, they are wasting time and money. At worst, a bad choice could jeopardize the recruiter or manager's job, perhaps even the success of the company. A lot is at stake.

Your mission is to neutralize their concerns by eliminating *fear—doubt* and *uncertainty*.

➤ Preparation—Understand the Meeting's Purpose

The employer believes you'll bring something to the organization. What exactly is that? Are you being interviewed because he has announced a specific opening, or did something in your approach pique his interest? To prepare for the meeting, you need to understand the reason for his interest.

If you're being interviewed for a specific job, he'll tell you and you'll know what to focus on. If it's a general nonspecific get-to-know-you interview as a result of your unsolicited approach, you need to focus on the requirements you uncovered while researching the company. If he's in line with your accomplishments, then that's likely the reason for the meeting.

Personally, I've always found being direct gets the best results. The easiest thing to do is simply ask, "How much time do you think we'll need" and "what's your agenda?" They'll tell you. If they don't tell you, it means they definitely have a pressing problem that your background indicates you can solve—but they don't want to show their hand. In that case, you'll need to focus on what you've accomplished over the past 5 years. This is more work, but it's not impossible.

If you ever find yourself in an interview where you're unsure of the agenda, quickly ask, "Where would you like to begin our conversation?" If he says, "Tell me about yourself," then you should ask, "Where would you like me to begin?" Where he wants you to begin is what he's most interested in. Focus on his interests.

Projecting the image of a stellar can't-do-without candidate comes with practice and preparation. There are 3 things you need to do:

1. Complete a T-account exercise.
2. Build your "story" book.
3. Rehearse your message.

T-Account Exercise

There's no substitute for this exercise. A sage headhunter taught it to me years ago. The exercise requires you to overlay your accomplishments on the employer's needs. This preps you to talk about your accomplishments, long-term goals, as well as strengths and weaknesses in the context of the specific job you're interviewing for.

I know this sounds too easy—too common sense—too logical, but it's not. In my experience, few job hunters spend time thinking about how their experience and skills relate to a job until they're actually asked. I've seen people blow it when they were asked the simplest questions: "What do you know about our company?" That is the perfect opportunity to explain what you've learned and how your experience makes you their perfect candidate. Too often, even the most senior people "wing it."

Draw a line down the middle of a page. List the employer's needs on one side and your skills and accomplishments that prove you can do the job on the other. In the interview, you'll be able to point out these compatible assets for the employer. You'll stand out as organized and prepared. Grab a blank sheet of paper and do it now. (You can recycle this exercise in your thank-you note.)

Analyzing Your Strengths and Weaknesses

All employers ask you about strengths and weaknesses. It's one of the few questions you can absolutely guarantee. Yet, it's numbing how little forethought most people give to this question. This might sound asinine, but I've actually had people who, when asked about weaknesses during an interview, either couldn't come up with any or replied, "I don't believe I have any." Candidates who say they have none—I guess they are, in their own mind, perfect—Mr. Employer will view them in a highly negative light. So much so, that once they state they have no weaknesses, the game is over. And I mean over. These are disastrous interview blunders! Assess your weaknesses in advance of an interview.

GUERRILLA MISSION

Strengths

Now that you've completed a needs analysis with the T-account exercise, you need to list your top 10 strengths as they pertain to the job you are seeking. Grab a piece of paper and list them in bullet form. Stop. Do it now. This is important.

Now look at your strengths. Which of those applies to the job for which you are being interviewed? If you were the interviewer, would that be enough? Would you spend your last dollar to acquire you? If your answer is yes, proceed to the next exercise on weaknesses. If you said no, congratulations for being so honest; you have just saved your interview from certain disaster. You're running these exercises because, like a pro sports coach, you understand that practice makes perfect and game day is no time to practice. Run through this exercise until you've listed 5 strengths to support the job's requirements.

Weaknesses

Run the same exercise, only this time list your weaknesses as they apply to the job. Now pick a weakness you've been working on and detail what you've done to correct it. Are you short-tempered? Don't mention that one! This is not true confessions time. Interviewers expect you to pick something "light." That's what candidates do. Please don't disappoint them. What you're going to do that most candidates don't think to do is demonstrate your follow-through. Right after you reveal your weakness, you're going to explain what you've done to correct the matter.

You might prepare an answer like this:

I was told a few years ago that my budgeting wasn't good enough. I had never received any formal training, so I immediately registered in a night class. On my last review, my supervisor noted how much improvement I'd made. My budgeting skills are now well above average. He did me a big favor.

Congratulations. In this example, you told the interviewer:

➤ What the problem was (budgeting)
➤ Why it was a problem (no training)
➤ What you did to correct it (night class)
➤ What the results were (improved skill level)

Moreover, you've also shown that you are open to constructive criticism and most importantly, that you are prepared to act on feedback. Most employees are not. If the interviewer is keeping score, you just received double bonus points because employers will hire someone with average skills and great attitude over a self-confessed superstar any day.

Build Your Story Book

Following the T-account exercise, you need to turn your strengths and accomplishments into memorable stories because everyone likes a good story. More importantly, people retain ideas more easily if they're presented in the form of a story. After hours and hours of interviewing, it's often difficult for interviewers to remember one candidate from another unless one of them—that'll be you—really grabs their interest with a great story.

Storytelling has other advantages:

➤ When you link ideas for the interviewer, you're far more likely to engage the listener's interest and leave a favorable impression.

➤ The conversational tone relaxes your interviewer and will turn an interrogation into a conversation.

➤ Storytelling appeals to an interviewer's "gut-feel" and innate ability to hire people with "promise."

➤ Given 2 people who are equally qualified on paper, an employer will tend to hire the best storyteller because the person is perceived to have superior communication skills.

Unlike the fairy tales you heard as a child, your stories are based on facts. They portray you as a modern-day hero—confident but not arrogant, decisive but not overbearing, driven but not maniacal. You must provide accurate illustrations of the significant goals you've achieved and the skills and training you mustered to achieve them. You get to play the part of the "hero" who invented the new product, closed the big deal, or in some other way vanquished the dragon.

Which accomplishments prompted the employer to want to meet you in the first place? Those are the stories to use. The key elements of each story relate to the requirements—be they in sales, marketing, engineering, or something else—you outlined in the T-account exercise.

For example, you have discovered from your research that the employer needs to be able to bring new products to market in a timely manner and you have 10 years' experience in new product development. Your story might sound something like this:

Mr. Employer, in the summer of 2009 our major competitor, in an attempt to run us out of business, began giving away a product that they claimed had the same features as our mainstay product. Not surprisingly, revenue plummeted 90 percent in our next quarter. The bottom fell out of our stock. Several of our key development and salespeople quit. In response, I led 2 small teams of 6 engineers on a mission to develop our next-generation product and to expose the weaknesses in the competitor's offering. Within five weeks, we discovered serious design flaws in the security layer of their software that made the user's data vulnerable to hackers. We staged a demonstration of our findings for our sales and marketing team. They designed a counterattack that stopped our competitor in its tracks. Meanwhile, my second team added major functionality to our core product. When the flaws in our competitor's product became front-page news, my team was ready with a bulletproof upgrade. We did all this in less than nine weeks. Company revenues surged 15 percent higher than our previous best quarter.

What is the interviewer likely to infer from this story?

➤ You rise to the occasion when confronted with difficult situations.

➤ You can lead under pressure.

➤ You can execute a strategy.

➤ You're a team player and a team captain (because you kept saying "we" not "I").

You're a ... you're a ... It'll be a long list of positive attributes leading them to conclude, "We've gotta have you on our team!" and that's what you want.

The interviewer will infer all positives and will start to ask "how" questions:

➤ How do you manage?

➤ How did you keep them focused?

➤ How—how—how.

Guerrilla, they're hooked. This is exactly how you want them to react. Now you get to lead them into a natural discussion on the similarities between what you've done and what they need. Make sure you prepare a few more anecdotes to reinforce your positive attributes.

Rehearsing Your Message

From your T-account, pick out instances where you used those skills successfully. Prepare 3 relevant stories for every interview. Use these to create analogies during the interview. Starting with your most relevant accomplishment, write a 2- or 3-paragraph story. Bulleting the sequence of events may make it easier to write the paragraphs. The act of writing forces you to organize your thinking and etch the details in your mind for easy retrieval. Now read the paragraphs out loud. Does your story sound like you're talking or does it sound like you're reciting something you've memorized? Your story must be delivered in a conversational tone.

Practice telling the story until your words and facial expressions appear natural. In an interview, your ability to retrieve information quickly is important. It'll boost your confidence and surprise the interviewer who'll expect the usual period of silence while inadequately prepared candidates contrive their answer.

Your ability to rapidly recall the details of a story affects whether you'll get an offer and if you'll be invited back. I recently watched a VP sales candidate crash and burn during an interview. While his answers were perfect and naturally delivered, he paused for 3 or 4 seconds before he answered each question. In an interview, that's a long time. For every moment an employer watches you think, you lose credibility. You need to be prepared to speak within one short breath after they stop talking. The employer must see you as "all together."

Interviews aren't real life. Everyone knows that, but it won't stop the interviewer from forming a real-life opinion on your candidacy. You can know your job better than anyone in the world, but if you freeze during the interview process, the interviewer isn't likely to care. If you can't just naturally "flick a switch" and perform like a Hollywood actor, you'll need to rehearse with the zeal of a drill sergeant. If you practice long enough, you, too, can deliver an Oscar-winning performance.

GUERRILLA INTELLIGENCE

Tales from the Trenches
Kevin Watson

Few hiring managers interview well. A manager may hire as many as 100 people in his lifetime or, put another way, spend a total of 400 hours of effort. Compare this with the 6,000 hours that he will spend at lunch, and it is obvious to see why so little emphasis is put on doing hiring correctly and why training is virtually nonexistent.

Recently, I had a headhunter phone to ask if I would be interested in looking at an opportunity. I received a link to their web site containing the job requirements and skill set required. It was a perfect fit!

So with all the appropriate preparation and an updated resume, I proceed to the interview. At the start of the interview, they asked if I had any questions. What questions could I have? The company is well known within the community, the balance sheet is fantastic, and I had a complete list of the skills and requirements for that position.

The interview proceeded as planned (both on their side and mine). I was to the point for every question asked. I gave specific examples to show I possessed all the skills they needed [based on the job description I had received]. As the interview wound up, I was confident that I proved to them I could manage and lead a development team.

There was only one problem. The job posted on the web site was already filled. The company had decided to split the original position into 2 positions. They had filled the position posted on the Web but never bothered to update the original job description.

I had interviewed for the wrong position!

It hit me like a 2 × 4 across the head. Most interviews are full of nonspecific questions that are designed to act like an atomic accelerator—shooting high-speed electrons at atoms to see what falls out. Would I have conducted any other business meeting that way? Would a salesman sit in front of a customer and explain to them the feature set of a product without first asking what they were trying to use the product for?

If the interview was approached like any other business meeting, the outcome would be quite different. First, the meeting would start by listing the requirements followed by solutions that fit the problem trying to be addressed. In my case, if I would have gone to the white board and ask these simple questions (and written the answers to them):

➤ What is the goal of this position?
➤ What are the responsibilities of this position?
➤ What do you hope this person will accomplish in this role?

(continued)

> ➤ Is this a new position? If no, what did the previous person do really well and what did that person do really poorly?

> ➤ How do you know if a person is successful in this position?

> ➤ What is the reporting structure—what about the "dotted lines?"

> ➤ Are there any direct reports? Does one of them want this position?

As the questions and answers begin to fill the white board, you now have a structure in which you can hang your experiences. If done correctly, your "white board" resume will fit exactly their specific requirements. Doing this at the start of the interview would have told me what position I was applying for and would have made me look like a leader rather than a follower.

_____

Kevin Watson, www.linkedin.com/in/kevinwatson/.

■ HOW TO ANSWER QUESTIONS

Answer questions with a 1-2 punch—a short answer followed by a long answer. For open-ended questions, I always suggest you say, "Let me give you the short version. If you need to explore some aspect more fully, I'd be happy to go into greater depth."

Answers of less than 30 seconds are generally insufficient, but answers over 3 minutes are too long. This is an important detail. In the first instance, you'll come across as light, lacking knowledge, depth, and insight—not the impression you want to be making. Long answers right off the bat, though, could brand you as being too technical or boring. You need to strike a fine balance and this 1-2 punch does it. In the end, a question like, "What was your most difficult assignment or biggest accomplishment?" might take anywhere from 30 seconds to 30 minutes depending on the detail—but let the interviewer draw the details out of you.

Always remember that the interviewer is the one who asked the question. Tailor your answer to what the person needs to know without a lot of extraneous rambling or superfluous explanation. Why give a sermon when a short prayer will do?

➤ Preparing for Typical Interview Questions

The interview isn't just about your stories. Beyond the purely technical questions specific to each job, I have listed the typical questions
interviewers ask. These are behavior-based interview (BBI) questions.
If BBI is new to you, don't panic. It was designed to reduce hiring
errors by focusing on a job hunter's past experience and behaviors instead of relying on an interviewer's gut-level decision-making ability.
BBI questions actually focus on the core components of your accomplishments. That's good for you.

If you have experience with traditional interviewing techniques,
you'll find the BBI different in several ways:

➤ The interview will be structured to concentrate on areas that
are important to the interviewer, instead of allowing you to concentrate on areas that you think are important. (The T-account
exercise and a thorough understanding of the job description will
give you all the clues you need.)

➤ Rather than asking how you *would behave* in a particular situation, the interviewer will ask you to describe how you *did behave*
in a similar situation.

➤ The interviewer will drill you for details. You'll have no time to
speculate. (Now you know why we've spent so much time detailing
your accomplishments.)

If you prepare reasonable answers to the following questions,
you'll be well on your way to acing your interview, no matter who
is conducting it.

Strengths

➤ What key factors have accounted for your career success to
date?

➤ What do you consider to be some of your most outstanding
qualities?

➤ What is your greatest strength or asset?

➤ In what areas have others been particularly complimentary
about your abilities? Why?

➤ During past performance reviews, what have been consistently cited as your major assets? Why?

➤ From a performance standpoint, what do you consider your
major attributes?

Weaknesses

➤ What aspects of your current position could be better performed, and what kind of improvement could you make?

➤ If we asked 2 or 3 of your peers who know you well to be somewhat critical of your performance, what 2 or 3 improvement areas would they likely identify? Why?

➤ If you could, what 2 things would you most like to change about yourself to improve your overall effectiveness—and why?

Job Performance

➤ What have been your last 3 performance evaluation ratings? Why?

➤ In what areas does your performance excel?

➤ Why, in your judgment, are certain businesses successful?

➤ In your judgment, what factors account for most business failures?

Personal Style

➤ What kind of operating style do you feel is not conducive to good performance? Why?

➤ What basic values and beliefs do you feel are important to good performance?

➤ How would you categorize the traits and attributes of a good manager? Why are these important?

Management Skills

➤ What are some of the techniques you use to motivate poor performers?

➤ Give me some examples of how you have used these techniques.

➤ What results did you get?

➤ How could these have been improved?

➤ What is the toughest decision you have had to make as a manager?

Communication Skills

➤ Give me an example of a complex communications problem that you faced.

➤ What made it complex?

➤ Why was it difficult to communicate?

➤ How did you solve this problem? Why?

➤ How might you have further improved the communications?

Integrity

➤ If you caught one of your most valued employees doing something dishonest, what would you do?

Assertiveness

➤ If your boss told you that you had a "stupid idea," but you knew it was a very good one, what would you do?

Risk

➤ What factors most influence your willingness to take a risk?

Analytical Skills

➤ What is, perhaps, the most complex business analysis you have had to make?

➤ What factors made it complex?

➤ How did you tackle this task?

➤ How did your result reflect the effectiveness of your analytical abilities?

Perseverance

➤ Describe a work situation where you knew you were right, but the odds of winning were such that you felt you had to abandon your position?

➤ What odds did you face?

➤ How great was the resistance?

➤ What approaches did you use?

➤ What factors persuaded you to abandon your position?

How did you do? I can't overemphasize the need to practice your answers to these questions. If you can, you should rehearse with a nonjudgmental friend. If you don't have any friends, rehearse in front of a mirror with a tape recorder. (Make a mental note to acquire some friends in the future.)

Ask and answer the questions one-by-one, and when you're finished, watch or listen to the tape. Do you sound confident? Are your answers complete? Would you hire you? Last, did you notice your facial expressions? Did you look happy, relaxed, and natural; or did you look like someone who needed to pass gas? Practice, practice, practice—until you feel confident and look terrific.

➤ How to Answer the "F" Question

If you where fired from your last job, you should expect to be asked why. What are you going to tell them? The truth! How you tell them is the important point. Use truthful, positive information to put yourself in a favorable light—and modestly explain what you learned from the experience. Outline the steps you've taken to upgrade your skills or change your behavior to ensure it won't happen again. If it was a personality issue, then briefly state the following, "I'm open to working overtime but can't work 70 hours a week." They'll conclude your former boss was a slave driver without your having to say so. If you don't make a big deal over it, neither will they.

➤ How to Answer the "L" Question

Many people have been answering this question lately. Layoffs happen all the time. It's a fact of modern-day life. It's not personal, so don't take it that way. Explain in 30 seconds or less how it came to be and why you where chosen: seniority, geography, nepotism, whatever the case. If the company went through 7 layoffs and you were in the last round, that's positive news you should impart. Practice describing your situation from the employer's viewpoint. Work through any feelings of anger or bitterness beforehand. You'll score points for professionalism.

■ DRESS FOR EXCELLENCE

I don't care how many times you've read "dress like the interviewers," it's wrong. You dress in the best clothes you have, no exceptions. Guys, there are only 2 colors when it comes to suits: navy blue and charcoal gray. Shoes are black with matching black socks (if you wear white socks, I'll find out and personally hunt you down). If you have body art, you should cover it.

Women should wear conservative business attire, appropriately buttoned. Perfume and jewelry should be kept to a minimum (only one pair of earrings).

A WAR STORY

Shari Miller

I had a candidate who lived in Fresno, California, and worked at a small family company—a very laid-back working atmosphere. He was going to be interviewing for a director of MIS for one of Sacramento's largest food chain stores. After the interview process was over, I found out just how much he really wanted the position. He was very self-conscious about his appearance. He was afraid they would think him too old (if I remember correctly, he was only in his late 30s) because he was prematurely gray. He also wore his hair in a ponytail. He had his hair cut and dyed, spent time in a tanning booth to look younger, more with it. He bought a corset to look slimmer than he actually was.

He also worried about what people would think if they saw him pull into the parking lot at corporate headquarters in his old junker, which would be spewing smoke after making the 3-hour drive from Fresno to Sacramento—so he rented a Lincoln Town Car. Looking like Fresno's version of George Hamilton, he arrived in Sacramento for the interview with his new hairdo, his nails manicured, looking trim and thinner, and wearing an Armani suit his wife had found at the Veterans' Thrift Store (if you can believe that). He was ready to show Sacramento what a farm boy from Fresno was all about. He was the forerunner to Extreme Makeover.

Shari Miller, deceased.

■ HOW TO RECRUIT AN INSIDE ADVOCATE

During your research, I hope you found the phone number of the interviewer's executive assistant. If not, call and get it now because the day before the interview you're going to recruit that person onto your team. Here's how to recruit your interviewer's most trusted confidant: the day before the interview, call the assistant and say:

> *Hello my name is [your name goes here] and tomorrow at [the time for the interview goes here] I am scheduled to meet with [the interviewer's full name goes here]. I just wanted to call and ensure that [interviewer's first name goes here] schedule is still intact.*

Wait while the assistant verifies it is. Thank the person and hang up the telephone. Making this call telegraphs the assistant 2 key subliminal messages that work in your favor:

1. You value your time.
2. You value their time.

Guerrilla, how many people do you seriously think would risk making that call? Not many. In my experience, candidates never confirm an interview once it's set up. By calling to confirm you indicate the interview is not the most important thing you'll do that day. What do you think that does to your leverage it increases it?

In sales school, rookies are taught to never confirm an appointment once it's set because it gives the other person an opportunity to back out. What they neglect to point out is that by risking rejection, you can actually strengthen your position. The other person assumes, "This guy must really be important." This enables you to walk into the meeting with confidence. This has never backfired on me.

Moreover, tomorrow the only person the interviewer's assistant will remember is you. You are likely the only person who has ever called to confirm. That speaks volumes about your self-esteem. To the assistant, your simple gesture is indicative of how professionally you'll interact with them if hired. Personal assistants, secretaries, and receptionists can have enormous influence on your success. Be rude even once and you'll torpedo your chances.

■ THE ABSOLUTE LAST THING YOU DO BEFORE BED

It is often the simple questions that trip people up, so before you turn in for the night, review your answers to the following 2 questions:

1. Why do you want this job?
2. Why do you want to leave your present company, or why did they leave you?

Most candidates stumble on those basic questions. Don't be caught speechless!

■ GAME DAY

What most candidates don't realize is that the job is already theirs. Guerrilla, the interviewer is seeing you because he (or she) wants to hire you. He has a problem you can solve and he acknowledged as much the second he agreed to an interview. The issue now is to convince him that he's not making a mistake. Essentially, it's up to you not to drop the ball.

The first few seconds will set the tone for the interview, so look the interviewer straight in the eye, smile, and say, "I've been looking forward to meeting you." If he asks why, go for it. The game's on and you have the ball. Most employers want "can do," "will do" employees. Start your meeting off like any other business meeting by laying out why you're there. Don't waste time with the idle chitchat about the weather or the "big game" last night. The employer will be grateful.

In order of importance, an employer will consider the following factors at a first interview:

1. Character
2. Relevant accomplishments
3. Drive
4. Initiative
5. Communication skills

Throughout the meeting, the interviewer will be determining whether you have what he needs, not only through your stories but also through your body language. Yes, body language.

■ THE SCIENCE OF BODY LANGUAGE

Sixty-five percent of all communication is nonverbal. There has been a lot of hullabaloo on the science of body language and its value in job interviews. What your gestures "say" about you could make a difference in your interview success. For example, are you lying when you tug at your ear or is your ear just itchy at the wrong time? A trained professional will know the difference. Your interviewer is probably not a trained professional, but many interviewers think they can read body language. I've read many of the books on the subject and few agree on what means what, so let me give you a quick primer on the subject. I promise this won't require a personality makeover.

Interviewing can make people nervous—on both sides of the desk. The interviewer has an hour or less to decide if she ever wants to see you again. Generally speaking, a blind date isn't this stressful. You want to put your best foot forward and appear to be the kind of person you really are, even when you're nervous:

➤ Relax and be yourself. Just be more polite!

➤ Offer a firm handshake. In the United States, 3 pumps up and down is sufficient.

➤ Maintain eye contact when you're talking, but don't stare. Focus on the interviewer's nose if direct eye contact bothers you. Avoid looking down into your lap.

➤ Sit facing the interviewer, not off to the side.

➤ Lean slightly forward and look attentive. It indicates you're interested in what the person is saying.

➤ Keep your hands out of your pockets and away from your face—especially your nose! Excessive gesticulation is distracting.

➤ Keep your 2 feet planted squarely on the ground. Crossing your legs may be misinterpreted as a "defensive move" and that you have something to hide.

If you can remember these points, you're covered in the body language department. If you forget some of this advice, don't panic. Focus on the interview: the minutia is not as critical as many of these books would have you believe. Oh yes, I almost forgot, tell the truth and your body language won't give you away.

■ YOUR GUERRILLA INTERVIEW STRATEGY

Your mission: to impress interviewers so much they handcuff you to the desk for fear you'll escape. Don't laugh! It could happen.

Not that long ago, I was interviewing with a client who was particularly impressed with the candidate I'd recruited. It had been a long and difficult project because of the rare skill set we were looking for, but the interview was going as planned. At one point, the president became so excited he dragged his 4 vice presidents in to meet the candidate as well. The interview ran for 6 hours—well past the allotted time. We had to order in lunch for the 7 of us. In the end, we only let the candidate go home after he promised to review our offer with his wife that night and call us first thing in the morning. (Yes, he signed on.)

This candidate understood the number one guerrilla job-hunting tactic and how to use it. Unusual? Yes! Rare? No. Similar events have transpired many times during my 22 years of recruiting. Okay, never with handcuffs—but you get the idea.

➤ Your Number One Tactic

Sell first. Buy later. Here's what I mean. No matter how much research you've done, no matter how eminently qualified you are, no matter how great the width of your smile, your first objective is to get them to like and want to hire you. In the beginning, it's not about you—it's about them. Your mission is to sell-sell-sell. Even if you've never sold a thing in your life, you can do this. Once they're sold on you—you get to buy while they sell-sell-sell. Let me explain.

Interviews have 3 distinct stages. During the first 2 stages, you sell. During the third, you turn the tables and make them sell you. Here's how the interview should unfold.

Stage 1: The Warm-Up

The warm-up general discussion is designed to get to know you. Let the interviewer lead. If he asks you the time-honored opening question, "Tell me about yourself," there's only one way to respond: "Where would you like me to begin? Where should I start?" By using this method, you subtly telegraph that your thoughts are well organized, and you want to understand the intent of the question. Be prepared to jump into your primary reason for being there. They have a need you can satisfy. Ply them with stories and analogies but don't be overbearing.

They'll question you about the specifics of those jobs that interest them. The more time they spend on a subject, the more relevant it is to the position, so don't be too quick to move the discussion to your interests. You're not running the show, they are—for now.

Listen carefully to the interviewers and be direct. Bring your success stories forward. By focusing on results, you demonstrate how you can make them money, save them money, and so on. Ensure that you're answering their questions completely. Ask, "Is there anything else you'd like to know about this?" or "Does that answer your question?" to make sure that you have delivered the details they need. Ask questions that are on topic and in line with theirs. Ask for clarification if you don't understand a question or need more details.

Stage 2: Detailed Discussion of Qualifications

This stage involves an in-depth technical discussion of your key skills as they apply to the position. Demonstrate your current industry knowledge by talking about their business, market position, and any new products their competitors have rolled out.

Many interviewers don't know how to interview to get the information they need to make a hiring decision. Guerrilla, it's your responsibility to ensure they get it. To take the lead tactfully, ask some "how" questions that will steer the conversation toward the strengths you want to emphasize:

➤ How has XYZ affected [insert pertinent area of company]?

➤ How are you dealing with [insert pertinent topic]?

➤ How do you think XYZ will affect the industry over the long term?

Be prepared to answer this question yourself and engage the interviewer in conversation. Prepare 3 "how" questions before you go. You don't have to agree with the interviewer's opinion but you do have to listen. Some interviewers will challenge you just to test the depth of your character. Have your facts ready and be prepared to drill down to the tactical level to explain the Who, What, Where, When, Why, and How of your major accomplishments. By discussing how they relate directly to the position, you demonstrate your ability to hit the ground running.

If the interviewer says something outrageous, bring the discussion back on track by saying, "That's interesting." Or "I hadn't thought of that," and then ask another question. Don't get into an argument.

I recently watched a candidate lose a job offer because he got into an argument with the president over a minor technical issue that wasn't even germane to the technology. In the ensuing moments, the candidate aptly demonstrated that he was not open to new ideas or anyone else's opinion. He answered the employer's biggest concern without being asked directly. They continued their search and hired someone else a month later.

Don't let that happen to you—even if you're right—you're wrong. By the way, the candidate was right, in terms of the technology discussed, but he approached the tête-à-tête as an absolute authority. In this case, my client wanted a leader, not a dictator. Not 15 minutes earlier, the candidate had been emphasizing his inclusive leadership style. The moral of the story: be ready to be tested.

Stage 3: Closing Discussion

Finally, after the interviewer has interrogated you and is satisfied that you're the real deal, he'll politely ask if you have any questions. He'll assume he's already answered them during the interview and won't expect any. This moment of truth separates the winners from the losers, so to speak. Asking the right questions will lead the employer to the inevitable conclusion that you're the right candidate.

■ TAKING CHARGE OF THE INTERVIEW

Your personal question period is an important event. It gives you a final opportunity to separate yourself from the pack. Here's where your copious research comes into play. When someone asks us deep, thoughtful questions, we think the person is smart and important, don't we? Think about this for a minute. You can turn this behavior into a strategy to create demand for you. If your interview didn't go very well or was only so-so, this is where you can make up ground and overtake your competition. If it went as well as I expect it will, here's where you ensure that *you* get the offer.

➤ Becoming Their Top Choice

By asking the right questions, you can learn the company's real weaknesses and map them to your accomplishments right in front of the interviewers. It's a curious thing, to watch employers start nodding their heads. When you see telltale side-to-side head movements, don't panic. It doesn't mean no. It means, "Yes." It signifies, "I can't believe this guy understands my problems." The interviewer is thinking, "I should have been selling this guy. Here he's been assessing me the whole time. I can't let this one get away!" Now watch the interviewer start to sell you and sell you hard. He's now handed control over to you. Once you are at this point, ask all your questions and carefully drill down on the answers.

Questions Designed to Separate You from the Pack

➤ *Can you explain to me how your business philosophy has changed/evolved over the past 5 years?* How does this compare to your competitor "X"? Their answer tells you what the company values most. It will tell you whether the company is product or market driven and where its weaknesses lie. If the company hasn't changed in 5 years, it is either a runaway success or blind: either way, your opportunity to make a real impact could be minimal.

➤ *How does the company deal with the inherent conflicts between quality and the timely delivery of new products?* This tells you how realistic the company is and whether its alpha- and beta-testing processes are well run. It also gives you insight into how the different departments operate. Anything less than total co-operation between kingdoms is a recipe for disaster—everyone works on "Internet time" now.

➤ *What industries or outside influences affect the company's growth?* This tells you how the company minimizes the downside and maximizes the upside. Many external influences can impact a company's success. A smart company will be able to recognize these external influences and leverage them.

➤ *What are 5 major short- and long-range goals and objectives?* How are success and progress being measured? How is the company doing against these metrics? This defines the company's vision and underscores its grasp of the market. Do you think it is geared for the long run and has the financial muscle to accomplish its goals? Is the product/service really spectacular or just average? How can your experience help the company achieve its goals?

➤ *From an overall effectiveness standpoint, what might improve or enhance the company's competitiveness?* This tells you whether the company knows its weaknesses; if it doesn't, it is headed for trouble. How do your strengths and interests play into this? Can you really contribute?

➤ *What are 2 or 3 characteristics that your company feels are unique to your company?* This tells you what kind of people the company attracts. This is a trick question: if the company hires no one but high-energy, motivated, positive people, it could be headed for trouble. A company needs people whose opinions conflict, especially on major issues like new markets or services.

➤ *What are the 3 main functional tasks of this position?* This tells you about the core responsibilities of the position. You need to make certain you have the authority to complete your mandate.

➤ *In what stage of the buying cycle is your product/service?* This tells you whether it's an early adaptor product/service or if it is seeing its sunset. Your ability to sell (if that's what you do) in a missionary role—to convert the nonbelievers—could be critical to the success of this company. If you like to build new products and play with state-of-the-art tools, a sunset firm will be dull and you'll soon be looking again.

➤ *What is your debt-to-equity ratio?* If they are a public company, this information is available in the annual report. Odd question, you might think, but in reality any company with a debt-to-equity ratio more than 3:1 could experience difficulty raising cash to launch a new product, no matter how hot the market. The dot-com bust proved that.

Like a good lawyer, you need to know the answers to these questions yourself. Your questions should lead the interviewer to focus on those areas that demonstrate your strengths.

The Killer Question

Here's how to leverage every interview you're on and get 5 more interviews. Ask this question during your interview:

"Ms. Smith, in my research I found the following competitors [name up to 5]. Can you please tell me what they're doing that keeps your executive team up at night?"

Why do you ask this? You're giving the interviewer the opportunity to brag first and then confess her concerns so that you:

➤ Can assess how you can best help them achieve their goals.

➤ You have the data points you need on their competitors to immediately turn approach them for a job as soon as you're finished with that interview.

Very guerrilla shocked? Look at it this way. Maybe they'll hire you. Maybe they won't. This is just a preliminary business meeting with no guarantees on either side, but the interviewer is definitely going to use everything you say to his or her advantage. You should do the same. If they confess their concerns with a competitor, why shouldn't you use that to your advantage? Get on the phone to the hiring managers at their competing firms and tell them, "I just came back from an interview at ABC Company and given what they told me about you and why you keep them up at night.... . I think I'd rather work for you. Can we have coffee?"

■ HOW TO ASK FOR THE JOB

The goal of every interview is to get an offer: an offer for the job or an offer to interview more. Your goal in the first interview is to be asked back. It is highly unlikely you'll be hired in one interview although I've had it happen. There are 2 closing questions—as we call them in sales—that are appropriate for your first interview:

1. Who will I meet in the second interview?

2. When would you like to schedule our next meeting?

   If you don't think the interview went well, then you'll want to try this next question. It will surface their concerns and give you an opportunity to deal with them; you just have to be brave enough to let them finish talking before you answer:

3. Is there any reason you wouldn't consider inviting me back for a second interview?

Don't interrupt and don't argue. If they have misunderstood something you said, say "I see. What gave you that impression?" Again, let them talk until you feel confident you can address their concerns.

When you book the second interview, ask the following 2 questions:

1. Are there any presentation materials I should bring?

2. Who, besides yourself, will make the final hiring decision? Will I be meeting with them as well?

At the end of the final interview, you want to ask:

➤ What challenges would you have me tackle first?

➤ Is there anything preventing you from extending an offer to me?

➤ When would you like me to start?

Throughout the interview process, you must maintain your enthusiasm for the job. Your objective is to get the offer and then think about whether you really want it. Many people mistakenly try to decide if they want the job during the interview. Big mistake! This will distract you during the interview, and your lack of focus will be apparent to the interviewer. Focus only on getting the offer.

■ CONCLUDING THE MEETING

When you're just about ready to go, ask one last question: "Is there anything else you think I should know about the company or this position?" This signals that you've finished. If they like what they've seen, they will say something to regain control. Tell them you're interested in meeting the key people you'll be working with if they think there's a good fit. Now shut up.

Go home and write them a memorable thank-you note. Use Interviewbest.com to construct a PowerPoint capturing the information you now recognize the hiring manager needs to know to hire you with confidence.

■ HOW TO HANDLE MONEY

There's only one way to handle money; defer the conversation until you know you want the job. Memorize the following line for when you're asked about salary expectations: "I like this company and I like the opportunity, but it's premature to discuss potential compensation until we've mutually agreed there's a good fit both ways. Wouldn't you agree?"

That's the only answer you need. It brands you as bright, confident, and self-assured—exactly what they want. If they come back with the old "We just want to make sure we're in the range" line, you must say, "I'm certain you'll be fair." That statement will stop them in their tracks. It accomplishes 2 goals. In their mind, it signifies money isn't the most important issue—which every employer likes to know, and it forces them to the bargaining table. You want them to get you to the table. You'll learn how to close the deal in Chapter 13.

GUERRILLA INTELLIGENCE

Soft Diligence

Steve Panyko

An essential phase of your job search is that time when you establish a cultural fit or shared values between the organization and yourself. This is the logical next step after "hard diligence" or the process of analyzing financial statements, history, and backgrounds on key players of the company.

As you go through your interview, you will seek to determine how the management team views and relates to their customers, to their employees, and to their shareholders and board of directors. These 3 directions of interaction are critical for you to understand and for you to be culturally aligned with the organization.

To determine the value placed on customers, you should ask questions like:

➤ Who is your best customer, and why?

➤ Who is your worst customer, and why?

➤ How have your customers affected your product development?

➤ How many times do you visit your customers?

The answers you get should never disparage the customer, should value the customers' input in determining product requirements, and should generally reflect a desire to meet with the customer more often than the pressures of the job currently allow. Responses outside that envelope are a red flag that the organization does not have good customer relationships and may believe they can be successful despite the customer.

Next explore the value placed on employees. First determine stability by asking average length of service, time since the last downsizing, rate of growth, and turnover rates. Once you have assessed stability, ask questions like:

➤ How often do you hold all-hands meetings?

➤ How are service anniversaries, critical accomplishments, and holidays celebrated?

➤ How do you encourage employees to participate in community projects?

➤ What emphasis is placed on training and staff development?

➤ Other than for cause, what reasons have caused employees to leave the company?

It is important that the answers to these questions portray a genuine caring for employees, the community they live in, and their families. A healthy organization has a consistent track record of growth and is obsessed with employee development. The latter should be referenced to company policy and not be a matter of one manager's attitude.

Finally, you need to assess the value the management team and the organization place on their stakeholders (shareholders

(continued)

and the board of directors). Probe how frequently the board of directors have toured the facility or seen product demos. Determine whether the board or investors have helped develop new business or champion new market opportunities. Look for contentious attitudes toward either investors or the board of directors. Ask questions like:

➤ In this position, will I have an opportunity to meet the board, and if so, what will they be interested in learning about me as a part of the organization?

➤ Does your sales and marketing organization view investors as a strategic partner in opening new markets?

➤ Has there been turnover on the board of directors, and if so, why?

These questions should paint the picture of the management team, staff, and investors all aligned to grow the business and learn from the marketplace. They should proudly discuss strategic relationships or distribution partnerships that have been co-developed with investors or members of the board of directors. If your responses portray isolation from stakeholders, be cautious about both the stability of the management team and their openness to utilize outside resources to help develop and grow the business.

Most people do a good job of assessing the "hard data" associated with the organization where they are seeking employment, and other parts of this book talk about how to use modern tools to perform this hard diligence. Do not underestimate the importance of "soft diligence." You must be comfortable that your values and attitudes toward customers, employees, and stakeholders are consistent with those of the managers and employees with whom you interview. If they are not, this often leads to long-term dissatisfaction with your job. If they are aligned, the opportunity for you is very real.

Steve Panyko has been a senior executive at AT&T Bell Laboratories, Motorola, Harris Corporation, and ITT. He has also been CEO of 4 private equity funded companies that he helped establish, fund, and take through successful exits. Now Steve works out of the Colorado Springs office of Perry-Martel International. www.linkedin.com/in/sfpanyko/.

■ SECOND AND THIRD INTERVIEWS

It is rare that anyone is hired on the first interview. It happens, but normally only at the most junior levels. Even presidents will want you to meet their senior executive team before making an offer, no matter how impressed they may be. No one wants to upset the delicate team dynamics they have in place. Directors, of course, will have you meet their vice president. The lower you are on the corporate hierarchy, the more likely you'll meet several people in the process.

You know that being invited back for second and third interviews means that the company is interested in you and you're interviewing well. Make sure you continue to sell yourself just as you did in the first interview. Don't assume the first person who interviewed you has passed on the details of that meeting.

Generally speaking, you need to ask everyone in the process the questions you asked the first interviewer. Plan your agenda so you know what you want to cover in the interview. Work on improving areas that may have been perceived as weak in the first interview. An employer's decision-making process is less rational than you might think. You want everyone you meet to like you. Once you've made it into the "acceptable" category, getting the offer is a matter of fit. Make sure you get a business card from everyone you meet. Thank-you notes need to go to each interviewer separately.

Tips for Other Types of Interviews

➤   *Telephone interviews:* Phone interviews are used to screen candidates out—not in! The screener's job is to decide whether you warrant an in-person interview. Your job is to convince them you do by sounding enthusiastic. Screeners don't necessarily know what the job entails and may not care by the time they get to you on their list. It is your responsibility to tell them how your skills and accomplishments fit the requirements.

When someone calls you to do a telephone interview, make sure you can actually take the call. If you can't speak at the moment, tell the caller and arrange for a time to return the call, or ask for a minute to walk into a conference room and change phones. Very few people will refuse you this time, and it could make the difference between receiving a so-so or a superstar rating. Take a few minutes to get ready by reading your resume and reviewing the company's ad.

➤   *Board or group interviews:* If you're faced with a panel of interviewers, the first thing you want to do is to walk to the end of the table and shake each of their hands and ask each participant for a business card. When you sit down, lay the cards out on the table so that each card faces its owner. When you begin to answer questions, you can address them by name. This will impress the interviewers and build your confidence.

When asked a question, look directly at the questioner when answering. Don't worry about the rest of the panel. If multiple people ask you questions at the same time, answer the first one completely before moving to the next. It is quite all right to ask the speaker to please repeat a question. Be genuine and relaxed, especially if you sense they are trying to irritate you. They may try to see how you react under pressure.

Chapter 13

Negotiating the Deal

How to Bargain with Confidence

> The worst thing you can possibly do in a deal is seem desperate to make it. That makes the other guy smell blood, and then you're dead. The best thing you can do is deal from strength, and leverage is the biggest strength you can have. Leverage is having something the other guy wants. Or better yet, needs. Or best of all, simply can't do without.
>
> —Donald J. Trump, *Trump: The Art of the Deal*

Congratulations. You've been through all the interviews. You like the organization and the job—it's a good fit. The organization likes you, too, and offers you the position, so now what? How do you make sure you get the best deal possible?

Guerrilla, you've been setting up the close from the first moment you walked into the employer's office. You looked sharp, acted smart, and came off as self-assured by not talking about compensation—a real "A+ Player." Carry that same behavior into the negotiations. Candidates who net the best results approach the negotiation process with a blend of positive attitude and preparation.

The information in this chapter is important to your financial well-being, whether you are an individual contributor or a senior executive. Some of the entitlements and strategies may not apply to your current situation, but the strategies and tactics are valid for every new hire. As you go through the chapter, think about how you can apply these techniques.

■ PROJECT A WINNING ATTITUDE

Unlike many business deals that are short-lived and transactional in nature, employment negotiations are relationship driven and can last a lifetime. It may be acceptable to thump your fist on the desk to gain a concession buying a car because you're not likely to see the salesperson again; however, you'll likely see the employer's negotiator every morning at the water cooler. You may get a small special consideration, but at what cost—being labeled a horse's ass? The uncompromising aloofness of a candidate who doesn't give a damn bespeaks such a wealth of self-confidence that the client may figure there's something to it, but if you don't deliver, you'll be dispatched with equal indifference.

In negotiations, flashy, bold, or arrogant behavior is a detriment. Approach the negotiations instead with detached enthusiasm coupled with the ability to walk away. If any old offer is acceptable, you have nothing to negotiate—but you must negotiate because you risk alienating the employer if you don't. After all, it's no fun for the fisherman when the fish jumps into the boat.

You don't want to appear so excited that they offer you less than top dollar. Conversely, don't run them off by appearing indifferent. As a headhunter, I never worry about the brash, ego-driven candidates—they're easy to close—it's the quiet ones I have to keep an eye on. Your leverage rests with your confidence in your ability to do the job. You don't need to sell. The employer must sell you. But first, you need to understand what you're buying.

■ PREPARING FOR THE OFFER AND NEGOTIATIONS

Research equates to power. That's absolutely the case now. Before you receive an offer, you need to create a checklist of your needs and expectations. Guerrilla, if you don't plan like this, you may find that in the rush and excitement of accepting the position, you forgot or missed important elements. Winning at this stage requires you to look beyond salary and deal with the complete package.

■ NEGOTIATE YOUR POWER BEFORE YOUR PAY

This may seem at first a little backward. Doesn't your title determine your salary? Well, actually, no. It's the depth of your responsibilities that determines how much an employer is willing to pay you. The greater your level of responsibility, the richer your pay packet. Therefore, it's in your best interest to negotiate your duties and responsibilities before tackling compensation. You and the employer must have the same understanding of your responsibilities and the specific performance standards that gauge your success.

Performance standards must be observable and measurable; they can't be subjective or your performance becomes open to interpretation, making your bonus subjective as well.

For example, a subjective clause in a contract might read, "Increase sales." An objective statement would read, "Increase sales by 15 percent in 12 months." Only the second clause can be measured.

If during the interview process you agree to shoulder more responsibility than the employer originally envisioned, document it at the time, so that when you negotiate compensation, you can both make an apples-to-apples comparison. By supersizing the responsibilities of the job (do you want fries with that?), you push compensation upward. The easiest way to negotiate the salary you want is to increase the responsibilities of the job. You must document the following:

➤ Title
➤ Reporting structure
➤ Authority
➤ Accountability
➤ Number of direct staff
➤ Specific performance standards
➤ Committee responsibilities if any

Any increase in authority or responsibility *that you can document* will amplify your compensation package. If the increase in responsibility is not documented and the "job description" stays the same, there's no justification to raise your salary. You and the employer need to have the same view of the position's scope before the offer is made. Your initial strategy is to increase the compensation package in light of the increased responsibility. That way, the employer's first offer is already inflated and probably closer to an acceptable level, requiring only minimum negotiation.

Once you have the details of the job finalized, it's up to the employer to come back to you with a reasonable offer. You have 2 choices here. You can either tell the employer exactly what it will take to close the deal or you can let him make an offer. After investing this much time in interviewing and negotiating, most employers will come back with a reasonable offer because they don't want to repeat the process with someone else. By the time it gets to this point, the employer already has a pretty good idea of what the market is paying for this position and what the company can afford. As a headhunter, my strategy is to aim for the absolute top dollar and settle a few bucks below. It's in your best interest to let employers think they've won. This shows that you are flexible.

> ### Establishing Your Bottom Line

Do you know what your bottom-line salary must be? "More" isn't a number. Most people have an idea of what they would "kinda like to make," but rarely do people know exactly what they need. Fewer still know what they want prior to the offer. Failure to establish your bottom line may place your current lifestyle at risk or at the very least leave money on the table. It's important to know those details but it's even more important not to tell the employer. Ideally, you want to start negotiating well above your minimum amount and if all goes well, never approach it. Guerrillas won't wait until the last possible moment; they'll tally up the cost of their lifestyle well in advance of the employer's first offer.

All employers think about salaries in ranges of high and low. Many subscribe to salary surveys. You can find out the inside skinny on thousands of companies—free—by going to Glassdoor.com. Your future employer's industry association will likely have a salary survey, too; pick up the phone and ask. If you can't get access to it, then do your own. Call their competitors. You'd be surprised how much information you can get from a human resources department if you tell them you are a researcher—which you are. Appendix 3 provides a detailed list for researching compensation requirements.

> ### Negotiating Benefits

Compensation is more than just your base salary, but employers will be focused primarily on the base salary because it's a fixed cost and in some cases, such as insurance, it determines the cost of other benefits. From your viewpoint, though, almost everything you don't have to pay for directly is money in your pocket.

Maybe you noticed that I did not list a cell phone as a benefit in Appendix 3. Companies will try to tell you it's a benefit; in reality it's an electronic dog collar. Many of the newer phones have geographic information systems (GIS) positioning technology making it too easy to track you down—via satellite—on your day off. Ask for a monthly allowance instead.

➤ Tuition Forgiveness

This is not the same as an education allowance. Tuition forgiveness deals with the money you already invested in your education. For example, you may have financed an advanced degree in nursing, and now each month you have a student loan just as you might have a loan for a car or house. If you're in a "hot area" like IT security or nuclear medicine, you may be able to get the employer to assume your education mortgage.

Now's the time to stop reading and turn to Appendix 3, if you haven't already. Take a hard look for any items you currently pay that you could switch over and have the employer cover. Insurance programs can be very costly and you pay for them with after-tax dollars—double ouch. The employer will gladly provide extra benefits if he thinks that you will accept a lower salary. Let him reason that way for now.

Remember, benefits are great, but they're not spendable dollars. You maximize your cash flow by having the employer pay for your benefits. Always maximize the employer's portion of the coverage because you're not taxed on benefits. Well, okay—in Canada benefits may be taxed; but in the United States, you're taxed on your gross salary, not your total package including benefits. Frequent flyer miles are the only exception; if the company gives them to you and you use them, the IRS will tax you.

Look at the list in Appendix 3, determine what you have now, and how much each item costs. What benefits can you reasonably expect the employer to pay for? What would you like them to pay for? Make a list now so you know what you're going to be negotiating for and the monetary value of each item.

Using a checklist ensures you won't have regrets later. It also demonstrates your business savvy. Be alert, employers may try to trick you by focusing on your "total compensation" instead of your salary. Instead of focusing on the $40,000 salary, the employer will try to sell you on the $52,000 package (base + benefits). In most employee/employer negotiation schemes, it's to the employer's advantage to load up the benefits component to lower base salary. Of course, guerrilla, you'll be prepared to counteract this. You want the highest possible salary and great benefits, too.

■ YOUR STRATEGY

Take the lead. Do not make the mistake of letting the employer define the issues for you. You must negotiate salary last. Why? Simple, the employer will be focused on the big number—your salary—to the exclusion of all else. We want to nibble—just a little—and then a little more. Talking about the little items first will earn you a string of rapid concessions on items like insurance, professional fees, and vacation. If the employer wants to be the hero on the salary front, who are you to deny them? A true winner gives wins away, so let them feel like they're winning. For the time being, focus on increasing the value of your benefits by 50 to 100 percent. It's still money for you and there's no ego involved in their giving away benefits.

If you are relocating and you already own a home, make sure you don't get stuck with two. Have a clause put in the employment agreement that states in effect that you'll endeavor to sell your house but if after 2 months the house is not sold at fair market value, the company is responsible for buying the former home outright or paying your mortgage until such time as the house is sold. This is one of those benefits you want to think about from the outset but only table as an "afterthought" just as you're reaching to sign the employment agreement. Essentially, you need to have all the other points of the agreement in writing before you try this. Don't worry, you're not going to shock the employer; they were just holding their breath hoping you wouldn't bring it up. Shame on you if they succeed.

On several occasions, I've needed to go above and beyond even this. I have gone so far as to negotiate the moving of a director's wine collection from France. In another case, we bought a manager a home and moved his daughter's horse.

Nothing, it seems, is beyond reason as long as the employer is convinced the company needs you. Remember, though, parity is important in an organization and some of the things you request may be denied because they would shake up the organization's existing compensation ranges and structures. If this is the case, don't push further—the organization isn't likely to budge and you will lose.

■ THE PSYCHOLOGY OF THE DEAL

After several go-rounds on benefits, you'll likely be close to settling in to negotiate salary. When you think that time has come, you may want to raise the following issues as much for the opportunity to secure them as to give them away:

➤ Signing bonus
➤ Severance
➤ Earlier-than-scheduled compensation review
➤ Guaranteed minimum first-year bonus

How you deal in the final negotiations will be a telltale sign for the employer on how well you will negotiate for the company. This is especially important if you are seeking a purchasing, marketing, or sales position. You don't want to cave, but you do want to be seen as being logical in your rationale and considerate of their position.

Throughout the negotiations, you may hear comments or questions like the following and you need to be prepared to deal with them in a logical and matter-of-fact style:

➤ If we make you this offer, will you accept it right now?
➤ What will it take for you to accept the offer?

➤ What other way can we structure this deal so that it would be acceptable?

➤ What do you think is fair-market compensation for someone like you in this city?

➤ How low can you go on each dimension of the compensation package?

My advice is to remain cool and stick to your agenda. An employer who is asking you these questions is trying to close you. The "psychology of the deal" dictates that you *never* accept an offer on the spot. If you say yes immediately, it weakens your position now and in the future. Always ask for a day to think about it even if you're ready to sign. You may want to use phrases like:

➤ I'm very interested in joining your team, and I'd like the night to think it over. Is that okay with you?

➤ I'm very interested in joining your team, and I'd like the night to discuss the details with my spouse. Do you mind? (This is especially relevant if it requires relocation.)

Your uncommon courtesy will buy you the night—or longer—to mull over the details and ensure you haven't missed anything.

■ BREAKING AN IMPASSE

When negotiations come to an impasse, and they always do, it's your responsibility to continue driving the deal. Be prepared to ask questions and keep the negotiations alive and moving forward. Asking the following demonstrates your sincere interest in coming to an agreeable offer:

➤ What flexibility do you have on: salary, signing bonus, annual bonus, or anything else?

➤ How about considering other dimensions of the package, beyond annual salary and job title? For example, signing bonus, annual bonus, vacation, retirement plan, and equity.

➤ What other differently structured compensation packages can you offer?

■ NAVIGATING THE GAUNTLET

Most people are reluctant to negotiate because they either feel greedy or have a hard time asserting themselves. Yet, these same people are quite effective when acting on behalf of their company. Guerrilla, if this describes you, it is okay. Your remedy is at hand—do it for your family. Think what a difference an extra $5, $10, or $20,000 could make in little Timmy's life. By negotiating for those you care about most, you'll negotiate a better deal. It's never just about you.

■ BODY LANGUAGE

You need to be conscious of your body language. Be aware of the messages you are sending. There are times when the negotiation can be a real grind. Don't get rattled. Don't let them see you sweat. Telegraph what you want the employer to see. If you are smiling and your palms are face up on the table, those are signs that you are open and receptive to what they are saying. If, instead, your eyebrows are furled and your fists are clenched, I have a pretty good idea what you're thinking. Drink lots of water. No coffee or alcohol. Take frequent bathroom breaks if you need to compose yourself.

■ ASK FOR A LITTLE—GET A LOT

If you are negotiating an hourly wage, remember that every dollar per hour represents $2,080 per year. Most employers like to talk salary. For salaries less than $50,000, focus the employer on the dollar per hour amount. Simplify and minimize the concession you need. For example, it's easier to get an employer to agree to an increase from $20 to $24 per hour than to get them to agree to a $48,000 salary when they budgeted $40,000. Which do you think is more palatable for the employer? Asking for $4 more per hour is nothing—$8,000 causes unnecessary headaches but it's still $8,000.

You may also run into one of the following scenarios and need to decide in advance your course of action (I have a few suggestions):

➤ The employer acts like they're doing you a favor.
➤ They appear cordial until you dig your heels in.
➤ Someone besides your future boss is doing the negotiations.

The employer wants to strike the best deal possible. All kinds of games may get played. Disarming the employer can be as easy as turning your hands palm-up on the table and saying to them, "You look a little tense, is everything all right?" That phrase will force even the most hardened negotiator to lighten up. Try it.

■ NEGOTIATE WITH THE FINAL DECISION MAKER

Before you start, make sure you understand whom you're negotiating with. Some employers use the timeshare-vacation approach. They send in the human resources manager or some junior functionary to have the preliminary discussion and isolate your hot buttons. After several hours of discussion, they suddenly need management approval. You don't want to discover at the last minute that your hard-fought concessions were all for naught and you're facing a new negotiator.

If the offer has come through a headhunter, you need to understand the recruiter's role in the negotiation. Typically, it's in his best interest to get you as much money as possible because his compensation is tied to yours. You'd be wise to gauge your recruiter's skill at negotiating before turning your life over. Many recruiters lack the depth of knowledge and breadth of skills necessary to negotiate a complete package. In some cases, he or she is more interested in closing the deal as quickly as possible. If this happens, the smart guerrilla remains firmly in the driver's seat.

Use your recruiter as a sounding board and a platform to launch trial balloons. If the employer gets agitated, it'll be with the recruiter, not you. If something goes wrong, just deny—deny—deny. The employer may step in to finish the negotiations and the recruiter will still get paid—it's all part of the game.

■ CLOSING THE OFFER

Get it in writing. Keep notes during the negotiations explaining what was agreed on. Date stamp your notes. When the final draft is completed, read it closely to make certain that the final offer reflects what you've agreed. If years down the road you notice a discrepancy, you won't be able to correct it. You get one shot at doing this right.

When the final deal is done, pay a lawyer to review the terminology of the contract or letter of employment for unforeseen pitfalls (e.g., noncompetition clauses that would force you to move to Alaska if you wanted to pursue your profession with another employer in the future). Employ the lawyer to read the terms and conditions for ambiguity only, not to renegotiate or add to the contract. Most lawyers are deal breakers not deal makers, and you don't want to kill your deal.

Finally, don't talk yourself out of a deal—know when to shut up. Once it's done, it's done. Move on quickly to another subject. I need to emphasize the importance of talking about anything but the deal once it's done. Talk about the weather or the "big game." Avoid anything that sensitive people can dispute.

GUERRILLA INTELLIGENCE

The Good, the Bad, and the Great!

Cindy Kraft

Jack and I started working together during the wind down of his CFO duties post-merger. Like many senior-level finance executives, he held a number of positions over the past 7 years and his positioning, through no fault of his own, was one of a job hopper. Added to his angst was the fact that his salary had taken numerous dives through the various moves.

Jack had set some high goals in anticipation of accepting a new position, including compensation, corporate culture, and relocating to a specific geographic area. He was resolute in his determination to make a *right* move rather than *any* move.

Jack built 2 foundational documents that served as the driving mechanisms in deciding whether or not to take the positions he was offered. The first document was value-driven. He identified his top 8 values and analyzed each position offered (including compensation and culture) against those values. The second document was a list prioritized around "must haves," "wants," and "frankly, don't care abouts" in his next role. This was his road map for entering into serious negotiations to get what he wanted.

The "must haves" list contained items he was unwilling to negotiate—they were the items that would "make or break" the deal; the "wants" list contained items he would be willing to negotiate in order to get a "must have"; and his "don't care abouts" were his ace in the hole. He put these items on the bargaining

(continued)

table and then magnanimously threw them out as he continued to negotiate in the things on his "must have" list.

Through the course of our 9-month journey, Jack received numerous offers that he turned down because they did not meet his requirements and/or his values. The decision to say no took great courage on his part as he remained firm in his desire to make the right move, not a move... despite the search taking longer than he anticipated.

With a clear and compelling value proposition, great patience, and hard work, Jack did indeed get his "right" job. He was able to relocate to his desired geographic location with the company paying his relocation costs as well as buying his house in this stalled housing market; ask for and receive the salary he desired, which was well above the salary from his previous position; and also obtain every one of his "must have" perks.

A compelling value proposition and the confidence to clearly articulating his value to prospects enabled Jack to powerfully negotiate his desired compensation... and get everything he wanted. Sweet!

Cindy Kraft, The CFO–Coach, www.cfo-coach.com, www.linkedin.com/in/cindykraft/.

■ HOW TO KILL YOUR DEAL

It goes without saying that I respect your judgment—you bought this book—but I need to caution you not to overdo it. It's easy to get caught in the euphoria of "doing the deal" when you do this type of negotiation only occasionally.

Guidelines for Successful Negotiation

➤ Don't immediately agree to the offer. You'll brand yourself as "light."

➤ Don't give ultimatums. If you adopt a take-it-or-leave-it attitude, they'll leave it.

➤ Don't be negative. Seek win-win resolutions instead; it'll disarm your opponent.

➤ Don't try to renegotiate a point that's already been agreed to. Trying to reopen a discussion once it is closed brands you as immature and may jeopardize the entire deal.

➤ Don't let the employer renegotiate anything unless you get a major concession.

➤ Don't discount the help. Let recruiters do their jobs. I once had a candidate who insisted on negotiating directly with the CEO instead of through me. The client and I wanted this guy badly and he knew it, but he never once asked about compensation. In the end, the candidate left $40,000 in base salary and $200,000 in options on the table, and that was just the initial package I'd been authorized to negotiate. The options alone turned out to be worth $1.6 million.

■ HOW TO MAXIMIZE YOUR DEAL

Here are some rules you should remember:

➤ *Focus on the package, not the salary.* Several years ago I recruited a general manager for a technology client. Our ideal candidate turned out to be unaffordable. His base salary was $60,000 above our top end. I convinced the candidate of the true potential of the technology. He took a cut in base pay in exchange for 250,000 options. It was a heck of a sales job because the options were underwater. Over a 4-year period, he drove the value of the company's stock to $72 from $2.50, netting himself a cool $16.8 million.

➤ *Only let them check your references after you've accepted the offer.* Never invest your reference's time for an offer you don't accept. You look foolish and the reference is less likely to help you the next time. Some people think it enhances their value, but that's rarely the case. Any employer who's read my booklet "Don't Hire a Liar" will know how to cut through the smoke and mirrors and get at the truth [FREE at perrymartel.com]. You have more to lose because they may find areas where you're not as strong as they thought, in which case they might lower the offer.

➤ *Measure your value against your true peers.* It never ceases to amaze me the number of people who undervalue their jobs. When you're conducting your salary survey, make sure you know what the comparative person is really responsible for. Titles by themselves are pretty meaningless. You may be a senior engineer responsible for 10 to 12 people while a similarly titled person is responsible only for herself. Should you be paid the same amount of money? Of course not. Make sure you appraise yourself fairly.

■ URBAN MYTHS

You will get a lower salary if a professional recruiter (headhunter) is involved. Wrong. In fact the opposite is more likely. Hiring managers have 2 distinct pots of money. Your wage is treated as a salary expense. The recruiter's fee comes out of a hiring budget. The two are completely separate.

The recruiter will receive a percentage of your salary for the first year. Wrong. If you are placed in a permanent position, the recruiter is paid whatever fee was agreed on with the employer up front. It does not come out of your check. As previously stated, it comes out of a different budget. You lose nothing.

GUERRILLA TIPS

➤ Expect to compromise. There are rarely absolutes; negotiating is a give-and-take on both sides. Seek win-win resolutions.

➤ Explore constraints and flexibilities. Seek to understand the employer's constraints, such as salary levels or equity positions for certain positions. Likewise, know your own constraints and flexibilities.

➤ Listen more than you speak. Listening is different from hearing. Seek to understand, not to be understood. Understand what is being said and why it is being said.

➤ Be sensible. You are looking for a relationship that ought to be equally beneficial. Recognize their constraints and requests, as you expect them to recognize yours.

➤ Offer solutions. It is your responsibility to offer solutions that can be the basis for negotiations. You know what you want. Don't make them guess continuously.

■ SUMMARY

You'd be surprised at the lengths to which some employers will go once they believe they have found their ideal candidate. It is absolutely essential to have the employer recognize your value before you begin to negotiate. If an employer understands your value and is convinced you can do the job, then the question becomes, "How much it will take to get you?" Deal from a position of strength and you might just hear Donald Trump say, "You're Hired!"

Chapter 14

Ready Aye Ready

Our deepest fear is not that we are inadequate. Our deepest fear is that we are powerful beyond measure. It is our light, not our darkness, that most frightens us. We ask ourselves, who am I to be brilliant, gorgeous, talented and fabulous? Actually, who are you not to be? You are a child of God. Your playing small doesn't serve the world. We were born to make manifest the glory of God that is within us. It's not just in some of us; it's in everyone. And as we let our own light shine, we unconsciously give other people permission to do the same. As we are liberated from our own fear, our presence automatically liberates others.

—MARIANNE WILLIAMSON

You are on the frontlines of a war—the war for talent. The first 100 days at your new posting will determine your success. Hold nothing back. Give your new employer all of you. Then . . . keep a watchful eye on your horizon.

Success in the global economy requires speed, innovation, and, most importantly people—bold, passionate, unique individuals who bring the right skills and attitude to a situation at the right time. People like you.

Praill and Zander landed 18 interviews, got 11 call backs, and received 7 job offers from choice companies . . . NEVER HAVING READ A NEWSPAPER, SURFED A JOB BOARD, GONE TO A NETWORKING EVENT, OR SPENT A PENNY ON CAREER COUNSELORS . . . and the offers just keep on coming! Once you set yourself up to be found on the Web, opportunities will come to you.

Today, Allan and Darryl have both been headhunted a number of times. As true guerrillas they understand better than anyone how to position and market their skills, to search the world, cold-call prospects, get their attention, raise their proposition above the background noise, and to keep at it tenaciously for however long it takes—be it weeks or months—and be intelligent enough to present their skill set in creative new lights until the persuasion works.

Keep Jay and I informed—E-mail your guerrilla stories to me at dperry@perrymartel.com and let me know if we can share your success with other guerrillas.

Remember, in a dog-eat-dog economy the guerrilla is king!

Bonuses

Appendix 1
Call Logs

Date: _____

NETWORKING CALLS

Follow-Up Time	Person	Phone Number	E-Mail	Referred

Agencies/Recruiters

Company	Person	Phone Number	E-Mail	Action

Web and Newspaper Ads

Company	Hiring Manager	Position	Phone Number	E-Mail	Action

Company	Web Site	Contact	Phone Number	E-Mail	Comments

Weekly Activity Plan

	[Objectives / Performance]			
	Week One	Week Two	Week Three	Week Four
Prospect / Cold calls				
Networking				
Contact search firms / agencies				
Answer ads				
Information interviews				
Thank you notes				
Research and read				
Job interviews				
TOTALS				

Appendix 2

eXtreme™ Makeover Resume Samples

Mark Smith

COMPANY
YOUR SLOGAN HERE

Co-Honoured as # 1 outstanding employee within company of 110 staff

Consistent achiever of 110% productivity awards

Developed & delivered a sales campaign that created 23% response rate from top Canadian CEOs in tough economic conditions

Developed & Managed a # 1 highest volume store for a 270 store chain between $4 and $5 million in revenue per year

Phone: xxxxxxxxxx
Cell: xxxxxxxxxxxx
Fax: xxxxxx
E: xxxxxx

Xxxxxxx
Any town

Summary

Dynamic sales operations manager. Accomplishments include:

➤ Integral part in making company best investment in Canada rated by Finance Forum.
➤ Key initial contact & presenter to help win $22 million US in venture investment.
➤ Merged multi-million dollar UK & US sales operations into 1 sales infrastructure.
➤ Produced the case studies & business proposals for many large contracts.
➤ Developed collateral that was integral to all corporate contracts.
➤ Key initial presenter with majority of business partners (i.e. Novell).
➤ Consistently created high response rate sales campaigns & lead generation programs.

CAREER DRIVER

Taking the surety of success, the passion to succeed, and the deft handling of economic drivers to build great organizations.

SPECIAL SKILLS

My start-up and management experience has honed the following skills:

➤ Execution – consistently delivering to fixed time schedules against very steep odds.
➤ Creation – business plans, case studies, marketing documentation, reports, collateral & presentations which always enjoy extensive internal/external usage.
➤ Service Excellence – in creating new clients & maintaining established relationships.
➤ Focus – efforts always stay targeted on what creates income and reduces costs.
➤ Management – finding & hiring people with the highest potential & then actualizing it.
➤ Achievement – delivering performance in the top 1% in all previous positions.
➤ Strategic Budgeting – creating best usage of finite resources.
➤ Communication – effective trainer in sales procedures, software, & product services
➤ Administered – SFA (Sales Force Automation) systems.

EMPLOYMENT HISTORY

*Consultant CRM solutions – **ABC Technologies** (2002-2003)*

Sales Operations Manager – DEF Networks, New York, (1998-2002)
➤ A leader in online interaction software & Internet phone technology.

• sales	• reporting	• collateral development	• customer service
• marketing	• training	• procedure development	• strategy

Manager – Consumers Distributing (1984-1998)

EDUCATION

Bachelor degree in Economics
Diploma in Business Administration
New York University, New York, New York

Microsoft Certified Professional
Microsoft Certified Trainer

PRODUCT EXPERTISE

• MS Excel	• MS Word	• MS PowerPoint	• Goldmine 5.7
• Working knowledge MS Project, Access, Visio, & Adobe Products		• Upshot	

Logos provided by Templatemonster.com.

311

Mark Smith
EET, B.A., PMP

XXXXX
President's Awards of Merit:
Excellence 1995

XXXXX
President's Awards of Merit:
Teamwork 1992

President's Award of Merit:
Administrative Excellence
1987

XXXXXXXX
XXXX
XXXXXXXX

Objective

To increase shareholder value by developing and delivering high quality products.

PROFILE

Fifteen years' experience in both the technical and business aspects of the technology industry, with a demonstrated ability to deliver.

How:

- Discover What the Customers Want;
- Drive Design, Development and Delivery;
- Act as Technical Evangelist Where Necessary.
- "Six Sigma" Methodology.

Examples:

➢ Created XXX's first OC3/OC12 FPGA, that was functional across multiple SONET-Ethernet interface 'Madonna Metro' products.

➢ Improved XXX's BMS100-Family product line integrity and robustness by 60%, achieved a cost improvement of $30M.

CAREER DRIVER

Inspiring and leading teams to develop breakthrough products, which solve customer demands and have real commercial value in the global market.

SPECIAL SKILLS

My experience has honed the following development know-how:

- Execution – regularly delivering to fixed time schedules against all odds.
- Experimentation - relentless probing for new R&D and product approaches.
- Expressive clarity – strategic development plans.
- Management - optimizing people and finances to meet objectives.
- Strategic Alliances – technical liaison throughout project life cycles
- Budget maximization - for effective use of finite resources.
- Leadership - of teams ranging from 6-30 people across multi-country-sites.

EMPLOYMENT HISTORY

XXXXXXXXX .   2001- present

Private consulting focused on bringing technology to market *"faster, better, cheaper."*

ABC Networks Limited   1983 - 2001

FPGA/Hardware Designer - Maddonna Packet Switching, xxxx, 1999 - 2001
Sr. Projects Leader - Technology (R&D) Organization, zzzz, 1999 – '94
Projects Leader - Technology (R&D) Organization, zzzzz, 1993 – '90
Task Force Leader - Quality – Customer Satisfaction, zzzzz, 1989 – '87
Analyst - Quality – Reliability Engineering, zzzzz, 1986 – '84
Functional Tester - Customer Service Operations, zzzzzz, 1983

EDUCATION

Project Management Professional (PMP), Project Management Institute, 2002
Bachelor of Arts, XXXX University, XXXX, Ontario, 1995
Major: Industrial-Organizational Psychology
Electronics Engineering Technologist, XXXXXXX College, XXXXXX, XX, 1983
Major: Telecommunications

**Mark
Smith**
EET, B.A., PMP

OBJECTIVE

To increase shareholder value by developing high quality commercial grade software products.

PROFILE

Over twenty years' experience in both technical and business aspects of the technology industry, with a demonstrated ability to develop new software products (9 to date) for both commercial and military markets.

How:

- Discover What the Customers Want;
- Drive Design, Development and Delivery;
- Act as Technical Evangelist Where Necessary.

CAREER DRIVER

Inspiring and leading teams to develop breakthrough products, which solve customer demands and have real commercial value in the global market.

"Mark is a visionary. He is able to create a vision for a product and deliver upon that vision..." (D.D.)

SPECIAL SKILLS

Experience has honed development know-how:

- Execution – regularly delivering to fixed time schedules against all odds.
- Experimentation - relentless probing for new R&D and product approaches.
- Expressive clarity – strategic development plans.
- Management - optimizing people and finances to meet objectives.
- Strategic Alliances - to bring products to market faster.
- Budget maximization - for effective use of finite resources.
- Leadership - of teams ranging from 8-55 people

EMPLOYMENT HISTORY

Company, Senior Manager of Development, (97- present)

- Recruited to turnaround the development of a legacy product line. Launched new technology road map and subsequent product, which catapulted **Company** to the front of the line in a new category.

Company, Vice President of Research and Development (96-97)
Company, Supervisor Of Technical Support (94-96)
Company, General Manager/Product Manager, Manager Engineering, Engineer (89-94)
Company, Research Associate (87-89)
Company, Software Engineer (86-87)
Company, Manager xxx (85-86)

Xxxxxxxxx
Xxxxxxxx
xxxxxxxxxx

address
address

EDUCATION

Bachelor of Computer and Systems Engineering
Nice University, 1985

Marcy Smith

AIR TRAVEL
COMPANY

Job Objective
Casual or Substitute teacher, on-call for K-6 children.

Personal Summary
Creative, energetic, resourceful, mother of two school-age children.

Special Skills
My courses in **Early Childhood Education** & **Psychology** with my work experience in the service industry has honed these skills:

- Training – delivered new employee indoctrination..
- Management – influence and optimize people to meet objectives.
- Budget maximization - for effective use of finite resources.
- Experimentation - relentless probing for novel solutions and approaches.
- Organization – canvass volunteers, build and motivate teams, direct outcomes.
- Project Management - evaluate programs, initiate projects, develop and execute strategies.
- Computer – Windows, Internet, Microsoft Office.

Education
University of Dallas – part-time, 2 years of Psychology
Heritage College, - Early Childhood Education, interrupted by maternity leave.
Dallas College - Science, 1993

Employment History

04/97 –	*Maternity Leave*
09/95 – 04/97	**Company**, Senior Customer Service Representative
-	Beneficial specializes in high-risk loans to middle income families. I was "Employ-of-the-Month" several times and as such was responsible for training new employees.
05/91 – 04/95	**Company**, Stewardess, Fly with me airways.
10/90 – 05/91	**Company**, Waitress
89-90	**Company**, Receptionist

Languages
Fluent in Spanish and English

Xxxxxxxxx
Xxxxxxxx
xxxxxxxxxxx

Community Involvement
City of Angels Community Health Care

Dotty Smith

COMPANY
YOUR SLOGAN HERE

Objective
To increase shareholder value through correct accounting practices.

Summary
Creative, energetic, experienced accounts payable professional.

Special Skills
Working in the accounts payable group at Future Electronics has honed these skills:

- Audit – keen sense for catching discrepancies.
- Organization – extensive expense audit and month-end reporting.
- Budget maximization - for effective use of finite resources.
- Organization -canvass volunteers build and motivate teams, direct outcomes.
- Customer Service – reduced claim errors and improved reimbursement times.
- Management – influence and optimize people to meet objectives.

Employment History
Accounts Payable Officer – **Company**, City, State   (1996 – 10/020)
  ➢ Audited and processed expense claims for 1100 sales people and senior management across North America. Acted as department supervisor to cover a maternity leave. Extensive background in expense auditing and the preparation of detailed month-end reports. Annual revenues ~$9.6 billion.

Receptionist - **Company** (08/95 – 02/96)
Receptionist/Clerk - **Company** (10/94 – 08/95)

Computer Skills & Formal Education
Excellent knowledge of Microsoft Office and Oracle Financials. Proficient in various packaged software applications including word processing, e-mail etc.

Nice Institute, in nice city - Office Systems - A.E.C.
Nice High School, in nice city - Diploma

Languages
Fluent in English and Spamnish.

Interests and Hobbies
Reading, music, interior design and travel.

Xxxxxxxx
Xxxxx
X

xxxxxxxxxx

Brian Perry

Summary

High-energy - results focused coax cable/fibre optic technician with 18 years experience.

ACCOMPLISHMENTS

- Developed Triolithic Return Alignment Technique.
- Responsible for rapid analyses and repair for critical users like: Client Headquarters, Client, ATM banking system, Internet, and traffic lights.
- Received Company *Service Award* for outstanding work on the ZZZ Rebuild.

Special Skills

Working in a fast-paced service-oriented environment has honed these skills:

- Technical Audit – keen sense for system-wide troubleshooting.
- Execution – exceptional track record for repair times - 25% faster than company average.
- Project management – working with state-of-the-art high impact systems.
- Customer relations – focal contact for commercial customers during critical system failures.
- Training – inspired team commitment to quality service and customer satisfaction.
- Budget maximization - for effective use of finite resources.
- Management – influence and optimize people to meet objectives.

Employment History

Company xxx/company zzz – *City, State*   *1985-2002*
- Joined as a maintenance technician troubleshooting cable lines and was promoted quickly through a series of increasingly demanding technical jobs including quality control and duty supervisor to become 1 of only 4 advanced network technicians who maintain Rogers' large and extremely complex network system throughout zzz and zzzzz.

Network Maintenance Technician	*1995-2002*
Quality Control Technician / Duty Supervisor	*1990-1994*
Maintenance & Senior Maintenance Technician	*1985-1990*

Education & Additional Training

Excellent knowledge of Microsoft Office and proficient in related software applications.

- Electronics Engineering Technician Diploma – Nice College, 1982-1984
- Electronics Engineering Technologist Program – Nice College, 1979-1981
- Fibre training and online courses on Company network 1995-2002
- Linear Circuits, Nice College, 1990
- Basic CATV Concepts, Nice College, 1988

Professional Certification

- **Security Clearance**
- Manhole Access License
- Skyvan Hydraulic Aerial Device License

Technical Skill Summary

Emergency cable locates; Trunk sweeps; Cable/fibre equipment transmitters/receivers and power supplies; Amplifiers, modulators, spectrum analyzers, video surveillance cameras; Use of OTDR, laptop computer and construction plans to pinpoint cable/fibre failures; Gas detectors, water pumps and other manhole equipment; system monitoring and manual checks including system channel signals, C.T.B., cross-modulation, carrier to noise and hum measurements: and Quality control.

Xxxxx
Xxxxxxxx
xx
xx

Mary Smith

COMPANY

Summary
Creative, energetic, experienced community builder, and public school educator.

Special Skills
Working within the education system and various community organizations at the municipal, provincial, and federal levels has honed these skills:

- Organization -canvass volunteers build and motivate teams, direct outcomes.
- Project Management - evaluate programs, initiate projects, develop and execute strategies.
- Leadership - community outreach, public speaking, consensus building.
- Management – influence and optimize people to meet objectives.
- Budget maximization - for effective use of finite resources.
- Teaching – assess students, develop curriculum, facilitate learning, test, and re-assess.
- Experimentation - relentless probing for novel solutions and approaches.

Employment History
Teacher - ABC School Board, City/State. (1995- present)
- Have taught: Junior Kindergarten, Kindergarten, Grade 1-2 split, Grade 2 and Grade 6 students across the Pontiac Valley. Physical Education Instructor at Eardley Elementary for one year.

Director - Company, self-directed Pre-school, Aylmer, Que. (1993-1995)
Teacher - Company Board of Education Adult Education & E.S.L., Ottawa, ON
Enumerator & Returning Officer - Company. - poll (1989/1993)
Executive Assistant to Minister of Education - Company Regina, Sask. (1984-1985)
Policy Advisor - Premier of Saskatchewan (1983-1984)
Director French Kindergarten - Company., Baie d'Urfe, Que. - 1982-1983
Lab Technician - Company, Lachine, Que. 1980-1982
Supply Teacher - Company, Beaconsfield, Que. (1980)

Education
University of Calgary, B.Ed. Early Childhood Education & Educational Psychology (1975-1980)
Mariannopolis College, C.E.G.P. Diploma – Languages and Psychology (1972-1974)
Additional post-graduate courses in Psychology & E.S.L. (U-Sask., Carleton, McGill) (1984,'91,'98)

Languages
Fluent in English and French

Community Involvement
Ottawa Twin Parent Association, Director/Counselor - for higher order of multiples, (1990-2000)
Aylmer Women's Forum, Coordinator – "Speakers Bureau" (1986- 1990)
South Hull School Committee, Chair - speakers, information meetings, (1997-2000)
Eardley School Committee, Chair develop and maintain daily volunteer base, (1993-1996)
Eardley School Committee, Parent Committee Representative, (1997-1998)
Literacy Council, Member/Volunteer - supporter and canvasser, (1997- present)
Medical Council of Canada, Volunteer, (1998-present)
Ottawa Board of Education, Volunteer Teacher, (1990-1991)
Spicer Commission, Volunteer – Youth Forum, (1991)
Member St. John's Ambulance
Volunteer Firefighter

Xxxxxxx
Xxxxxxx
xxxxxxxxxxxxxx

Thomas Weishaar

rain·mak·er – one whose influence can initiate progress or ensure success.

Cell: +1.610.909.2000
Office: +1.610.989.9720
Home: +1.610.989.9668

http://www.weishaars.com
tom@weishaars.com

SUMMARY

Technology sales and busdev executive. Milestones include:

- sold a two-year global software contract to General Electric valued at $10,000,000+

- developed a *Global Strike Team* to rapidly engage senior level management at numerous Level 1 financial institutions including ANZ, Commonwealth Bank, National Australian Bank, Commerz Bank, Abbey National, Royal Bank of Scotland, Deutsche Bank, Wells Fargo, ABN Amro, etc.

- initiated leveraged worldwide partnership/ relationships with Logica (London), WiseKey (Geneva) and TC TrustCenter (Hamburg) Ernst & Young (Ottawa)

- Licensed 80,000+ copies of StreetSigns to Palm Computing.

- closed multiple million-dollar agreements with OEM's: IBM, Fujitsu/ICL and Sun.

- closed unique Software Licensing Agreement with Coopers & Lybrand centered on a transactional pricing model for it's customer, Chase Manhattan Bank.

- invented the first full sized folding keyboard for the Palm Pilot . Generated orders for over 10,000 units during the first month.

CAREER DRIVER

An opportunity which will allow me to promote the promise of developments in the new age of high technology to business for an organization that has an aggressive mind-set.

EMPLOYMENT HISTORY

TWA, President (2001 – present)
➢ *Private consultancy with a mandate to push the envelope for business development and leverage market entry in the fast-changing high-tech world.*
•strategy   •sales   • business development
•marketing   •OEMs   • contract negotiations

Vice President Strategic Business Development - KYBERPASS Corporation (1999 –2001)
Founder &Vice President Sales & Marketing - TREKWARE CORPORATION (1997 – 1999)
Director Global Business Development - JETFORM CORPORATION (1992 – 1997)
Senior Account Executive - EGGHEAD SOFTWARE (1989 –1992)
Manager of National Accounts, Financial Services- METRIPLEX CORPORATION (1986 - 1989)

EDUCATION

St. Michaels College
Manhattan College

Appendix 3

Compensation Checklist

Compensation Checklist	Staff	Management	Executive	Current	Offer
Compensation					
Base salary	X	X	X		
Annual bonus	Rarely	X	X		
Equity	-	-	X		
Stock options	Rarely	Negotiable	X		
Commissions	Depends	Depends	Depends		
Profit sharing		-	X		
			Subtotal		
Incentives					
Retirement benefits		X	X		
Deferred compensation			X		
Financial planning assistance			X		
Income splitting			X		
Signing bonus	Rarely	Occasionally	X		
			Subtotal		
Benefits					
Bridge the healthcare plan*	Rarely	Negotiable	X		
Cafeteria plan	Rarely	Negotiable	X		
Paid vacation		X	X		
Company car		Negotiable			
Automobile allowance		Negotiable	X		
Medical		X	X		
Dental		X	X		
Life		X	X		
Disability		X	X		
Travel		X	X		
			Subtotal		

Compensation Checklist	Staff	Management	Executive	Current	Offer
Perks					
Paid parking	Negotiable	x	x		
Professional dues	Negotiable	x	x		
Onsite daycare		x	x		
Home office		x	x		
High-speed Internet		x	x		
Technology tools		x	x		
Continuing education	Negotiable	Negotiable	x		
Tuition forgiveness**	Negotiable	Negotiable	x		
Wellness programs		Negotiable	x		
Training days		Negotiable	x		
Club memberships		Negotiable	x		
Travel consideration		Negotiable	x		
Sabbaticals		Negotiable	x		
Flex-time (Flexible work hours)	Negotiable	Rarely	Negotiable		
			Subtotal		
Relocation Assistance					
Moving expenses	Negotiable	Negotiable	x		
Realtor fees	Negotiable	Negotiable	x		
House-hunting trips	Negotiable	Negotiable	x		
Short-term housing	Negotiable	Negotiable	x		
Short-term living allowance	Negotiable	Negotiable	x		
Bridge loan		Negotiable	x		
Low interest loan			x		
Forgivable loan			x		
Company purchase of home		Negotiable	x		
Spousal career assistance		Negotiable	x		
			Subtotal		
Severance					
Lump sum severance		Negotiable	x		
Insurance continuation		Negotiable	x		
Outplacement		Negotiable	x		
Relocation assistance			x		
			Subtotal		

* Often a new employer cannot place a new employee and dependents on medical insurance for a given period of time ranging from 30 days or longer. In such cases, you may be eligible for Consolidated Omnibus Budget Reconciliation Act (COBRA). Although you are no longer at the last employer, you may be eligible to receive continuation of the same coverage at a group rate, except that the premiums come out of your

pocket. So, it still is a heavy monthly expense. You may be able to have your new employer "bridge" the cost under COBRA. In other words, pay your premium until you can be placed on their policy. To learn more about COBRA, visit www.cobrainsurance.com.

** Tuition forgiveness—depending on the shortage of a particular skill set (healthcare professionals, high-level security clearances, and high-demand management and executive people are three examples). It's negotiable at all levels. Skill set shortage really drives the deal; what's hot today may not be tomorrow.

Valuing the Deal

Valuing the deal is as simple as seeing how the new offer compares to the old. Add up the two columns and see how you're doing. The value is in the total amount from the first five sections. The section on "severance" is career insurance and shouldn't be factored into the package. While in some cases your salary may only have gone up say, 10%, the value of your benefits may have soared by 50% to 100% or more. At the end of the day it's as much about purchasing power as it is about how much you get to keep.

What's your total current situation: _____

What's the total for the new offer: _____

About the Authors

Jay Conrad Levinson is the author or coauthor of the more than 32 books in the biggest series of books on marketing in history. His books appear in 60 languages and are required reading in many MBA programs worldwide.

Jay taught guerrilla marketing for 10 years at the extension division of the University of California in Berkeley. He was a practitioner of guerrilla marketing in the United States—as senior vice-president at J. Walter Thompson, and in Europe, as creative director at Leo Burnett Advertising.

He has written monthly columns for *Entrepreneur* and *Inc.*, a syndicated column for newspapers and magazines and online columns published monthly on the Microsoft and GTE web sites.

Jay has served on the Microsoft Small Business Council and the 3Com Small Business Advisory Board. In addition to books, he has produced a videotape, an award-winning CD-ROM, a newsletter, and has started a consulting organization and web site.

David E. Perry is a veteran of more than 996 executive search projects, with a 99.8 percent success rate. Called the "Rogue Recruiter" by the *Wall Street Journal,* he is a student of leadership and its effect on organizations, ranging from private equity ventures to global technology corporations.

David is frequently quoted on trends and issues regarding executive search, recruiting, and HR in leading business publications including the *Wall Street Journal,* the *New York Times, Globe and Mail, CIO, Fortune, IT World, Canadian Business, EETimes, HR Today,* and appears regularly as an executive search and labor market analyst for CBC News World.

David is the author of *Guerrilla Marketing for Job Hunters: 400 Unconventional Tips, Tricks, and Tactics to Land Your Dream Job*

(Hoboken, NJ: Wiley, 2005) and *Career Guide for the High-Tech Professional: Where the Jobs Are and How to Land Them* (Franklin Lakes, NJ: Career Press, 2004).

As an advisory board member and HR Policy Advisor of the Canadian Advanced Technology Alliance (CATA), David has developed an extensive knowledge of leadership, innovation, and technology. This ever-evolving expertise keeps him at the pulse of most innovative and successful leaders. David is immediate past Chair of the Canadian Technology Human Resources Board and was on the board of the Software Human Resource Council.

Keynotes and conference presentations have included CeBIT, Performance Institute in Washington, DC, CATAAlliance Conference, Canadian Academy of Engineering, Canadian Information Processing Society, Canadian On-Line Information Summit, and the 2009 Innovation Summit.

David graduated from McGill University in 1982 with a BA in Economics and Industrial Relations. As a Commissioned Officer, he graduated first in his class and was awarded the Sword of Honor. He has been recognized as one of the "Top 40 Under 40" Entrepreneurs. He lives in Ottawa with his wife and business partner, Anita Martel, and their 4 children. He recruits globally.

Index

Free Job-Search Resources